AFRICAN CHRISTIAN THEOLOGY

AFRICAN CHRISTIAN THEOLOGY

Samuel Waje Kunhiyop

ZONDERVAN

African Christian Theology
Copyright © 2012 by Samuel Waje Kunhiyop

Samuel Waje Kunhiyop has asserted his right under the Copyright, Designs, and Patents act 1988 to be identified as the Author of this Work

Original Edition © 2012 by HippoBooks

This edition of African Christian Theology is published in arrangement with Langham Publishing

ISBN 978-0-310-10711-8 (softcover)

Requests for information should be addressed to:
Zondervan, *3900 Sparks Dr. SE, Grand Rapids, Michigan 49546*

Cover design: projectluz com
Book design: To a Tee Ltd, www.2at.com

Printed in the United States of America

19 20 21 22 23 24 /LSC/ 12 11 10 9 8 7 6 5 4 3 2 1

CONTENTS

FOREWORD

D r Samuel Waje Kunhiyop has scratched where the African church is itching. Too much of our theological reflection in Africa is informed by Western thinkers and their understanding of Scripture. Ignorance and ethnic arrogance have resulted in the African worldview and African religious beliefs being dismissed as primitive and heathen. Yet these beliefs underlie the way African Christians understand their world and relate to their creator. And biblical interpretation and application has much to do with world view and native religious belief systems.

Indigenous African theologians have attempted to provide a corrective, but their work often reflects the effects of a different kind of ethnocentrism and cultural clash, rather than the biblical orthodoxy that is native only to the kingdom of Christ and not to any particular region of the earth. The kingdom of God is itself the corrective needed for each and every culture for salvation and redemption.

Dr Kunhiyop makes a significant contribution by allowing the Christian Scriptures to speak to African traditional beliefs. African religious beliefs are taken seriously and are subjected to the scrutiny of the infallible and inerrant word of God, the Holy Bible, with a view to informing the faith and conduct of African Christians. It is inculturation theology, which is gaining popularity on the continent, with a difference. And the difference lies in Dr Kunhiyop's high view of the Bible.

African Christian Theology will be a helpful tool in mitigating the harmful effects of syncretism in the African church. As such, it will also have implications for African society as a whole, not only spiritually but also in terms of socio-economic development. It is the sort of book that is needed by African pastors and is warmly recommended for seminaries and Bible schools as a foundational text in systematic theology.

Aiah Foday-Khabenje
General Secretary
Association of Evangelicals in Africa

ACKNOWLEDGEMENTS

It is simply impossible to write a book of this nature without the contributions of others. First, I am grateful to Gerry Breshears, my theology professor at Western Seminary, Portland, Oregon, for planting the seed of this book in my mind. During my postgraduate studies, he asked me, "Sam, do you think there should be an African theology?" This was in 1987! I don't remember how I answered him, but the question has stuck with me ever since. This book is the result.

I am indebted to Pieter Kwant, the director of HippoBooks, who encouraged me to write a simplified and abridged theological book which covers the major themes of systematic theology. I thank HippoBooks for awarding me a grant to cover the basic costs of research. I am very grateful to Isobel Stevenson and Suzanne Mitchell for the excellent and professional editing they have done. They have been co-labourers in the vineyard of our Lord and Saviour Jesus Christ.

I would like to thank the South African Theological Seminary, Rivonia, for giving me sufficient time to write this book. I am particularly thankful to Drs Reuben van Rensburg (Principal) and Kevin Gary Smith (Vice-Principal), who gave me moral support and encouragement for the research.

I am very thankful to Dr Frank Jabini, who read the first draft and provided valuable comments. I am also grateful to Prof. Danfulani Kore and Drs Sunday Agang and Tshilolo Liphadzi, who gave me important personal encouragement.

I am grateful to Dr Ruth Cox, veteran missionary to Nigeria, who read the first draft and made helpful comments and corrections.

Thank you to all my students and colleagues for the encouragement you have given me over the years. I am also grateful to all my friends and supporters, particularly in the USA and Nigeria, who prayed for me during the writing of this book. These include Ron and Carol

Speers, Bruce and Beth Welker, Stan and Ruth Guillaume, Dave and Joy Dawson, Mark Perraut, Robert and Mary Rieck, Larry and Deborah Tornquist and Stephen Kemp.

I am deeply grateful to my wife, Yelwa, who gave me emotional support and encouragement. Her belief in me has always given me the necessary strength to persevere.

To the glory of God, the Father of our Lord Jesus Christ, who has given me the undeserved opportunity to write my understanding of his holy word to the present generation of African Christians.

INTRODUCTION

To speak of an African Christian theology often raises critical questions and scepticism. What is the goal of such a project, and why in particular is the word *African* included in the title of this book?

To some, the word *African* signals a rejection of anything that has links to the West, colonialism and economic imperialism, and thus an African Christian theology is perceived as reactionary and hostile to any theology developed in the West.[1] However, I have no intention of being reactionary. My goal is to articulate a theology that originates from an authentic search for the meaning of Scripture in order to apply it to African life today.

Others who see themselves as defenders of evangelical and biblical Christianity suspect that African Christian theology must inevitably be liberal and syncretistic. But *African* is no more a synonym for *liberal* than *American* is a synonym for *evangelical*. Scripture is always interpreted within a context, and Africa is the context in which I seek the true meaning of Scripture.

Still others are concerned that a specifically African theology will be little more than a study of comparative religion, in which Christian theology is grouped with Islamic theology, African Traditional Religion, Buddhism and Hinduism. This is the way Christianity is already studied at many African universities. Aylward Shorter, for example, states, "African Christian theology must grow out of a dialogue between Christianity and the theologies of African Traditional Religion."[2] He understands *dialogue* to be a "serious exchange, a confrontation of beings, a

---

[1] Samuel G. Kibicho's book, *God and Revelation in an African Context* (Nairobi: Acton, 2006) is an example of a theology developed in reaction to a missionary presentation of Christianity in Africa.

[2] Aylward Shorter, *African Christian Theology: Adaptation or Incarnation?* (Maryknoll: Orbis, 1977), 1.

meeting of meanings, values, attitudes and understandings".[3] Samuel G. Kibicho also objects to any portrayal of Christianity as superior to African Traditional Religion.[4] He believes that both are equally valid.[5] Yet while there is a place for a comparative approach imbued with a deep appreciation of the values and practices of various religions, that is not what will be attempted in this book. I write as one who is convinced that Christianity based on biblical revelation stands above all other religions.

My own understanding of African Christian theology is that it should take the African situation seriously while seeking to be true to the explicit teachings of Scripture. It should affirm the inspiration, infallibility and authority of all sixty-six books of the Scriptures for life and practice, while upholding the positive values in Africanness.

When Wilbur O'Donovan set out to write a book on Christian theology that would seek to answer the real questions raised by African Christians, he was guided by the conviction that "theology must be truly Christian but also truly African in expression".[6] He hoped that his work would encourage other "African authors to present the results of their own study in written form".[7] As a former student of Wilbur O'Donovan, I see this present book as a modest response to this desire.

Every Christian theology – whether written for the West or for the Japanese, Chinese, Latin Americans or Portuguese – evolves from questions concerning how the Bible speaks to particular contexts. Thus this book is written to address questions that arise from the African context and to apply the word of God to them. However, it is critical to remember that an African Christian theology does not stand alone but

---

[3] Ibid., 4.

[4] Kibicho argues that a pluralistic understanding of revelation would help "Christianity to be more inclusive through the shifting of the accent from an indiscriminate exclusiveness. Such a theology would thereby help Christianity to be more truly universal as it would include within its circle of recognition and acceptance other monotheisms – even Judaism" (*God and Revelation*, 181).

[5] In the preface to his book, *God and Revelation in an African Context* (2006), Kibicho writes, "The Gikuyu people, alongside other peoples of all generations with good genuine religions, had a sound saving knowledge of the One True God before Christianity was introduced to them. This is so because the Divine Spirit responsible for this inspiration is not restricted to Christianity" (15, see also 171, 183, 340).

[6] Wilbur O'Donovan, *Biblical Christianity in African Perspective* (Carlisle: Paternoster, 2000), 5. The view of Benezet Bujo, an African theologian, is also pertinent. He states, "It is important that Christianity show the Africans that being truly Christian and being truly African are not opposed to each other, because to be a true Christian means to be a true human, since it was Jesus himself who was truly human and who humanized the world." *African Theology in Its Social Context* (Maryknoll: Orbis, 1992), 84.

[7] Ibid., 3.

is part of the larger context of the Christian story. God's dealings with humankind began at creation and have continued to the present day in the context of the universal church of Jesus Christ. An African Christian theology therefore needs to interact with truths that apply to all peoples, tribes and nations, such as in the subjects of revelation, sin, God, the spiritual world, the community of God and the end times. In fact, this book follows the logical order of many traditional Christian theologies. I have not set out to reinvent the wheel.

What, then, are the issues that must be addressed by a specifically African Christian theology? First, an African Christian theology must take seriously the religious world view of the African. Africans unquestioningly believe in a Supreme Creator of the universe and humanity. There is no ethnic group in Africa that does not have a specific name for a Supreme God. There are also other religious beliefs about such topics as the spirit world (populated with good and bad spirits), the creation of the universe, the problem of evil, divine revelation, sins, sacrifices, purification, cleansing, death, judgement, and life after death. These beliefs provide an important bridge to a meaningful discussion of a theology that makes sense to Africans. Though an African Christian theology does not depend solely on African religious traditions, to attempt to write one that does not take into account the continent's religious legacy and traditions will be futile and unproductive.

> The [African] church is composed largely of people who come out of the African religious background. Their culture, history, world views and spiritual aspirations cannot be taken away from them. These impinge upon their daily life and experience of the Christian faith. So the church which exists on the African scene bears the marks of its people's backgrounds. No viable theology can grow in Africa without addressing itself to the interreligious phenomenon at work there.[8]

Second, these religious beliefs and the African world view are not lost when Africans become Christians. They need to be examined critically. They affect everyday life, whether in terms of marriage, farming, career choices or even such mundane matters as travelling. Dreams, for example,

---

[8] John Mbiti, "The Encounter of Christian Faith and African Religion", *Christian Century* (August 27–September 3, 1980): 817–820. Also available at www.religion.online.org.

are not thought of as merely arising from psychological causes but are understood as a real way by which God or the gods reveal themselves. Once Africans become Christians they do not become Jewish, American or Asian. Even though they may change their names from Chaka to Titus, from Jabulani to Abraham, from Nandi to Rebecca, or from Ladi to Grace – they are still African or Zulu or Bajju.

Third, theology must "scratch where there is an itch". For centuries, the development of Christian theology in Africa has been controlled exclusively by the West. Theological teaching materials like textbooks, catechisms and manuals and the philosophy and methodology used in the training of African pastors and church leaders have been Western in orientation. The issues raised and discussed are often irrelevant to African Christians. For example, countless books have been written on arguments to prove the existence of God, a critical issue for the Western mind, but these are completely unnecessary and even wasteful to Africans who, because of their foundational beliefs, already accept that God exists. If Africans have no problem believing in the existence of God, why burden them with proofs of God's existence? The location of the "itch" for Christians in New York in the USA will not be the same as that for Christians in Bukavu in the Democratic Republic of Congo. The critical issues for Africans must be addressed in concrete terms.

Fourth, for Africans there is an intimate balance between the abstract and the practical. Purely abstract thinking is regarded as irrelevant. Thus theology from a purely conceptual perspective has no essential value to most African Christians. It is not that Africans are unable to do abstract thinking, for all humans are capable of abstraction. The point is that for most Africans, abstract thinking should be situated in concrete reality and should be productive and relevant. Theology must therefore speak to the real issues of life, and that is what this book attempts to do.

Fifth, and finally, Christian theology must also be comprehensible to all Christians, not just to a select group of intellectuals. Much of what is termed *theology* is really incomprehensible to most Christians. The majority of Africans do not even know what the word *theology* means, and books written on theology are often so complicated and difficult to read that they are beyond the understanding of the layperson. Given that the basic task of theology is to help Christians make sense of the Bible, this is simply unacceptable. To that end, this book seeks to articulate a theology that ordinary Christians can understand and apply to their faith.

Survey of Contents

The approach followed in this book is similar to that in most traditional Christian theologies but with direct application to the African situation.

- *Chapter 1* discusses the foundations of African Christian theology, dealing with the basic issues such as its definition, nature, formative factors, and African presuppositions and convictions. The role of history, philosophy and ethics in theology is discussed briefly.

- *Chapter 2* discusses revelation. In traditional African religious thought, dreams and visions are the major means by which the gods and ancestors reveal what is required of humanity. So this chapter deals with the questions of how God has revealed himself to us, and whether he continues to reveal himself today.

- *Chapter 3* discusses the debate on the nature of the African knowledge of God before the arrival of Christianity and the significance of the Trinity in forming a complete and biblical picture of God. Africans have a concept of the spirit world, but how does this relate to the Bible's teaching on the Holy Spirit, Satan, and angels and demons? How does the spirit world interact with our daily lives?

- *Chapter 4* discusses creation and the fall. There are various creation myths in Africa. The idea of original sin is not common, and sin is thought of mainly in terms of offences committed against the gods, ancestral spirits and the communal laws, traditions, taboos and so on. This chapter examines the biblical data on the creation of men and women in the image of God, how humanity fell into sin, the origin of sin and evil in the world and their consequences.

- *Chapter 5* provides a survey of African scholarship on Christ and salvation, critically reviewing the popular themes of Christ as founder, ancestor, elder brother, diviner and proto-ancestor. The person and work of Christ in relation to salvation, and the consequences of that salvation, are discussed from a biblical perspective. It is important to do this, for while the idea of substitutionary atonement is quite common in African Traditional Religion (and can even involve human sacrifice), the concept of a god dying on behalf of humanity is very rare. The idea of a god sending his son to die on behalf of the sins of humankind is non-existent.

- *Chapter 6* clarifies the work of the Holy Spirit in salvation. Many African Christians mistakenly think that as a sign of salvation all believers will experience the Spirit through speaking in tongues or other unusual experiences. This chapter explains who the Spirit is, what the Spirit does, and what evidence of the Spirit we should or should not expect to see in all believers.

- *Chapter 7* discusses personal Christian living. The true test of Christianity is living it out. What people really believe is evident by the way they live their lives. This chapter emphasizes contemporary Christian teachings that are popular in the church in Africa such as holistic salvation, blessings and curses, generational curses, the use of the phrases "the blood" and "the name of Jesus", prayers and reverence for ancestors.

- *Chapter 8* examines the concept of the church, the community of God. The chapter briefly presents the view of community in Africa, which provides a platform for studying the Bible's teaching on the nature, marks, mission and organization of the church, and the relationship between the church and society.

- *Chapter 9* focuses on the beliefs and practices of the community of God. Churches have different beliefs and practices according to their history and tradition, and this chapter covers those that are pertinent to African Christianity, including spiritual gifts, church discipline, pastoral ordination, the role of women in ministry and the remuneration of church workers. It is critical to examine these practices in light of Scripture.

- *Chapter 10* discusses the African concepts of death and the afterlife and examines the Bible's teaching on eternity, judgement, the second coming of Christ, the tribulation, heaven and hell.

How to Get the Most Out of This Book

1. **Get a Bible.** The main tool of theology is the sixty-six books of the Bible. To get the most out of this book, you therefore need to have a Bible. In every chapter and for each topic discussed, all relevant passages in the Bible are surveyed in order to present what the Bible in its entirety teaches on the subject. Though the New International Version is the main translation used here, any translation (for example, the New American Standard Version, Authorized / King James Version, The New Living Translation, Revised Standard Version or the Good News Bible) may be used. If possible, consult more than one version, as one translation may provide a better understanding than another. An understanding of the original Hebrew and Greek languages is not required but will aid further in understanding the meaning of the Scriptures.

2. **Know your situation.** As this book seeks to deal with African issues, you need to be familiar with your own particular setting, whether you are African, European, Asian or American. John Mbiti's *African Religions and Philosophy* remains the most comprehensive book on the African religious and philosophical background.[9]

3. **Answer the questions at the end of each chapter.** You may also have questions of your own that need to be answered. Check your answers with what this book says on the topic but, most importantly, subject your answers to the scrutiny of the Scriptures.

4. **Use the additional reading list provided at the end of each chapter.** These lists are included to help you study further and increase your understanding of the relevant issues.

5. **Read the key biblical passages on each topic.** This will help you to become familiar with what the Bible in its entirety says about a subject.

6. **Pray that God will transform your life and thinking as you read and study his word.**

---

[9] John Mbiti, *African Religions and Philosophy* (2nd ed.; Oxford: Heinemann, 1969).

1

THEOLOGY

What Is Theology?

The root meaning of theology is *the study of God*. The word was originally used by ancient Greek poets to refer to myths about pagan gods, but in the second century AD Clement of Alexandria used it when speaking of the true knowledge of God. In the fifth century, Augustine of Hippo in North Africa used the term to refer to the study of temporal rather than eternal matters. He did not see these as separate but as complementary. Both were meant to serve wisdom, the acquisition of which was the ultimate goal of all philosophy.

It was only in the twelfth century that *theology* gained a more technical meaning. Peter Abelard, a medieval French philosopher, taught that theology was sacred learning as a whole, as distinguished from secular disciplines such as the sciences. Theology deals with how we understand God and his revelation to his creation. While it is concerned with matters of faith and with eternal happiness as our ultimate goal, it is also a "self-conscious scholarly enterprise of understanding".[1]

Over the centuries, Christians have tended to emphasize either the scholarly or the spiritual side of theology. In the main, universities have taken the academic route while seminaries have been more concerned with the spiritual side, focusing on faith, prayer, virtue and passion for God. Average Christians have tended to shy away from the scholarly side, regarding it academic and therefore non-spiritual. There have been misrepresentations, mistrust, suspicion and even name-calling on both sides of the divide.

---

[1] Edward Farley, *Theologia: The Fragmentation and Unity of Theological Education* (Philadelphia: Fortress, 1942), 31.

The true meaning of theology, however, lies somewhere between the two extremes. It is an intellectual and spiritual search for answers to questions about divine revelation and the human condition. It studies both God's revelation of himself and our own condition as beings composed of a body, mind and spirit. Then it seeks to apply the truths that emerge to men and women today. Theology is useless if it confines itself merely to ideas. It has to be vitally concerned with everyday life and the issues that affect God's creatures. Indeed, it is as much interested in real life as it is interested in correct belief, for doctrine and practice are intimately related.

Philosophy and Theology

Philosophy and theology have always been cousins. Traditions in philosophy have shaped and challenged Christian doctrine and ethics as the theologians of each era have examined the faith in light of contemporary thought. This is not a new phenomenon. Early Christian theology was influenced by the thinking of Plato and Aristotle; eighteenth- and nineteenth-century theologians had to wrestle with the challenges posed by the Enlightenment and philosophers like Immanuel Kant. Today, we have to respond to the serious questions posed by postmodernism.

Some people become very nervous when they are told that philosophy plays a significant role in the development of a meaningful and relevant theology. This is because they define philosophy as human wisdom in opposition to the word of God. Others dismiss philosophy as merely human – and often useless – speculation. While it is true that philosophy has sometimes been used to discredit the word of God, the fact that something is used wrongly does not mean that it is inherently wrong. For example, the devil quoted Scripture to tempt Jesus (Matt 4:1–11), but this does not mean that we cannot quote or use Scripture ourselves. Moreover, even critical philosophy has been used by God to open our eyes to some of our own blind spots. It has sometimes led to the dismantling of some harmful beliefs and practices in the church that contradict the Christian faith. For example, philosophical enquiry into the rules of logic and evidence has helped Christians to identify the falsehood and lies that underlie many stories and confessions that are used to promote the belief and practice of witchcraft.

The root meaning of the word philosophy is *the love of wisdom*. The recognition that *both* philosophy and theology are committed to a rigorous intellectual search for wisdom and truth is the basis for a working relationship between them. Philosophy pursues truth by seeking to clarify concepts and issues. It is concerned with "critical reflection on justification and evidence. Philosophy evaluates arguments and assesses presuppositions and truth claims".[2]

We should not see reason as automatically opposed to faith. The ability to reason is one of the characteristics of God, and we can reason because God created us in his image (Gen 1:26).[3] We are rational beings, just as God is rational. God himself invites us to use our reasoning ability: "'Come now, let us reason together', says the Lord" (Isa 1:18, NIV '84). Reason, illuminated by the Holy Spirit, enables us to understand God's truth in the Holy Scriptures. What God opposes is self-sufficient, unaided-by-the-Spirit reason, as used by secular philosophers.

Here is a list of some areas in which theology benefits from its interaction with philosophy:

- *Logic*: Philosophers study logic in order to be able to distinguish between good and bad arguments. Logic helps us avoid fuzzy thinking when we recognize that "what is historically untrue or logically contradictory can neither possess religious value nor make theological sense. Error is error and nonsense is nonsense in every realm of thought."[4] Over the centuries, philosophy has helped to purge theology of inconsistencies and make it more coherent.

- *Hermeneutics*: What we know is influenced by how we interpret things, and hermeneutics is the philosophical study of the nature of interpretation. As theologians, we have to interpret God's revelation of himself in Scripture and also in nature, which is the revelation he has made available to all created beings. The fact that we are fallen

---

[2] Norman Geisler and Paul Feinberg, *Introduction to Philosophy: A Christian Perspective* (Grand Rapids: Baker, 1980), 19.

[3] Herbert Schlossberg and Marvin Olasky, *Turning Point: A Christian Worldview Declaration* (Downers Grove: Crossway, 1987), 110.

[4] Arthur Holmes, *Philosophy: A Christian Perspective. An Introductive Essay* (Downers Grove: Inter-Varsity Press, 1977), 23. He elaborates: "If God cannot contradict himself, neither can general revelation contradict special revelation, neither can scientific truth contradict biblical truth, and neither can valid philosophical reasoning contradict valid theological reasoning. Just as careful logic cannot allow contradictory truths without forfeiting the laws of thought, so a consistent theism cannot allow contradictory truth without forfeiting the veracity of God" (24).

and need God's grace to rightly understand the things of God does not excuse us from using our minds to study them and clarify our ideas about God and the things of God.

- *Apologetics*: Philosophy can help us provide a reasoned defence of the Christian faith to the unbelieving world. People who might not be willing to listen to direct biblical preaching might respond to the gospel when confronted with philosophical reasoning that is in agreement with the Bible.

- *Systematic theology*: Theologians use tools and terms provided by philosophy when seeking to clearly explain how different parts of the teaching in the Bible fit together. For example, the word "Trinity" is not found anywhere in the Bible. But theologians use it as a quick way of expressing the concept that God is one yet three. This concept arose because inductive study of the whole Bible led theologians to conclude that God exists as the Father, the Son and the Holy Spirit. They then made a deduction that these are not three gods, but one God in three persons. In the same way, an inductive study of the Bible leads to the conclusion that Christ exhibited both human and divine qualities. Philosophy has helped theologians wrestle with the problem of how the omnipotent (all-powerful), omniscient (all-knowing) and unchanging God can be united to human nature, which is finite, mortal and not all-knowing. Our answers to this question are not complete, but they are better than they would be if we had not been able to use the tools of philosophy (like induction and deduction) to shape our teaching on this issue.

- *Philosophical theology*: Christian thinkers have to wrestle with issues that the Bible does not address directly. For example, the Bible assumes that God exists; philosophy looks for proofs of his existence. It also has to wrestle with the relationship between the sovereignty of God and human freedom, and with the problems posed by pain and suffering in this world. It can also be used to help African Christians ask meaningful questions about the nature and activities of the spirit world as it interacts with our world.

Ethics and Theology

The relationship between ethics and theology is similar to the relationship between dance and music. As a Hausa proverb states *idan ganga ya canja, rawa zai canja* [If the beating of the drum changes, the dance will change]. In the same way, any change in our theology affects our world views, beliefs and values, and thus our ethics. Christian ethics and morality are the end result of theology. That is why we cannot say that the theoretical issues of theology are only important for scholars, teachers, students or professors in the classroom. Theology affects the way we behave in real-life situations.

God demands that his people should be holy as he is holy. Theology, as the study of God and his revelation, helps us to interpret what this means so that we can live holy lives in this world. This too underscores the close relationship between theology and ethics; one cannot study one without addressing the other. As Ray Sherman Anderson states, "It is the right hearing of the Word and the obedient response to the claim on one's personal and social life this Lord brings that constitute the basis for a theological ethics."[5] Karl Barth puts it this way: "Ethics as a theological discipline is the auxiliary science in which an answer is sought in the Word of God to the question of the goodness of human conduct. As a special elucidation of the doctrine of sanctification it is reflection on how far the Word of God proclaimed and accepted in Christian preaching effects a definite claiming of man."[6]

Thus Christian theology is critical for ethics. Our behaviour must be consistent with our theological position.

Church History and Theology

God's work in redemption did not cease with his revelation in Scripture and the incarnation of his Son, Jesus Christ. God has been at work through the Holy Spirit throughout history to preserve his creation, to save humankind and to build his church. He has promised that he will be with his people till the end of time (Matt 28:20). There are therefore many lessons to be learnt from the history of the church, both oral and

---

[5] Ray Sherman Anderson, *The Shape of Practical Theology: Empowering Ministry with Theological Praxis* (Downers Grove: InterVarsity Press, 2001), 143.

[6] Karl Barth, *Ethics* (trans. Geoffrey W. Bromiley; Philadelphia: Seabury Press, 1981), 3.

written. These lessons can help us to create a theology that is consistent with the Bible and with what God has been doing in and through his church. For example, the many failed predictions of doomsday across church history must affect our eschatology. Thus it is important that theologians be aware of the traditions, beliefs and customs of the church throughout the centuries.

What Shapes Theology?

Theology is shaped by at least four factors: revelation, experience, reason and tradition.

- *Revelation*: God's unveiling of himself and his will to his creation is the primary source for Christian theology. Without this, theology would be purely speculative, with no sure foundation. God's revelation is given in two forms. There is his *general revelation* of himself through history, nature and the human conscience, and there is his *special revelation* of himself in the Holy Scriptures. Both forms of revelation are important in theology, but the Scriptures have the dominant, authoritative, judging and evaluative role. All other factors that are brought into Christian reflection must yield to the finality of the revelation of God in his word.

- *Experience*: Human experience provides the theologian with many topics for discussion. We have to be able to deal with the suffering caused by natural disasters such as hurricanes, earthquakes, tornadoes, tsunamis, epidemics, floods and famines, as well as with the suffering that arises from human errors or actions, including plane and car crashes, rape, abortion, war and terrorism. In Africa, we have to address issues such as HIV/AIDS, wars, genocide, witchcraft, occultism and spiritism. While these matters are not explicitly dealt with in Scripture, we need to be able to square them with our theological beliefs. If we ignore human experiences, our theology will be boring and irrelevant.

- *Reason*: Theology involves applying our minds to God's revelation of himself to us, and so it requires us to use our minds, our human reasoning. There is some dispute about how far we can trust our reasoning. Historically, Roman Catholic theologians have viewed human reason as reliable in formulating theology, whereas Protestants have been more inclined to regard it as suspect because our minds have been corrupted by sin. But, as pointed out above, human reason is still a key tool in theology. Without it, we could not begin to make sense of theological statements. However, our reason must be subject to the word of God.

- *Tradition*: Roman Catholics and Protestants have disagreed on the role of tradition in theology since the days of the Reformation. It used to be that Catholics held that the Bible and tradition together were the main sources of revelation, whereas Protestants argued that the Bible was the only source of revelation. However, at the Second Vatican Council (1962–1965), the Roman Catholic Church radically changed its position, stating that there was only one source of revelation – the Bible, although it added that the Bible must be interpreted within the tradition of the church. The Protestant charge that Catholics hold to two sources of revelation is therefore no longer valid, and Catholics and Protestants seem to be coming closer together in their views of the Bible than before.

  Protestants, in turn, have recognized that God has been active throughout church history, and that "we are all prone to approach Scripture in the light of inherited or acquired traditions".[7] Protestants accept traditions that are in agreement with the teachings of the apostles and the New Testament church. For example, we accept the theological statements on the Trinity formulated by early church councils such as the Council of Chalcedon (AD 451). We still quote the Nicene Creed (AD 325) which says that Jesus was "very God of very God and very man of very man", a clear summary of the Bible's teaching that Jesus was 100% God and 100% human. Tradition in this sense is Scripture rightly interpreted. Theology does not blindly accept tradition but assesses its correctness or otherwise in light of Scripture.

---

[7] Carl F. H. Henry, *God Who Speaks and Shows* (vol. 4 of *God, Revelation and Authority*; Waco: Word, 1979), 289.

Fundamental Principles

No system of theology is developed in a vacuum. Theologians always approach their task with certain presuppositions, and it is important to be aware of what these are because they will shape the outcome of our thinking. Evangelical theologians are guided by the following five fundamental principles, each of which will be explored in more detail in later chapters.

1. Revelation is the basis of theology

As stated above, revelation is our starting point when doing theology (see chapter 2). Although general revelation is important, we give priority to God's special revelation of himself in Scripture. The Scriptures have their source in God and, properly interpreted, are the ultimate authority for Christian life and theology.

2. The triune God is the focus of theology

The general belief in the existence of God and the supernatural that permeates African Traditional Religion and much Western spirituality is inadequate when it comes to Christian theology. Theology must be focused on the personal God revealed in Scripture and affirmed by historic biblical Christianity. "A vague theism [belief in the existence of a god] is futile. The cutting edge of faith is due to its definiteness. ... The Christian has made a decision for God, who has spoken – in nature, in history, in the prophets, in Christ."[8]

The nature of the triune God is discussed in more detail in chapter 3. At this point, it is enough to affirm that there is only one God, not many gods, and that he exists in three persons – God the Father, God the Son and God the Holy Spirit – each of whom is equally God. Where they differ is in their roles.

Among the implications of the Christian understanding of the triune God is that God is not confined to those areas of life we define as "spiritual". God's participation in creation, his personal revelation in the incarnation of Jesus Christ, and the Holy Spirit's continuing work in the

---

[8] William Temple, *What Christians Stand For in the Secular World* (Philadelphia: Fortress, 1965), 9.

life of believers demonstrate that God is personal and has an intimate relationship with all aspects of his creation.

3. Salvation is rooted in the work of Christ

Moral philosophy cannot forgive failure or save the lost. It cannot instil in people the ability to live with failure. This is not because philosophy – or philosophers – lacks kindness or compassion, but because it lacks any foundation for grace. It is only through biblical revelation that we can know of God's saving grace in forgiving moral offenders (sinners). He justifies us by faith, bringing us into a right relationship with himself, and sanctifies us by transforming our moral and spiritual character (see chapters 5 to 7). Sanctification affects every aspect of our existence – spiritual, physical and emotional – including marriage, politics and technology. Theologians thus have the right to engage with the whole of human existence, including matters relating to sexual and political morality and the environment. We are also called to share in God's activity of restoring sinners to the "congregation of the righteous", the "communion of saints" – "God's people".[9]

4. The redeemed community is the context of theology

The "idea of community is at the heart of biblical theology".[10] The focus of biblical revelation is the story of how God formed a covenant people (see chapter 8). When God called Abraham, the idea of a community was central to his call. In Genesis 12:2, God said to Abraham, "I will make you into a great nation, and I will bless you; I will make your name great, and you will be a blessing." In the book of Exodus, community was again stressed in the liberation of the Israelites from Egypt: "I will take you as my people, and I will be your God" (Exod 6:7). "The legislation that fills the pages of Exodus, Leviticus and Deuteronomy illustrates this mix of the practical necessities of community formation and people trying to give their religio-moral convictions a communal expression."[11]

---

[9] Arthur H. Jentz, Jr., "Some Thoughts on Christian Ethics", *Reformed Journal*, 30 (1976): 55.

[10] R. K. McClough, "Community Ethics", in *New Dictionary of Christian Ethics and Pastoral Theology* (Downers Grove: InterVarsity Press, 1995), 111.

[11] Bruce C. Birch and Larry L. Rasmussen, *Bible Ethics in the Christian Life* (Minneapolis: Augsburg, 1989), 29.

The theological concept of a redeemed community is developed in the New Testament. God worked through Jesus Christ to create for himself a community called the "body of Christ" (1 Cor 12:27), a "city set on a hill" (Matt 5:14), the "temple of the Holy Spirit" (1 Cor 6:19). The classic text is Matthew 16:18 where Jesus says, "I will build my church." Beginning with a group of disciples, this redeemed community has blossomed over the ages despite its human failure to always mirror the life of Jesus Christ. Hayes notes, "The community, in its corporate life, is called to embody an alternative order that stands as a sign of God's redemptive purposes in the world."[12] This community has become one that is no "longer divided by former distinctions of ethnicity, social status or gender (Gal 3:28)".[13]

The African church should seek to develop and enhance this community in accordance with the biblical guidelines set out in chapter 8.

5. An eternal perspective is the hope of theology

Christian theology is concerned not just with the present but also with the future. Though Christ's salvation is complete, evil still afflicts creation. The only hope that sin will be finally and eternally removed lies in the Bible's teaching concerning the end times, the consummation of all things, when Christ will set up his kingdom from which evil will be removed, and there will be peace and righteousness. Jesus proclaimed this kingdom throughout his earthly life.

This view of the future has implications for our present life. The Apostle Peter wrote, "Since everything will be destroyed in this way, what kind of people ought you to be? You ought to live holy and godly lives as you look forward to the day of God and speed its coming. That day will bring about the destruction of the heavens by fire, and the elements will melt in the heat" (2 Pet 3:11–12). The Apostle John similarly states, "All who have this hope in him [Christ] purify themselves" (1 John 3:3). An eternal perspective means that believers should not be materialistic: "Since, then, you have been raised with Christ, set your hearts on things

---

[12] Richard B. Hayes, *The Moral Vision of the New Testament: Community, Cross, New Creation; A Contemporary Introduction to New Testament Ethics* (San Francisco: HarperCollins, 1996), 196. Hayes also observes, "The church is a countercultural community of discipleship, and this community is the primary addressee of God's imperatives. Thus, the primary sphere of moral concern is not the character of the individual but the corporate obedience of the church" (196).

[13] Ibid., 32.

above, where Christ is, seated at the right hand of God" (Col 3:1). Christians are urged not to focus on physical things because "everything in the world – the lust of the flesh, the lust of the eyes, and the pride of life – comes not from the Father but from the world" (1 John 2:16).

Believers should focus on eternal things not only because worldly pleasures are transient but also because all actions will be judged: "For we must all appear before the judgement seat of Christ, so that each of us may receive what is due us for the things done while in the body, whether good or bad" (2 Cor 5:10).

In Conclusion

African Christian theology is both a scholarly discipline and a deeply spiritual endeavour. As a scholarly discipline, it pursues its task with the best academic tools to achieve its goals. As a spiritual endeavour, it involves personal commitment, devotion and character formation. Ultimately, all theological assertions must yield to Scripture, the inspired and infallible word of God.

Though the word of God is forever settled in heaven (Ps 119:89), theology never claims finality. Every age and context will always have to study the word of God afresh and submit itself in total obedience to the eternal truths.

Questions

1. What is your understanding of the meaning and purpose of theology?
2. How does theology affect the Christian life?
3. What is the role of Scripture in theology?
4. What is the role of human experience in theology?
5. Discuss the meaning and significance of tradition in theology.
6. Edward Farley defines theology as "a term for an actual, individual cognition of God and things related to God, a cognition which in most treatments attends faith and has eternal happiness as its final

goal."[14] Discuss this definition and what it means for a study of African Christian theology.

7. Summarize in your own words the foundations of African Christian theology.

Further Reading

Millard J. Erickson. *Introducing Christian Doctrine*. 2nd ed. Grand Rapids: Baker, 2001.

Edward Farley. *Theologia: The Fragmentation and Unity of Theological Education*. Philadelphia: Fortress, 1942. (Reprint: Eugene; Wipf & Stock, 2001).

Norman Geisler and Paul Feinberg. *Introduction to Philosophy: A Christian Perspective*. 2nd ed. Grand Rapids: Baker, 1987.

Trevor Hart. *Faith Thinking: The Dynamics of Christian Theology*. Downer's Grove: InterVarsity Press, 1995.

John S. Mbiti. *African Religions and Philosophy*. Oxford: Heinemann, 1969.

Bernard Ramm. *Protestant Biblical Interpretation: A Textbook of Hermeneutics*. 3rd ed. Grand Rapids: Baker, 1980.

David Tracy. *The Analogical Imagination: Christian Theology and the Culture of Pluralism*. New York: Crossroad, 1981.

---

[14] Edward Farley, *Theologia: The Fragmentation and Unity of Theological Education* (Philadelphia: Fortress, 1942), 31.

2
REVELATION

Christians believe that God has taken the initiative to reveal himself to humanity, and that without this self-disclosure, no one would be able to know anything at all about God. We also believe that God has revealed himself in two different ways, namely *general revelation* and *special revelation*.

Over the last century, there has been extensive debate about the similarities and differences between the Christian understanding of revelation and the nature of God as set out in the Bible and the understanding of God and revelation in African Traditional Religion. One reason this has attracted so much attention is that the question of who God is and how he reveals himself to human beings is central to nearly all religions. Nigel Cameron goes so far as to say, "The central question of religion is that of revelation."[1] It is thus critical that when we discuss revelation we also understand it from an African perspective.

Traditional African peoples believe that God, the gods and ancestral spirits unveil themselves and what they want human beings to do through dreams, appearances and visions. Though such an unveiling can be given to anyone, it is more commonly given to elderly men and women, diviners, soothsayers and native doctors. Dreams, visions and revelations are never taken for granted. They are understood to mean that the gods want to send a special message that needs to be heeded. A diviner can interpret the messages.

When Africans convert to the Christian faith, this deep belief in traditional means of revelation is not discarded. Dreams and visions are still believed to be God's way of providing guidance and direction in matters of life and even death. Revelation is thus an important issue for us to grapple with. Just how important is illustrated by an incident in

---

[1] Nigel M. de S. Cameron, "The Idea of Revelation", in *Theological Dictionary of the Bible* (ed. Walter A. Elwell; Grand Rapids: Baker, 1996), 676.

Northern Nigeria in the 1930s. At that time, Islam was making inroads among the Maguzawa people, who worshipped idols and followed the Bori cult that celebrated spirit possession. A spirit could be summoned by clapping hands or beating a drum. The possessed person would then go into a trance and foretell the future or be able to heal some disease. When Muslim preachers came to the town of Malumfashi in 1935 to convert the people to Islam, a Bori practitioner known as Baba Hassim went into a trance and warned his family not to accept Islam but to wait for the religion that would be brought by a white man. Some two years later, a missionary team led by the Rev. and Mrs A. V. Ireland and the Rev. and Mrs H. K. Germaine brought the gospel to the town. The people accepted it, and are still Christians today. Clearly, this was a form of divine revelation before the coming of Christianity. In other words, it is an example of what theologians refer to as general revelation (in contrast to the special revelation contained in the Scriptures).

General Revelation

God has made himself known to all people at all times and in all places through nature, conscience (the ability to know good and evil) and history. Though this revelation is not as specific as special revelation, it is nevertheless divine.

Modes of general revelation

Nature

Genesis 1:1 states that "In the beginning God created the heavens and the earth". It therefore makes sense that his stamp should be on his product. Many passages in the Bible attest to this fact.

Job 36:24 – 37:24 contains Elihu's vivid depiction of natural phenomena, including

> rain that waters the earth, the thunder and the lightning that
> strikes terror in the heart, the fury of a thunderstorm, and the
> brilliant shining of the sun following the storm's departure. The
> text suggests that these natural phenomena attest the power,
> majesty, goodness, and severity of the creator God and that the
> data are there for all to behold (Job 36:25). Moreover, God's

address to Job (esp. Job 38:1–39:30) conveys the idea that natural phenomena (lightning, thunder, rain, snow), the daily rising of the sun, the majestic constellations in the heavens, and the complexity and harmonious interrelationships among the animal kingdom all attest the existence and glory of God.[2]

Psalm 19:1–5 depicts the glory of nature that testifies to divine glory. All creation bears the signature or rubber stamp of God and should lead us to praise and glorify him. As James M. Boice states, "There is enough evidence of God in a flower to lead a child as well as a scientist to worship him. There is sufficient evidence in a tree, a pebble, a grain of sand, a fingerprint, to make us glorify God and thank him."[3]

Paul Tillich comments that the traditional belief has been that "these voices of the universe are not heard by human ears; they do not speak in human language. But they exist, and we can perceive them through the organs of our spirit."[4] But, he adds, that is not the only way nature speaks to us. It also speaks "through every scientific book, through every laboratory, through every machine. ... The technical use of nature is the revelation of its mystery. The voice of nature *has* been heard by the scientific mind and its answer is the conquest of nature."[5]

But what does the psalmist mean when he says that "They have no speech, they use no words; no sound is heard from them. Yet their voice goes out into all the earth" (Ps 19:3–4)? Does he mean that no one is able to fully understand this glory of God in nature, or that no ethnic group or nation is excluded from understanding this glory portrayed in nature? The meaning seems to be somewhere in between. Everyone, from every part of the universe, regardless of their language, education and background, is surrounded by nature in such a manner as to be able to appreciate the glory of God. But not everyone actually appreciates this glory of God in nature. It is particularly evident to those who are believers.

---

[2] B. A. Demarest, "Revelation, General", in *Evangelical Dictionary of Theology* (Grand Rapids: Baker, 1984), 944–45.

[3] James M. Boice, *Foundations of the Christian Faith: A Comprehensive and Readable Theology* (2nd ed.; Downers Grove: InterVarsity Press, 1986), 31.

[4] Paul Tillich, *The Shaking of the Foundations* (New York: Charles Scribner's Sons, 1948), 78.

[5] Ibid., 79.

Acts 14:15–17 contains some of what Paul preached to Gentiles in Lystra. He told them that rain, fruitful seasons and joy are all pointers to the God who has graciously given these things. In response, the people of Lystra needed to turn to "the living God who made heaven and earth".

Further evidence of God's revelation of himself in nature can be found in Psalms 8, 104 and 147, as well as in Job 38 and Matthew 5:48.

The human conscience

Romans 2:14–15 deals with the internal evidence of general revelation, which is the moral law or conscience embedded in all men and women. Regardless of where they live and who they are, all have a rudimentary concept of right and wrong that can be said to be "bearing witness". This is a reflection of God's nature and should direct people to their creator. But the Jews broke the Ten Commandments that were written on stone, and the Gentiles broke the moral law God had written in their hearts (see Rom 1:32). All of humanity rejects the revelation embedded in our consciences. All will be called to account for what they have or have not done.

History

God's revelation of himself through history can be inferred from several passages in Scripture. In fact, Ernest G. Wright, Old Testament scholar and archaeologist, argues that God's revelation is to be understood primarily through his mighty acts in history, including his sending of Christ to be "a light for revelation to the Gentiles" (Luke 2:32). We see evidence of this in passages like Daniel 2:21, which states that God "changes times and seasons; he deposes kings and raises up others. He gives wisdom to the wise and knowledge to the discerning." There is also evidence in Acts 14:16–17, which says that "in the past, he let all nations go their own way. Yet he has not left himself without testimony". There are no people without this divine witness (see also Acts 17:24–29).

Response to general revelation

Two passages throw light on the human response to general revelation.

Acts 17:22–31 contains Paul's address to a group of Athenian philosophers. He began by referring to the "Unknown God" whom the people worshipped. This, he claimed, was the very God he was preaching. Then he pointed out that an Athenian poet had correctly understood something about this God, purely on the basis of general revelation (17:28). This text suggests that humankind can to some extent understand what God has done through nature, history and the conscience. Because men and women are made in the image of God, they can use their God-given reason to reflect on God and his creation. But this does not mean that all individuals necessarily do so. According to Paul Helm, "At best Paul is saying that all men *ought* to recognize that God testifies to himself through nature and human affairs, and this is obviously inconsistent with the view that God so reveals himself in nature that all men know that he exists on the basis of that revelation alone."[6] What they can understand if they do think about God is that he is a) the creator and ruler of the universe (17:24), b) self-sufficient (17:25a), c) the source of life and all good (17:25b), d) present in the world (17:27), and e) the source and ground of human existence (17:28).[7]

Romans 1:18–21 is a passage in which Paul addresses the issue of how human beings have responded to the revelation that God has provided. They have deliberately rejected, distorted and misconstrued it. They actively suppressed the awareness of truth they did have by rejecting conscience as a guide to God. They should also have been able to see that history shows marks of divine actions and control. But they denied this. This rejection of the knowledge of God attracts his wrath.

To sum up: The Bible teaches that God has given the world a true revelation of himself through nature, history and our consciences. Thus we can agree with the great sixteenth-century theologian John Calvin, "There is within the human mind, and indeed by natural instinct, an awareness of divinity."[8] This universal awareness of God is also sometimes referred to as a "sense of divinity" and a "seed of religion".

General revelation and salvation

An important question that arises as soon as we speak of general revelation is whether such revelation is able to lead to a saving knowledge of God.

---

[6] Paul Helm. *The Divine Revelation* (Westchester: Crossway, 1982), 13.

[7] Demarest, "Revelation, General", 945.

[8] John Calvin, *Institutes of the Christian Religion, 3, Book 1* (ed. John T. McNeill; trans. and indexed by Ford Lewis Battles; Philadelphia: Westminster Press, 1960), 43.

Evangelical scholars tend to say that it does not. Based on the doctrine of total depravity (which holds that our body, mind and spirit are all corrupted by sin), they argue that we are unable to interpret or respond to the revelation of God properly.

But does this mean that we are not responsible for our failure to respond? No, for as Calvin says, "although we lack the natural ability to mount up unto the pure and clear knowledge of God, all excuse is cut off because the fault of dullness is within us. And, indeed, we are not allowed thus to pretend ignorance without our conscience itself always convicting us of both baseness and ingratitude."[9] Millard Erickson makes the same point: "Thus it is apparent that in failing to respond to the light of general revelation which they have, men are fully responsible, for they have truly known God, but have wilfully suppressed that truth. Thus in effect, the general revelation serves, as does the law, merely to make guilty, not to make righteous."[10]

Other scholars, such as Karl Rahner, Hans Urs von Balthasar, Joseph Di Noia and Gavin D'Costa, as well as evangelical scholars such as Clark Pinnock and Gerald McDermott, are more optimistic about the extent to which we can know God through natural revelation. In his book *A Wideness in God's Mercy*, Pinnock calls for "a greater appreciation of how wide God's mercy is and how far-reaching God's salvific purposes are. An optimism of salvation is replacing the older pessimism."[11]

The Second Vatican Council (Vatican II; 1962–1965) took an equally optimistic view of the general revelation of God. One of the Vatican II documents states, "Those also can attain to everlasting salvation who through no fault of their own do not know the Gospel of Christ or His Church, yet sincerely seek God, and moved by grace, strive by their deeds to do His will as it is known to them through the dictates of conscience."[12] Following in the footsteps of thirteenth-century theologian Thomas Aquinas, Roman Catholic theologians argue that it is possible to construct a natural theology based solely on general revelation.

---

[9] Ibid., 68–69.

[10] Millard J. Erickson, *Introducing Christian Doctrine* (Grand Rapids: Baker, 1992), 173.

[11] Clark H. Pinnock, *A Wideness in God's Mercy: The Finality of Jesus Christ in a World of Religions* (Grand Rapids: Zondervan, 1992), 12. He also asserts, "I oppose the fewness doctrine which accepts that only a small number will be saved, and I maintain that God's universal salvific will enables Christians to have deep hopefulness for the nations" (13).

[12] *Lumen Gentium* (1964), 16.

Whichever position we take on this, we need to recognize that what we know of humanity indicates that people do not respond positively to general revelation. We can argue about whether they could or should do so, but the fact is that they do not. More than that, they actively suppress and reject the knowledge they could have (Rom 1:21). But this wilful suppression does not eradicate their knowledge of God:

> Human beings cannot entirely suppress their sense of God and his present and future judgment; God will not let them do that. Some sense of right and wrong, as well as of being accountable to a holy divine Judge, always remains. In our fallen world all whose minds are not in some way impaired have a conscience that at some points directs them and from time to time condemns them, telling them that they ought to suffer for wrongs they have done (Rom 2:14ff); and when conscience speaks in these terms it is in truth the voice of God.
>
> Fallen humankind is in one sense ignorant of God, since what people like to believe, and do in fact believe, about the objects of their worship falsifies and distorts the revelation of God they cannot escape. In another sense, however, all human beings remain aware of God, guiltily, with uncomfortable inklings of coming judgement that they wish they did not have. Only the gospel of Christ can speak peace to this distressful aspect of the human condition.[13]

General revelation and African Traditional Religion

Africans have not been excluded from the general revelation that was made available to all. They have enough revelation to be able to glorify God. We can catch glimpses of this in African Traditional Religion. Not only did Africans recognize the existence of a Supreme Being, they also demonstrated some aspects of the goodness that comes from God. All African societies valued kindness, honesty and love, and prohibited murder, rape, lying, cheating and adultery.

Some African theologians have suggested that this African knowledge of God is equivalent to the particular revelation given to Israel and in the Bible. John Mbiti, for example, states,

---

[13] J. I. Packer, *Concise Theology* (Wheaton: Tyndale House, 1993), 12.

Since the Bible tells me that God is the Creator of all things, his activities in the world must clearly go beyond what is recorded in the Bible. He must have been active among African peoples as he was among the Jewish people. Did he then reveal himself *only* in the line of Abraham, Isaac, Jacob, Moses, Samuel and other personalities of the Bible? Didn't our Lord let it be clearly known that "before Abraham was, I am!" (John 8:58)? Then was he not there in other times and in such places as Mount Fuji and Mount Kenya, as well as Mount Sinai? The decision word here is "only". The more I peeped into African religious insights about God, the more I felt utterly unable to use the word "only" in this case. In its place there merged the word "also". This was an extremely liberating word in my theological thinking.[14]

Similarly, Samuel G. Kibicho asked, "Is there not possibly a full salvatory knowledge of the One True God in the Gikuyu concept of God in both its pre- and post-Christian periods?"[15] His conclusions are even more radical than those of Mbiti, for he argues for "the possibility of the full and salvatory revelation or knowledge of God outside, and independently of, the historical Christian revelation".[16]

Mbiti is correct when he says that the God of the African is the same God who revealed himself to Israel. But he exaggerates when he claims that this *general* revelation in which Africans shared is the same as the *special* revelation given to Israel. Kibicho's position is equally questionable and shows the consequences of overreacting. Because he links colonial enslavement with Western missionaries, he rejects the missionaries' views on revelation. Yet the mere fact that missionaries' interpretations were sometimes wrong does not mean that their view of biblical revelation was automatically wrong. The question is, what does the Bible say about humanity's relationship to God? African theologians

---

[14] John Mbiti rejects the distinction between general and special revelation, claiming that "it is not a biblical distinction". ("The Encounter of Christian Faith and African Religion", *Christian Century* [August 27–September 3, 1980]: 817–820. Also available at www.religion.online.org.)

[15] Samuel G. Kibicho, *God and Revelation in an African Context* (Nairobi: Acton, 2006), 169.

[16] Ibid., 171. He says that the "Spirit of the One God, who was in Jesus of Nazareth and through whom alone God brings men and women everywhere to saving knowledge of, or faith in, himself, seems to have been no less fully present and accessible in the Kikuyu community of faith, independently of the Christian revelation in both the pre- and post-Christian periods of Kikuyu history" (171–172).

and laypersons must study the Scriptures for themselves and draw their own conclusions. This is something that Kibicho does not do. His main concern is to prove Western missionaries wrong.

So what can we say about African Traditional Religion? First, we need to agree with Mbiti that African names for God like Modimo and Olodumare were full of meaning and referred to the Creator God who revealed himself to our ancestors. But what was known about this God was less than his full revelation of himself in Scripture. Secondly, we can also agree with Mbiti that "God's revelation is not confined to the biblical record".[17] As Christians, we would argue that God's revelation is fully and completely revealed in Jesus. But what we know of Jesus is recorded in the Bible. Thirdly, we can agree with Mbiti that God's general revelation of himself prepared the way for and "undergirded the spreading of the gospel like wildfire among African societies which had hitherto followed and practised traditional religion ... there is a Christian Yes to African religiosity".[18] But while we can agree that the religious background of Africans makes them willing to accept Christianity, this is not at all the same thing as claiming that African Religion is the same as the faith prescribed in the Scriptures. That simply is not the case.

The Scriptures make it abundantly clear that all religions without Jesus as the only way end up in unrighteousness and suppression of the truth. Thus African Traditional Religion cannot be said to be on a par with the particular religion of Israel, which was revealed by God through his own inspired prophets.

The fact that there are aspects of African Traditional Religion that are right and others that are wrong fits with what we know of general revelation. It offers a "shadowy and outline form"[19] of the truth about God. But even when it is right, it is not enough for salvation. After all, Scripture makes it clear that "all our righteous acts are like filthy rags" (Isa 64:6). Africans fall short of God's standards because they, too, do not recognize and worship God as he requires. Thus the universal judgement that Paul refers to in Romans also applies to Africans. They, too, stand condemned and in dire need of the salvation that is provided in Christ Jesus through the shedding of his blood.

---

[17] Mbiti, "Encounter of Christian Faith and African Religion", 3.
[18] Ibid., 4.
[19] Cameron, "The Idea of Revelation", 680.

General revelation and our ancestors

If the general revelation that was given to Africans could not save them, what is the fate of those Africans who never had an opportunity to respond to the gospel? Are they lost eternally? This question applies equally to all others who have no opportunity to respond to the gospel before facing the judgement of God.

In answering this question, there are a number of points that need to be stated clearly to avoid confusion. First, God is righteous and fair. Nobody will receive an unfair judgement from God. Fallible human beings do make errors of judgement, but God is infallible and righteous.

Secondly, every human being is guilty of sin and deserves eternal condemnation (Rom 3:10; 6:23). No human being can stand before God and say that he or she is innocent.

Thirdly, everybody will be judged based on the revelation that he or she received. Even those who never heard the gospel proclaimed had an awareness of God and what he required. Everyone received enough revelation to warrant a response to it. This is true of those who lived in Africa, and also of those who lived in Old Testament times and did not know about Jesus Christ but had access to God's revelation through the prophets (Isa 1:1; Jer 1:2; Hos 1:1; Heb 1:1).

Fourthly, and finally, only God knows the ultimate destiny of every created being. God has intimate knowledge of all that he has created and will make judgements based on that knowledge which finite and fallible humans do not have. Consequently we cannot rule out the possibility that some who have never heard the gospel may be saved.

Special Revelation

Special revelation refers not to God's revealing of himself in nature but to his unique and personal unveiling of himself through words, acts and events, and ultimately through his personal incarnation in Jesus Christ. This revelation is faithfully and accurately recorded in the Scriptures – the sixty-six books of the Bible.

> The special revelation in sacred history is crowned by the incarnation of the living Word and the inscripturation of the spoken word. The gospel of redemption is therefore not merely a series of abstract theses, unrelated to specific historical

events; it is the dramatic news that God has acted in saving history, climaxed by the incarnate person and work of Christ (Heb 1:2), for the salvation of lost humankind.[20]

Old Testament concept of revelation

The Hebrew word for *revelation* means "unveiling" and refers to God's allowing people to see more of his character and work. The writer to the Hebrews speaks of God's revelation when he says that God "spoke to our ancestors through the prophets at many times and in various ways" (Heb 1:1). The "various ways" mentioned in the Scripture include *mighty acts* such as creation, the flood, the parting of the Red Sea, and the giving of law at Sinai. God also had *direct communication* with people such as Adam and Eve, Noah (Gen 6:13; 7:1), Abraham (Gen 12:7; 18:1–2), Moses (Exod 33:11; Num 12:6–8), Samuel (1 Sam 3:10–14) and David. He revealed himself in *dreams and visions* to people like Jacob (Gen 28:11–16), Joseph (37:5–7) and Solomon (1 Kgs 3:5) as well to his prophets who repeatedly proclaimed, "This is what the LORD says" (Isa 29:22; Jer 2:2; Ezek 3:1). He sent his *angels* to men like Gideon (Judg 6:11–14) and Daniel (Dan 9:20–21; 10:10). He wrote his commandments on tablets of stone (Exod 24:12) and made use of a donkey (Num 22:22–31), birds (e.g. the raven and dove in the flood – Gen 8:6–9) and even of Satan.[21]

In the context of Hebrews 1:1, the writer is referring to the ancestors of the Jews, but we can extend these words to apply to all our human ancestors who experienced divine revelation before the incarnation of the Son of God. After all, God did reveal himself to people outside the nation of Israel (Gen 41:1–7; 2 Sam 24:11; 1 Chr 9:22; 2 Chr 16:7; 29:30; Dan 2:3, 31–35; Amos 1:1). The point that the writer of Hebrews is making is that God revealed himself to humanity before the coming of Christ.

---

[20] Carl F. H. Henry, "Revelation, Special", in *Evangelical Dictionary of Theology* (ed. Walter A. Elwell; Grand Rapids: Baker, 1984), 946.

[21] For a thorough study of revelation in Scripture, see B. B. Warfield, *Biblical Foundations* (London: Tyndale Press, 1958), 11–42 as well as the articles in G. Kittle and G. Friedrich, eds., *Theological Dictionary of the New Testament* (10 vols.; Grand Rapids: Eerdmans, 1964–76). See also Charles R. Swindoll and Roy B. Zuck, eds., *Understanding Christian Theology* (Nashville: Thomas Nelson, 2003).

New Testament concept of revelation

The ultimate revelation of God is, of course, the Lord Jesus Christ (Col 2:3, 9; John 5:39). The writer of Hebrews underscores this in Hebrews 1:2, where he says, "but in these last days he has spoken to us by his Son, whom he appointed heir of all things, and through whom also he made the universe". John 1:18 also speaks of the personal unveiling or incarnation of God through the Son: "No one has ever seen God, but the one and only Son, who is himself God and is in closest relationship with the Father, has made him known."

Revelation and the Canon of Scripture

Though revelation precedes Scripture and is not quite the same as Scripture, the two are intimately connected. Without revelation, there would be no Scripture. Scripture is the record of God's special revelation.

We are told how Scripture came to be written in 2 Peter 1:20–21: "No prophecy of Scripture came about by the prophet's own interpretation of things. For prophecy never had its origin in the human will, but prophets, though human, spoke from God as they were carried along by the Holy Spirit." Prophets spoke or wrote God's word because they had the divine push to do so. Paul can thus describe Scripture as God-breathed (2 Tim 3:16). Its source is God.

We are also told the purpose of Scripture: "All Scripture ... is useful for teaching, rebuking, correcting and training in righteousness, so that the servant of God may be thoroughly equipped for every good work" (2 Tim 3:16–17). The Scriptures properly interpreted are the ultimate authority and standard for the Christian life and for theology.

The sixty-six books included in our Bibles constitute what is called the "canon of Scripture". (Roman Catholics also include the books of the Apocrypha in the canon – see below.) The word "canon" comes from a Greek word that means "a rod", and "especially a straight rod used as a rule".[22] Thus the "canon of Scripture" is the lists of books considered to be inspired by God and accepted as such by the church. They are the "measuring rod" for Christian teaching.

In AD 397 a church council known as the Council of Carthage produced the official list of books that the church accepted as inspired

---

[22] F. F. Bruce, *The Canon of Scripture* (Downers Grove: Inter Varsity Press, 1988), 17.

and belonging to the collection called the Holy Scriptures.[23] Those who drew up this list were guided by the very specific principles set out below. However, it is important to stress that even before this council agreed on the list of books that constituted the canon, God had already established the status of these books, which were widely recognized as inspired.

The Old Testament canon

At the Council of Jamnia in AD 90, Jewish rabbis ratified an official list of thirty-nine books that constituted the Hebrew Bible. These books had long been divided into the following three groups:

- *The Law*, also known as the Torah or Pentateuch, consists of the five books associated with Moses (Genesis, Exodus, Leviticus, Numbers and Deuteronomy).

- *The Prophets* are composed of the Former Prophets (Joshua, Judges, Samuel and Kings) and the Latter Prophets (Isaiah, Jeremiah, Ezekiel and the Twelve – Hosea, Joel, Amos, Obadiah, Jonah, Micah, Nahum, Habakkuk, Zephaniah, Haggai, Zechariah and Malachi). Christians often categorize these books as the Histories, Major Prophets and Minor Prophets.

- *The Writings* are made up of Psalms, Proverbs, Job, Song of Solomon, Ecclesiastes, Ruth, Lamentations, Esther, Daniel, Ezra-Nehemiah and Chronicles.

The Law (Torah) was considered the final rule of faith and practice for the Israelites, God's people (Deut 31:24–26; Josh 1:7–8). The writings of the prophets were also regarded as authoritative (Isa 8:16; Jer 36) and the Psalms and other books constituting the Writings were quoted as divine revelation (e.g. 2 Sam 7:14 and 1 Chr 17:13 quote Ps 2:7). This belief was upheld by New Testament writers who quoted from the books of the Law (e.g. Rom 4:3 and Gal 3:6 quote Gen 15:6), the Prophets (e.g. Rev 7:17 quotes Isa 25:8) and the Writings (e.g. Rom 4:6–7 quotes Ps 32:1–2; Heb 1:5 quotes Ps 2:7).

---

[23] For a detailed discussion of canonicity, see Henry C. Thiessen, *Lectures in Systematic Theology* (rev. Vernon D. Doerksen; Grand Rapids: Eerdmans, 1979), 50–61; and Wayne Grudem, *Systematic Theology* (Grand Rapids: Zondervan, 1994), 54–72.

When determining which books the church should recognize as constituting the Old Testament, the Council of Carthage was guided by the following principles:

1. *Was the book written by a prophet?* Many of the books of the Old Testament claim prophetic origin (Hag 1:3; Zech 1:1, 4; 7:12). The requirement for prophetic authorship was bolstered by appealing to Hebrews 1:1: "In the past God spoke to our ancestors through the prophets at many times and in various ways." It was also noted that Peter writes of the "prophetic message" (2 Pet 1:19) and says that men "spoke from God as they were carried along by the Holy Spirit" (2 Pet 1:20–21).

2. *Was the book written during the prophetic period?* In other words, was it produced between the time of Moses and Artaxerxes?

3. *Did people recognize the book as inspired?* Though the primary test of the canonicity of the Old Testament books was their inspiration by God, it was expected that the people of God would have recognized these books as inspired and accepted them as such. Such a requirement is legitimate, for the Old Testament gives a test for distinguishing a true prophet from a false one (Deut 18:21–22) and Jesus called on people to judge whether he was from God (John 7:17).

4. *What was the testimony of Christ?* Jesus endorsed the divine authority of the Old Testament (Matt 23:35; Luke 24:44; John 10:35) and drew on it in his teaching ministry (Matt 21:42; 26:54; John 5:39).

5. *Was it inspired?* The most critical test of canonicity was whether there was evidence that the book was God-breathed. Did it have the characteristics of divine inspiration described in 2 Timothy 3:16–17 and 2 Peter 1:20–21?

After examining all the books carefully, the Council of Carthage accepted the same thirty-nine books as the Jewish Council of Jamnia.

The New Testament canon

The New Testament canon is made of twenty-seven books, divided into the Gospels, the Letters (or Epistles), and the book of Revelation. The very specific criteria for accepting a book as part of the New Testament Holy Scriptures are listed below:[24]

---

[24] Thiessen, *Lectures in Systematic Theology*, 60.

1. *Was it written by an apostle or someone close to Jesus?* Books written by John, Matthew, Luke, Mark, Peter, James, Jude and Paul all passed this important test of apostolic authority. Books that claimed to be part of the Holy Scriptures but were written by unknown writers were not accepted. These included the so-called *Gospel of Peter*, the *Acts of Peter* and the *Acts of Paul*.

2. *Was it consistent with the apostolic teaching?* For example, the book called Tobit, which is in the Apocrypha, states that "Almsgiving saves from death and purges away every sin" (Tob 12:9). This is clearly inconsistent with the biblical teaching that one is not saved by works but only by grace through faith in Jesus Christ (Eph 2:8–9).

3. *Was it universally accepted throughout the Christian community?* For a book to be accepted, it had to receive the approval of the universal church. Books that were accepted by only a few local churches were rejected.

4. *Did the contents of the book have a spiritual nature?* The book should not merely be historical but should also reveal a spirituality consistent with the apostolic faith.

5. *Did the book have evidence of inspiration by the Holy Spirit?* There had to be internal evidence that the book was the product of the Holy Spirit, and not merely a human product.

Apocrypha and pseudepigrapha

The pseudepigrapha (a word that means "spurious writings") were generally written between 200 BC and AD 200 by authors writing under assumed names like Adam, Enoch, Moses or Ezra. The contents of these books are mainly fanciful and heretical, and so the Christian community does not regard them as canonical.[25]

The status of the books collectively known as the *Apocrypha* is disputed. The Roman Catholic Church accepted these books as canonical at the Council of Trent in 1548. Protestants, however, consider them to be non-canonical because their contents are sometimes factually wrong and because they teach heresies such as saying prayers for the dead to

---

[25] Robert Saucy, *Scripture: Its Power, Authority, and Relevance* (Nashville Thomas Nelson, 2001), 221.

help them escape purgatory (2 Macc 12:41–45), justify cruelty to slaves (Sir 33:25–27) and reveal contempt for women (Sir 22:3).[26]

Progressive revelation

God did not disclose all of his special revelation of himself at one time. Instead he did so gradually, beginning with the Old Testament and ending with his ultimate revelation in Jesus Christ and the completion of the New Testament canon. The Scriptures thus begin with Genesis and conclude with Revelation. Comprised of sixty-six books, the Scriptures are complete and contain all that God wants to reveal about himself to humanity.

Revelation and illumination

The fact that God's revelation of himself in inspired Scripture is complete does not rule out the work of the Holy Spirit in which he continues to illuminate the minds of believers, giving them new insights into the word and mind of God as they study the word of God and pray to him. "The same Spirit who inspired the prophets has been promised to *illuminate* the minds of those who seek to understand the meaning of divine revelation (John 14:26; 1 Cor 2:10–14)."[27]

Moreover, although the inspiration of Scriptures has come to an end, God's work in nature, history and the hearts of men and women continues. He uses dreams, visions, inner workings and direct messages to both unbelievers and believers for his glory and his purposes.

Illumination is thus God's continued guidance and direction to his children through the ministry of the Holy Spirit. Passages which speak about such guidance include Luke 4:1; Acts 8:29; 10:19–20; 11:12; 13:2; Romans 8:4, 14 and Galatians 5:16, 18.

But illumination is not the same as the original revelation given by God that resulted in the writing of the Holy Scriptures. This is an important point for African Christians to note, for one often hears of Christians and ministers receiving some "special revelation" from God. Phrases such as "the message of the Lord", "words of knowledge" and

---

[26] Saucy, *Scripture*, 222–226.

[27] Richard M. Davidson, "The Bible: Revelation and Authority" (paper presented at the Symposium on the Bible and Adventist Scholarship, Juan Dolio, Dominican Republic March 19–26, 2000), 19. Available online at www.aiias.edu/ict/vol_26B/26Bcc_017-055.pdf

"the word of the Lord" are bandied about, along with a great emphasis on what God is doing or revealing to the church through his chosen vessels. But it is critical that we distinguish between illumination and revelation. All "illumination" must be scrutinized and subjected to the authority of the Scriptures. If we do not do this, we may be deceived by false "revelations" or "messages from God".

The Inspiration of Scripture

Scripture is inspired in the sense that God breathed his word to the writers of Scripture. The initiator of Scripture was God, and he ensured that his word was properly and truthfully recorded. There are, however, different understandings of the exact nature of this inspiration.

The *mechanical dictation theory* holds that the writers of Scripture were passive while the word of God was communicated through them. However, this seems to be unlikely, for while God speaks through the writers of Scripture, we also see evidence of each writer's own style, imagination and personality. The writers were thus more than mere puppets, manipulated by God.

The *intuition theory* holds that certain human beings have great insight, and that inspiration represents "the intensifying and elevating of the religious perceptions of the writers".[28] But this type of inspiration is what produces devotional books and hymns. It has more to do with the illumination of the Holy Spirit, in which he helps people to understand the truth of Scripture, than with inspiration.

The *dynamic theory* holds that the writers of Scripture were guaranteed to transmit truth in matters of life and faith but not on historical and scientific matters. Closely related to this is the theory that *the ideas of Scripture are inspired, but not the actual words*. This view contradicts 2 Timothy 3:16, which specifically states that "all Scripture", thus including the exact words, is inspired.

Another approach is to say that *the Bible contains the word of God*. In other words, the Bible is not the word of God but *becomes* the word of God when God encounters the reader through it. But the Bible insists that it is inspired (2 Tim 3:16–17; 2 Pet 1:20–21) whether or not people experience that personal encounter with God as they read it. Moreover

---

[28] Thiessen, *Lectures in Systematic Theology*, 63.

this "modern tendency to veer toward a doctrine of revelation whose locus is to be found in an immediate existential response, rather than in an objectively conveyed Scripture, thwarts the theological interest in biblically revealed doctrines and principles from which an explanatory view of the whole of reality and life may be exposited."[29]

Finally, there is the *verbal plenary theory*, which holds that all Scripture, not just part of it, is inspired by God. This includes the whole of the Old Testament, which was the only Scripture known in the days of the New Testament church (see, for example, Luke 24:27, 32, 44–45; Rom 1:2; 3:2; 2 Pet 1:21).

The key Bible passage that provides explicit teaching on the concept of inspiration is, as quoted above, 2 Timothy 3:16: "All Scripture is God-breathed." Thus the *words* of Scripture are inspired; God directed the human authors to communicate what he intended. There cannot be communication without words, so the words must have been inspired, not just the ideas. The fact that God breathed his word through human beings indicates that there is also a human aspect to the Scriptures. In speaking his word to human writers, God used human language (Hebrew, Greek and Aramaic), personality and style.

Peter writes, "For prophecy never had its origin in the human will, but prophets, though human, spoke from God as they were carried along by the Holy Spirit" (2 Pet 1:21), making it clear that God was the initiator and origin of revelation and that he used human agency in bringing about his word. The authors of the sixty-six books of the Bible were not angelic or mystical beings, but real people with their own histories, traditions, customs and languages. The writer of Esther, for example, reveals the secular nature of the historical context of the book by not mentioning the name of God in the book. The author of Jonah highlights the reluctance and prejudices of the prophet as he was sent to deliver God's word to the Ninevites.

Likewise, in the New Testament, John's Gospel reveals his personality and world view in a way that distinguishes it from Matthew's. Paul's writings differ from Peter's in terms of style and the issues that interested him. Thus inspiration was a divine–human process. This dual aspect gives us the assurance that Scripture is not only of divine origin but also takes the human condition seriously.

---

[29] Henry, "Revelation, Special", 948.

The Nature of Scripture

The Bible consistently presents itself as truthful, inerrant and infallible.
Truthful. The fundamental meaning of the word translated "truth" in
the Old Testament is firmness and reliability. It also means "conformity
to reality, that is, truth as opposed to what is false".[30]

The Bible attaches great importance to truth. The Israelites were told
how to distinguish true prophecy from false prophecy (Deut 13:1–5).
One of the criteria was whether the prophecy was fulfilled (Deut 18:20–
22). Thus when Elijah brought the son of the widow of Zarephath back
to life, the woman declared, "Now I know that you are a man of God
and that the word of the Lord from your mouth is the truth." The fact
that his words had come to pass was a clear indication that his words
were true.

The truthfulness of Scripture flows from the nature of its author, for
God is described as true, dependable, reliable and faithful. Romans 3:4
states, "Let God be true, and every human being a liar. As it is written:
'So that you may be proved right when you speak and prevail when you
judge'" (see also John 17:3). Jesus too insists, "I am the way and the
truth" (John 14:6).

Bible passages that teach the truthfulness of Scripture include
Matthew 5:17–20 and John 10:35. In Matthew 5:17 Jesus asserts that
every part of Scripture must be fulfilled: "Do not think that I have come
to abolish the Law or the Prophets; I have not come to abolish them
but to fulfil them."

Jesus' words say it all: "your word is truth" (John 17:17). The words
spoken and written in Scripture are true. There is no falsehood or deceit
in its content.

Inerrant. Logically, if the Scriptures are true, they cannot be wrong. If
there are errors in Scripture, the Scriptures cannot be true.

Infallible. "Infallible" means "incapable of error". However, the word
is applied differently by Protestants and Roman Catholics. Among
Roman Catholics, it refers to the teaching that the pope, in his capacity
as head of the church, is infallible when he speaks on matters of faith
and morals. Among Protestants, however, only the Holy Scriptures

---

[30] Swindoll and Zuck, *Understanding Christian Theology*, 81.

are regarded as infallible. The Scriptures cannot mislead in what they assert. For example, when the Bible teaches that Jesus is the only way of salvation, it means that there is truly no other way of salvation apart from Christ. If the Bible were to assert that which was false, it would lead people astray. However, it is completely trustworthy.

The Authority of Scripture

Authority is that which is binding upon a person. In this sense, the Bible, properly interpreted, presents what is binding upon a person as directed by God. It is the final authority for Christian faith and conduct. This point is stressed in Isaiah 8:20, in the context of dealing with mediums and spiritists: "Consult God's instruction and the testimony of warning. If anyone does not speak according to this word, they have no light of dawn." In other words, everything must be judged by the word of God. Paul makes the same point when he states that "all Scripture is God-breathed and is useful for teaching, rebuking, correcting and training in righteousness, so that the servant of God may be thoroughly equipped for every good work" (2 Timothy 3:16–17).

Paul was, of course, speaking of the Hebrew Scriptures, which Jesus and the apostles constantly quoted as having final authority in regard to the issues early believers were struggling with. But the same point applies to the New Testament Scriptures. Even before these books were accepted as part of Scripture there is evidence that they "held a place unparalleled among religious and philosophic movements of the ancient world. Their community authority was 'a unique characteristic of the Jewish ethos'."[31]

The authority of Scripture outweighs that of human philosophy (Col 28:8), human knowledge (1 Tim 6:2), and human tradition (Matt 15:1–9). However, this does not mean that philosophy, knowledge and tradition are always bad. For example, traditions springing from the right interpretation of Scripture can be good. Thus the Creed of Chalcedon (AD 451) holds that Jesus is "very God of very God and very man of very man" and is acceptable because it is consistent with the teaching of Scripture.

---

[31] Bruce C. Birch and Larry L. Rasmussen, *Bible and Ethics in the Christian Life* (Minneapolis: Augsburg, 1988), 25.

The Interpretation of Scripture

If we are to take Scripture as our authority, it is vital that we understand what it means. We thus need to know something about hermeneutics, which is the study of how we interpret meaning, if we are to avoid being misled.

Over the centuries, Christians have adopted several approaches to interpreting Scripture.[32] However, before looking at them in detail, it is important to remind ourselves of an important principle:

> The Bible cannot be studied as any other book, coming merely "from below" with detached, sharpened tools of exegesis and honed principles of interpretation. At every stage of the interpretive process, the book inspired by the Spirit can only be correctly understood "from above" by the illumination and transformation of the Spirit, leading to a personal relationship with the Author of the Word.[33]

1. Allegorical method

The allegorical method is one of the oldest forms of interpretation. The major proponent of this approach was Origen of Alexandria (c. AD 185–254) who taught at the famous Catechetical School of Alexandria in Egypt. As an aside, it is worth noting that this was an important institution in the days of the Roman Empire, and that Christian thinkers such as Clement of Alexandria (c. 150–215), Cyril of Alexandria (c. 376–444) and Augustine of Hippo (354–430) were all African.

Origen was taught the allegorical method by Clement, who was himself deeply influenced by the Jewish scholar Philo, who used the allegorical method to remove things that he considered offensive in the Jewish Scriptures.

The allegorical interpretation teaches that the true meaning of a passage is spiritual rather than literal. It believes that "beneath the letter

---

[32] For more advanced rules of biblical interpretation, see the following works: Robert Traina, *Methodical Bible Study: A New Approach to Hermeneutics* (Grand Rapids: Francis Asbury Press, 1952); Bernard Ramm, *Protestant Biblical Interpretation: A Textbook of Hermeneutics* (Grand Rapids: Baker, 1970); Gordon D. Fee and Douglas Stuart, *How to Read the Bible for All Its Worth: A Guide to Understanding the Bible* (Grand Rapids: Zondervan, 2003); and A. Berkeley Mickelsen, *Interpreting the Bible* (Grand Rapids: Eerdmans, 1963).

[33] Davidson, "The Bible, Revelation and Authority", 15.

(*rhete*) or the obvious (*phanera*) is the real meaning (*hyponoia*) of the passage".[34] This approach is justified by quoting 2 Corinthians 3:6: "The letter kills, but the Spirit gives life" and misinterpreting it to mean that the ordinary meaning of Scripture is not useful or edifying. The spiritual meaning, which is given by the Holy Spirit, is to be preferred.

The problem with this method is that "it obscures the true meaning of the Word of God ... The Bible treated allegorically becomes putty in the hand of the exegete. Different doctrinal systems could emerge within the framework of allegorical hermeneutics and no way would exist to determine which were the true."[35]

An example of allegorical hermeneutics is the interpretation that the forbidden fruit in the garden of Eden was not fruit from a tree but was actually sexual intercourse. This misguided but popular interpretation leads people to believe that God condemns sexual relations in marriage, which contradicts other passages of Scripture (e.g., 1 Cor 7:1–2).

2. Mystical method

Those with a mystical approach to Christianity tend to have little interest in the physical realities of this world and instead focus primarily on direct, personal, intimate communion with God.[36] This is not wrong, for there is an element of mysticism in our faith. Believers do have a direct relationship with God through the indwelling of the Holy Spirit. But there is a problem when God's word is disregarded in the search for personal illumination. Scripture should not be interpreted solely in terms of how it feeds into a focus on private prayer, reflection and an intimate relationship with God. Harold Brown issues the following warning:

> Mysticism tends to do away with the need for intermediaries
> between the believer and God. The church cannot exist at
> all without a measure of mysticism, but as soon as mysticism
> begins to gain ground, it begins to do away with need for
> the church's ministers and their services. In the extreme case,

---

[34] Bernard Ramm, *Protestant Biblical Interpretation: A Textbook of Hermeneutics* (3rd ed. Grand Rapids: Baker 1980), 30.

[35] Ibid.

[36] Harold O. J. Brown, *Heresies: The Image of Christ in the Mirror of Heresy and Orthodoxy from the Apostles to the Present* (Grand Rapids, Baker, 1984), 285. Reissued as *Heresies: Heresy and Orthodoxy in the History of the Church* (Peabody: Hendrickson, 2005).

the mystic may dispense with the Scripture and even with the incarnate Christ himself, and seek to relate directly with an uncreated, absolute godhead.[37]

3. Spirit interpretation

Both the mystical approach and the approach that focuses on Spirit interpretation place far greater emphasis on personal communication with God than on serious study of the word of God. This is the approach of preachers who insist that the Holy Spirit has revealed the meaning of a Bible passage to them so that that they have no need to investigate any further.

The obvious weakness with this method is that it disregards what the Holy Spirit himself has already communicated in Scripture. The Spirit is not opposed to serious study of the Scriptures; he uses such study to bring forth the truth of Scripture. In both the Old and the New Testament we read of men and women who studied the Scriptures to understand what God was saying to them, and of God instructing his people to carefully study and interpret the Scriptures (see, for example, Josh 1:7–9; Ezra 7:10; Acts 17:11–12; Titus 2:1; 2 Tim 2:15). Phrases such as "devoted himself to the study and observance of the Law of the Lord" (Ezra 7:10), "examined the Scriptures" (Acts 17:11) and "correctly handles the word of truth" (2 Tim 2:15) all indicate that understanding the Scriptures involves serious study.

4. Literal-grammatical interpretation

The literal-grammatical method of interpretation also has ancient roots. It was championed by the School of Antioch, which was a rival of the Catechetical School of Alexandria. Its supporters include John Chrysostom (c. 349–407), Martin Luther (1483–1546) and John Calvin (1509–1564).

In this approach, the normal grammatical meaning of the text is used when interpreting Scripture. This is by no means the same as an overly literal interpretation. For example, when Jesus said "I am the door", we know that he did not mean that he was a wooden board mounted on hinges and nails. He was speaking metaphorically. The literal-

---

[37] Brown, *Heresies*, 285–286.

grammatical understanding recognizes this and looks for the normal meaning of the words in the sentence and the context in which they were uttered.

> The literal interpretation as applied to any document is that view which adopts as the sense of a sentence the meaning of that sentence in usual, or ordinary, or normal conversation or writing. The issue is not over a narrow, unimaginative literalism as against a fanciful, imaginative allegorism. The issue is whether a document is to be fundamentally approached in the normal, customary, usual way in which men talk, write and think; or whether that level is to be taken as preliminary.[38]

Literal-grammatical interpretation is not done in independence of the Holy Spirit. Those who follow this method look to him for illumination in understanding and applying what they read. They recognize that the ultimate purpose of interpretation is a changed life, and it is only the Holy Spirit who can transform a life.

The following basic principles apply when using the literal-grammatical method of interpretation.

1. *Learn to understand God's intended meaning of Scripture.* God has revealed himself to us by communicating in human language. Our beliefs and practices must therefore be based on a proper understanding of this divine communication. Gordon Fee observes, "Since God chose to communicate himself to us through human speech in historically particular circumstances, we are locked into a hermeneutical process that demands by its very nature that we listen carefully first of all to what is intended; for there alone lies our hope of hearing what God himself wants us to hear."[39] Christians need to work hard to understand what God has spoken in his word. Some need to learn the Bible languages of Hebrew or Greek to help them understand the meaning; others may have to rely on consulting different translations of God's word to determine what it says.

2. *Read the whole counsel of God.* Rather than indulging in selective reading, we should examine the whole of scriptural teaching on any

---

[38] Ramm, *Protestant Biblical Interpretation*, 53–54.
[39] Gordon D. Fee, *Gospel and Spirit: Issues in New Testament Hermeneutics* (Peabody: Hendrickson, 1991), 43.

given topic. Hayes observes that those "who seek to attend to the entire range of canonical witnesses are on firmer theological ground than are those who base their normative positions on a limited sample of canonical evidence."[40] Those who read the whole of Scripture will have a firmer grasp of the meaning of Scripture as a whole.

It is important not to read only those passages that favour our own position on a particular subject, but to study all that Scripture has to say on a subject before coming to a conclusion about what God teaches. For example, on the question of whether or not a Christian should participate in war, it is not enough to examine passages such as "Love your enemies" (Matt 5:44) and "Put your sword back in its place ... for all who draw the sword will die by the sword" (Matt 26:52). One must also study Luke 22:36 ("if you don't have a sword, sell your cloak and buy one") and the Old Testament passages that deal with war and represent God as a warrior.

3. *Allow the context to define the meaning.* The context embraces the historical context of the biblical author, or in other words, the time and culture within which the text was written. It also refers to the literary context, that is, the meaning that the words, phrases, sentences and paragraphs have in relationship to one another. Bible students must beware of "proof-texting", proving a point by quoting a scriptural text regardless of its context. This is a common cause of erroneous interpretation and irrelevant application.[41] Many errors would be avoided if Bible students focused on identifying meanings directly from the passages they are reading.

To give some examples from different parts of the Bible: a) The book of Esther does not mention the name of God, but that does not mean it is not inspired by God. His existence and power to save are very evident in the prayers and salvation of the Jews at that time. b) When James talks about the role of works in salvation, he is not undermining salvation by grace. His letter was written to believers who had already exercised faith and needed to demonstrate their faith by good works. Understanding that context eliminates any conflict between James and Paul. c) In Mark 9:1 Jesus promises that

---

[40] Richard B. Hayes, *The Moral Vision of the New Testament: Community, Cross, New Creation; A Contemporary Introduction to New Testament Ethics* (San Francisco: HarperCollins, 1996), 292.
[41] Mickelsen, *Interpreting the Bible*, 99.

"some who are standing here will not taste death before they see the kingdom of God come with power." This verse could easily be misinterpreted as a promise that some of Jesus' disciples would not experience death until the kingdom of God is revealed at the end of time. However, a closer look at the context, namely verses 9–10, indicates that the promise was fulfilled just a few days later at the Mount of Transfiguration. There Peter, James and John saw Christ in the glory of the kingdom.

4. *Read Scripture obediently and reverently.* God's word must be approached with reverence (Isa 66:2). The main reason for spending time studying it is so that we can obey the Lord; it is not so that we can win intellectual arguments. Psalm 119:11 states, "I have hidden your word in my heart that I might not sin against you." We read that Ezra "devoted himself to the study and observance of the Law of the LORD, and to teaching its decrees and laws in Israel" (Ezra 7:10). We need to do the same if the Bible is to shape and judge both our theology and our ethics. Like David, we must pray diligently and earnestly for understanding (Ps 119:33–40; see also Prov 2:3–7). Then we must accept by faith what the Scriptures say (John 5:46–47).

The Uses of Scripture

In many African cultures magical objects such as amulets and charms are popular as a means of protection from harm or evil. Christians can be tempted to use the Bible in a similar fashion. Some Christians place their Bibles on their pillows to ward off evil spirits at night. Others place a copy of the Bible in the glove compartment of their car to avert accidents. However, this is not the way God intended his book to be used. He intended us to use it for the following purposes.

1. For instruction in godliness. The Scriptures teach us how to live godly lives.

2. For correction (2 Tim 3:16). Knowledge of Scripture enables us to recognize wrong teaching about God.

3. For instruction in fighting against Satan and temptation. Christ used the word of God against Satan when tempted by the devil (Matt 4:1-11).

4. To know and understand the will of God. All that God requires of us has been revealed and recorded in Scripture (Mic 6:8).

5. For training (Josh 1:7–8). A primary means of training for ministry is gaining knowledge of the word of God. This involves meditation, reflection and application (Ezra 7:6). Paul calls this "training in righteousness, so that the servant of God may be thoroughly equipped for every good work" (2 Tim 3:16–17).

6. For doctrine or theology. Doctrine must be derived from the Holy Scriptures. Evangelicals recognize "the role of Scripture as *the* control on our theological formulation, as the definitive source for our knowledge of God, as the record and interpreter of the biblical history, and as the depository of the teaching of the living Jesus Christ."[42]

7. For guidance in all areas of life (Ps 119:105; Prov 30:5–6; Isa 8:20; John 17:17; 2 Thess 3:14; 2 Tim 3:16–17; Heb 4:12).

Revelation Today

Does God still reveal himself? If so, in what sense and forms? Can African Christians still expect God to continue to guide, lead and reveal himself through dreams, appearances and visions? Or does God now limit his revelation to what is recorded in the Scriptures?

We have already argued that God has revealed himself through nature, history and conscience, and that this revelation is available to all people in all places. There is no indication that this general revelation has ceased. However, we have also argued that God has revealed himself especially through Jesus, as truthfully recorded in the Holy Scriptures.

The general revelation Africa had before Christianity was introduced to the continent served as a bridge to the special revelation in Jesus Christ and to the sixty-six books of the Bible, which is the complete and final revelation of God. There will never be a sixty-seventh book of Scripture.

General revelation must therefore submit to this special revelation, properly interpreted, as the final judge in all matters of life and practice. So dreams and visions can still be used by God to demonstrate his power and will for Christians, but such revelation does not, and cannot,

---

[42] Cameron, "The Idea of Revelation", 680.

supersede the Scriptures, which are the primary way in which God's Spirit now communicates with us. "All other perceived communications from him should be gauged by Scripture and by the spiritual discernment of seasoned saints."[43]

Clark Pinnock puts it well:

> Revelation has not ceased. A phase of it has ceased, the phase that provided the gospel and its scriptural witness, but not revelation in every sense. ... We have in us the Spirit of revelation who causes the letter of the Bible to become charged with life and to become the living voice of God to us. ... Indeed, indications are that the Spirit continues to address us through one another, and through special gifts [such as prophecy].[44]

Paul speaks of this ongoing revelation in Ephesians 1:17, where he writes of "the Spirit of wisdom and revelation" and in 1 Corinthians 14:26, where he says that "When you come together, each of you has a hymn, or a word of instruction, a revelation, a tongue or an interpretation."

J. Rodman Williams agrees that God is still revealing himself:

> God desires to give the Christian believer an enlarged revelation of His Son. ... Also, God gives revelation to an individual for the upbuilding of the Christian community ... God, the living God, is the God of revelation. He is ready to grant through His Spirit a spirit of revelation and wisdom for a deeper knowledge of Christ and also through revelation and prophecy to speak to His people. God has not changed in His desire to communicate directly with those who belong to him.[45]

But, Rodman stresses,

> All such revelation is wholly subordinate to special revelation. *There is nothing to be added*: God's truth has been fully declared. Accordingly, what occurs in revelation within the Christian community is *not* new truth that goes beyond the special revelation (if so, it is spurious and not of God). It is

---

[43] Larry D. Hart, *Truth Aflame: Theology for the Church in Renewal* (rev. ed.; Grand Rapids: Zondervan, 2005), 69–70.

[44] Clark H. Pinnock, *The Scripture Principle* (2nd ed.; Grand Rapids: Baker, 2006), 189–190.

[45] J. Rodman Williams, *God, the World and Redemption* (vol. 1 of *Renewal Theology*; Grand Rapids: Zondervan, 1988), 43.

only a deeper appreciation of what has already been revealed, or a disclosure of some message for the contemporary situation that adds nothing essentially to what He has before made known.[46]

The Old Testament throws light on this ongoing revelation. For example, although the Israelites had the Mosaic law, they continued to receive personal revelations from God. Moses had been given the Ten Commandments, yet God continued to reveal himself personally to him on various issues. And the fact that the law had been written down by Moses did not preclude God's revelation of himself to Gideon and others. God's ongoing revelation is therefore still valid even when Christians have the whole of the Scriptures. The critical factor is that this ongoing revelation must be consistent with the Holy Scriptures. No divine revelation will contradict the Scriptures or add to them.

Thus, it appears that there is both continuity and discontinuity in relation to revelation. God continues to reveal himself sovereignly for his own purposes. However, in matters of belief, practice and theological investigation, the Bible, as the final revelation of God, must be the standard by which we judge what is right and wrong, what is moral or immoral, what is true and what is false.

Questions

1. Is the God of pre-gospel Africa the same as the God of the Scriptures?
2. Can a person be saved without hearing the gospel?
3. How is "revelation" understood by believers and churches in Africa today?
4. What is the difference between revelation and illumination?
5. What does Hebrews 1:1–2 teach with regard to dreams and visions?
6. What are the various ways in which God communicates with his people? What biblical evidence supports your answer?

---

[46] Ibid., 44.

Further Reading

F. F. Bruce. *The Canon of Scripture*. Downers Grove: InterVarsity Press, 1988.

Gordon D. Fee and Douglas Stuart. *How to Read the Bible for All Its Worth: A Guide to Understanding the Bible*. 3rd ed. Grand Rapids: Zondervan, 2003.

Paul Helm. *The Divine Revelation: The Basic Issues*. Vancouver: Regent College Publishing, 2004.

Michael Kyomya. *Interpreting Scripture*. Jos, Nairobi and Accra: HippoBooks / Grand Rapids: Zondervan, 2010.

A. Berkeley Mickelsen. *Interpreting the Bible*. Grand Rapids: Eerdmans, 1963.

J. I. Packer. *Knowing God*. Downers Grove: InterVarsity Press, 1973.

Bernard Ramm. *Protestant Biblical Interpretation: A Textbook of Hermeneutics*. Grand Rapids: Baker, 1970.

Robert Traina. *Methodical Bible Study: A New Approach to Hermeneutics*. Grand Rapids: Francis Asbury Press, 1952.

3

GOD AND SPIRITS

Africans who come to the Christian faith already have a belief in the existence of God and the spirit world. Martin Nkafu Nkemnkia states, "The reality of God does not constitute a problem for African thought. The question about God is not: 'Who is God?' since he always dwells among the people and all that one has and knows comes from God, such as descendants, cattle, harvest, etc. The question to be asked is how one can live without losing one's union with God."[1] Evidence for the African belief in God can be seen in the variety of names for God among all African peoples, as well as in religious beliefs and practices, rituals and sacrifices.

What is the African God like? Nkemnkia says, "God, for the Africans, remains a being of whom everything is asserted; of whom and in virtue of whom everything acquires a meaning. There is only one such being and he is accountable to no one."[2] Writing about African Traditional Religion, Geoffrey Parrinder notes, "God is believed in by everybody as the creator of all things, the almighty and all-knowing, the giver of life and breath, the final judge of all men. Although he is a great and distant God, yet his name is daily heard in salutations, blessings, proverbs and riddles."[3] God is viewed as supreme, all-powerful, all-knowing, loving and caring. He is also omnipresent, and can thus be worshipped "at any place, at any time, where and when the need arises".[4]

---

[1] Martin Nkafu Nkemnkia, *African Vitalogy: A Step Forward in African Thinking* (Nairobi: Paulines Publications Africa, 1999), 144.

[2] Ibid., 145.

[3] Geoffrey Parrinder, *African Traditional Religion* (Westport: Greenwood Press, 1970), 34. John Mbiti, who has written more on this subject than anyone else, says, "Families or individuals turn to God in acts of worship anywhere, without being bound to the feeling that God should be worshipped at a particular place." (*Concepts of God in Africa*, 243).

[4] John Mbiti, *Concepts of God in Africa* (New York: Praeger, 1970), 243. In the preface of the book, Mbiti notes that he researched 270 tribal communities in Africa.

However, while there is a concept of a Supreme Being, "the worship of that Supreme Being is conspicuously absent."[5] The only exceptions seem to be among the Akan[6] and the Gikuyu of Kenya, of whom Samuel G. Kibicho makes the claim that they "have always believed in the one Almighty God, the creator and ruler of all men and all things ... According to its own traditions, Gikuyu belief was a monotheism right from the beginning. The Gikuyu do not worship idols or natural phenomena and no evidence of their ever having worshipped idols in the past has been found."[7] But more usually we encounter "a whole array of lesser gods and the long line of ancestral spirits to whom prayers are offered and who are, indeed, regarded as the more responsible for the day-to-day factors of life."[8] Some scholars have argued that worship offered through intermediaries such as ancestors and other divinities is actually worship of the Almighty God himself, even though the worshippers are not conscious of this.

Is the Supreme Being whom Africans acknowledge the same as the God of the Bible? John Mbiti believes this to be the case. So does Bolaji Idowu, who argues on the basis of general revelation that God has revealed himself to Nigerians and is worshipped by them.[9] But this is to go too far. At most, the beliefs and practices of African Traditional Religion convey only a faint and incomplete understanding of who God is. The only true source of knowledge about God is his personal revelation of himself in Jesus Christ and the recording of that revelation in the inspired, inerrant and infallible Holy Scriptures. Indeed, Scripture insists that knowledge of a personal and sovereign God combined with worship of him through other divinities boils down to idolatry: "For although they knew God, they neither glorified him as God nor gave thanks to him, but their thinking became futile and their foolish hearts were darkened. They exchanged the truth about God for a lie, and worshipped and served created things rather than the Creator" (Rom 1:21–25).

---

[5] Byang H. Kato, *Theological Pitfalls in Africa* (Kisumu, Kenya: Evangel, 1975), 34.

[6] Harry Sawyer, *God: Ancestor or Creator?* (London: Longman, 1970), 6.

[7] Samuel G. Kibicho, *God and Revelation in an African Context* (Nairobi: Acton Press, 2006), 18–19.

[8] Sawyer, *God: Ancestor or Creator?*, 6.

[9] Bolaji Idowu, *Towards an Indigenous Church* (London: Oxford University Press, 1965), 24–26.

The God of the Scriptures

The Bible teaches that God is self-existent. When Moses asked God who he was, God simply replied, "I AM WHO I AM" (Exod 3:13–14). The psalmist regarded any questioning of the fact of God's existence as foolishness (Ps 14:1), and most Africans would agree. There is thus no need to explore the proofs of the existence of God in this work.

What is important is to seek to understand more about God. The only way to achieve such understanding is to examine his revelation of himself in his written word. When we do this, we discover that God exists in Trinity, is both transcendent and immanent, and is sovereign, omnipotent, holy, just and loving.

God exists in Trinity

The doctrine of the Trinity distinguishes the Christian concept of God from that of all other religions, including African Traditional Religion. Whereas some of these religions are monotheistic, none share Christianity's claim that God is one and eternally exists in three persons.

Some who reject this teaching argue that the word "Trinity" is not found anywhere in the Bible. This is true. But careful reading of the Scriptures shows that this idea is present throughout the whole Bible.

The Bible insists that God is one. In the Old Testament, this is explicitly stated in Deuteronomy 6:4: "Hear, O Israel: the LORD our God, the LORD is one." The New Testament reaffirms this: "There is no God but one" (1 Cor 8:4; compare Jas 2:19). On this point, Christians, Jews and Muslims are in full agreement.

However, the Bible implies that God is also three. This is not the same as saying that there are three gods or divinities. Rather, it is saying that "God is not simply a unity but a triunity – that is, God is one but coexists in three persons, Father, Son and Holy Spirit. He is differentiated within himself."[10]

The existence of plurality within the Godhead is hinted at in a few Old Testament passages. For example, in Genesis 1:26 God says, "Let us make mankind in our likeness"; in Genesis 11:7 he says, "Come, let us go down and confuse their language", and in Isaiah 6:8 he asks,

---

[10] Donald G. Bloesch, *God, Authority and Salvation* (vol. 1 of *Essentials of Evangelical Theology*, San Francisco: Harper, 1982), 35.

"Whom shall I send? And who will go for us?" The *us* and *we* in these passages may be an example of the royal "we" that signals the status of the speaker, but in light of the New Testament revelation it implies more than this. Proverbs 30:4 makes it even clearer: "Who has gone up to heaven and come down? Whose hands have gathered up the wind? Who has wrapped up the waters in a cloak? Who has established all the ends of the earth? What is his name, and what is the name of his son? Surely you know!" In the Old Testament, the listener would have known that God's name was Yahweh (translated LORD), but the name of his Son would only become known with the coming of Jesus Christ.

All three members of the Trinity work together. All three are involved in creation (Gen 1:1; Ps 102:25; Job 33:4; Luke 1:35; Col 1:16), baptism (Matt 3:16–17), the atonement (Heb 9:14), the Great Commission (Matt 28:19), the grace (2 Cor 13:14) and in the entire work of salvation (1 Pet 1:2).

The Father is the First Person of the Trinity. The Father is a distinct member of the Godhead. Jesus specifically distinguishes between himself and the Father (John 6:27) and Paul speaks of God the Father and Jesus Christ as separate but equal (Rom 1:7; Gal 1:1). The Father is not the same as the Son or the Holy Spirit, whom he sent into the world (John 14:16). We need to emphasize that these are distinct beings because the heresy called modalism teaches that the three persons of the Godhead are simply different manifestations of God. Those who hold to this belief claim that God the Father was active in the Old Testament, then revealed himself as the Son in the New Testament period, and now reveals himself in the church period as the Holy Spirit. But they are wrong. So are the Unitarians, who assert that Jesus and the Holy Spirit are just emanations of God. Neither modalism nor unitarianism is supported by Scripture.

The Son is the Second Person of the Trinity. Jesus Christ, the Son of God who offered himself as a sacrifice for the sins of the whole world, is fully human yet also fully God (Phil 2:6–11). His humanity is seen in his birth, his human personality and the fact that he experienced the same things as we do: growth, hunger, taste, desire, suffering and *death*. His complete deity is testified to by John 1:1–2: "In the beginning was the Word, and the Word was with God, and the Word was God. He was with God in the beginning." Jesus himself claimed, "I and the Father are one" (John 10:30), thereby both distinguishing himself from the Father and asserting the unity between himself and the Father.

The church has tried to summarize its belief in Jesus Christ's perfect deity and perfect humanity in formal creeds. The Nicene Creed (AD 325), for example, asserts,

> We believe in one God, the Father Almighty, Maker of all things visible and invisible. And in one Lord Jesus Christ, the Son of God, begotten of the Father, the only-begotten; that is, from the substance of the Father, God from God, light from light, true God from true God, begotten not made, of one substance with the Father, through Whom all things came into being, things in heaven and things on earth, Who because of us men and because of our salvation came down and became incarnate, becoming man, suffered and rose again on the third day, ascended into heaven, and will come to judge the living and the dead; And in the Holy Spirit. But as for those who say, There was when He was not, and, Before being born He was not, and that He came into existing out of nothing, or who assert that the Son of God is from a different hypostasis or substance, or is created, or is subject to alteration or change – these the catholic church anathematizes.[11]

Likewise, the Creed of Chalcedon (AD 451) reads, "In agreement, therefore, with the holy Fathers, we all unanimously teach that we should confess that our Lord Jesus Christ [is] one and the same Son, the same perfect in Godhead and the same perfect in manhood, truly God and truly man".[12]

Theological positions that deny, revise or reduce either the deity or the humanity of Jesus are thus contrary to Scripture. Such positions include

---

[11] Quoted from J. N. D. Kelly, *Early Christian Doctrines* (London: A & C Black, 1960), 232.

[12] Quoted from Kelly, *Early Christian Doctrines*, 339–40. The creed continues:
...the same of a rational soul and body, consubstantial with the Father in Godhead, and the same consubstantial with us in manhood, like in all things except sin; begotten from the Father before the ages as regards His Godhead, and in the last days, the same, because of us and because of our salvation begotten from the Virgin Mary, the Theotokos, as regards His manhood; one and the same Christ, Son, Lord, only-begotten, made known in two natures, without confusion, without change, without division, without separation, the difference of the natures being by no means removed because of the union, but the property of each nature being preserved and coalescing in one prosopon and one hypostasis – not parted or divided into two prosopa, but one and the same Son, only-begotten, divine Word, the Lord Jesus Christ, as the prophets of old and Jesus Christ Himself having taught us about Him and the creed of our fathers has handed down.

Arianism, which claims that Jesus was only a created being and not fully God; Nestorianism, which denies the unity of the two natures (divine and human) in the person of Christ; Monophysitism, which states that the two natures of Christ were fused into one; Apollinarianism, which teaches that Christ had a human body and soul but that his human mind was replaced by the divine Logos; and Ebionism, which claims that Jesus was a spirit-man who became superhuman at his baptism, when God adopted him as his Son. Although these heresies have Greek names, they are not ancient history, for many of them are still alive today. There are still those who teach that Jesus was only a man who was mightily used of God, and others who hold that he was only a prophet who lived a particularly holy life. Few preachers in Africa emphasize the two natures (divine and human) united in the person of Christ.

We need to be aware of this when we interact with the various metaphors scholars have used when talking about Christ in African terms. He has been described as Priest, Prophet and Potentate (Douglas W. Waruta), as the Master of Initiation (Anselme T. Sanon), our Chief, our Ancestor and Elder Brother (François Kabasele Lumbala), our Healer (Cécé Kolié) and our Liberator (Laurenti Magesa). Though these images are powerful, we must take care that in using them we do not detract from the deity of Christ.

The person and work of Christ are discussed in more detail in chapter 5.

The Holy Spirit is the Third Person of the Trinity. He is distinct from the Father and the Son. He too is a person and shares the attributes of *complete* deity (John 14:16–17). He is eternal (Heb 9:14), omnipresent (Ps 139:7–10), omniscient (1 Cor 2:10–11) and omnipotent (Luke 1:35). His role is discussed in more detail in chapter 6.

It is sometimes suggested that some Bible passages teach that the Son and the Holy Spirit are lower in status than God the Father. For example, Jesus himself says that the Father is greater than the Son, and that he does the will of the Father (John 12:50; 14:28). Jesus never says that the Father does his will. But this is not necessarily a proof of subordination, as an illustration from real life may help to explain. In my seminary, the principal, the dean and I all have doctorates. Our doctorates have the same value and status. We all have equal qualifications. But when it comes to the running of the seminary, the principal and the dean are my superiors, and I receive orders from them, but not vice versa. In the same way, the three persons of the Godhead are equal, but when it comes to the work of redemption they have different roles. The Father sent the Son, the Son died and rose again in obedience to the Father, and the Holy Spirit was sent by the Father and the Son.

God is transcendent and immanent

God is both distant (transcendent) and near (immanent). While he is above all creation, he is also constantly present and active in history and in his creation, which is totally dependent on him for sustenance. African Traditional Religion knows God as transcendent, but knows far less of his immanence. It is spirits with whom traditional believers interact, rather than with God himself.

God is transcendent in that he is sovereign and distinct from his created universe. He is "wholly other", self-sufficient, and independent. His thoughts are far above ours (Isa 55:8–9). His exaltation and holiness highlight our own sinfulness and the distance between us and God.

Yet God is also near to us, and this is called his immanence. He is near to us through his constant revelation of himself in nature, conscience and history, and through his special revelation of himself in the Holy Scriptures through which he still speaks to us today. He has repeatedly promised to be with his people. Yet he is also with all people: "'Who can hide in secret places so that I cannot see them?' declares the LORD. 'Do not I fill heaven and earth?' declares the LORD" (Jer 23:24). Paul also proclaims God's immanence when he says that "in him we live and move and have our being" (Acts 17:28).

The Trinity helps us to understand God's nearness. The supreme example of it is the incarnation of Jesus Christ when "the Word became flesh and made his dwelling among us" (John 1:14). He made the presence of God real and intimate, and promised, "I am with you always, to the very end of the age" (Matt 28:20).

God is also immanent through the Holy Spirit, who was "hovering over the waters" at creation (Gen 1:2). God freely gives his Holy Spirit to those who believe him (John 16:7), and this brings him close to us.

Isaiah 57:15 is a verse that brings out both the distance and the nearness of God: "I live in a high and holy place, but also with the one who is contrite and lowly in spirit." Psalm 113:5–6 echoes this: "Who is like the LORD our

God, the One who sits enthroned on high, who stoops down to look on the heavens and the earth?" Jesus himself indicates his immanence and his transcendence when he tells those around him, "You are from below; I am from above. You are of this world; I am not of this world" (John 8:23).

God is sovereign and provides for creation

The most explicit teaching of Scripture is that God is sovereign over his entire creation. In other words, "he has absolute authority and rule over his creation".[13] In order to be able to exercise such sovereignty, he has to be "all-knowing, all-powerful and absolutely free".[14] There is no rival or competitor, no spirit or thing, that can undermine his sovereign and loving provision for his creation. "His kingdom rules over all" (Ps 103:19).

The Scripture passages that follow testify to different aspects of God's sovereignty, omnipotence and care:

God's rule over all things: "Yours, LORD, is the greatness and the power and the glory and the majesty and the splendour, for everything in heaven and earth is yours. Yours, LORD, is the kingdom; you are exalted as head over all. Wealth and honour come from you; you are the ruler of all things. In your hands are strength and power to exalt and give strength to all" (1 Chr 29:11–12). Similarly, Isaiah 6:1–3 pictures God sitting on his throne, high and lifted up.

God's rule over all nations: "LORD, the God of our ancestors, are you not the God who is in heaven? You rule over all the kingdoms of the nations. Power and might are in your hand, and no one can withstand you" (2 Chr 20:6).

God's care for all creation: "All creatures look to you to give them their food at the proper time. When you give it to them, they gather it up; when you open your hand, they are satisfied with good things" (Ps 104:27–28; see also Matt 6:25–34; 1 Tim 6:13; Heb 1:3).

God's omnipotence: "I know that you can do all things; no purpose of yours can be thwarted" (Job 42:2).

---

[13] James M. Boice, *Foundations of the Christian Faith: A Comprehensive and Readable Theology* (2nd ed.; Downers Grove: InterVarsity Press, 1986), 117.
[14] Ibid.

God's provision for us: "And God is able to bless you abundantly, so that in all things at all times, having all that you need, you will abound in every good work" (2 Cor 9:8; see also Phil 4:18).

God's ability to save us: "Therefore he [Jesus] is able to save completely those who come to God through him, because he always lives to intercede for them" (Jude 24–25; see also Heb 7:25).

But although God has no rival, there does seem to be some opposition to his sovereignty. How else can we explain the evil and suffering that beset the creation that God declared to be good? This paradox has led some to see God as weak. As Pink observes, "A god whose will is resisted, whose designs are frustrated, whose purpose is checkmated, possesses no title to deity and, far from being a fit object of worship, merits nothing but contempt."[15] So what does the Bible have to say about the work of the devil, evil spirits and evil forces that are opposed to God's sovereignty?

1. *Suffering, pain and evil are real.* The Bible never attempts to deny the suffering caused by earthquakes, tsunamis, famine, disease, murder, rape and the like.

2. *Suffering has various causes.* Sin is the ultimate cause of all suffering and evil. When Adam and Eve sinned, the whole of creation was affected, which explains why we now have to endure natural disasters such as earthquakes and the ravages of disease. Sinful behaviour can also cause suffering, as when people are murdered or a drunken driver kills or maims others. At times we suffer because God allows us to be endure spiritual attack, as was the case with Job.

3. *God is greater than the devil.* "The one who is in you is greater than the one who is in the world" (1 John 4:4). Satan is allowed to act under the sovereignty of God (Job 1).

4. *Suffering and pain have an expiry date.* God's dealings with creation should be defined not only by what is happening in the present but also by what he plans for the future (Rom 8). Evil will not continue for ever for those who love Jesus Christ. There will be no pain, evil and suffering in the new heavens and the new earth in which "the sound of weeping and of crying will be heard in it no more (Isa 65:1; see also Rev 21:1–4).

---

[15] Arthur W. Pink, *The Nature of God* (repr.; Chicago: Moody, 1999), 34.

God is holy, just and loving

God is holy (Lev 19:1–2; Isa 6:3; 1 Pet 1:15–16). The Hebrew and Greek words translated "holy" or "holiness" come from a root that means "to set apart". God's holiness sets him apart from all that he has made, for as Revelation 15:4 says, "you alone are holy." God's holiness means that he is unique and the standard of all morality. It is a constant source of praise. Thus in both Isaiah and Revelation the seraphim who are worshipping God cry out, "Holy, holy, holy is the LORD Almighty" (Isa 6:3; Rev 4:8). God's people should imitate them: "Sing the praises of the LORD, you his faithful people; praise his holy name" (Ps 30:4). Christ also taught that prayer should begin, "Our Father in heaven, hallowed [holy] be your name" (Matt 6:9).

God's holiness is so important that God requires his people to share it. In the Old Testament he commanded the Israelites to be holy just as he is holy (Lev 11:45; 19:21). Jesus repeats this command when he tells his followers to "be perfect, therefore, as your heavenly Father is perfect" (Matt 5:48; see also 1 Pet 1:15). His words show that perfection and holiness are synonyms.

Consistent with God's holiness is his justice; his judgements are fair. If God as a holy God did not deal justly and fairly with all his creation, he would not be perfect and therefore not holy.

God's perfect justice would not be good news for us were it not that God is also loving. His justice condemns sinners, but his love led him to send his Son to die for the sins of those sinners. Those who believe and receive this gift of love are saved and freed from condemnation. However, those who refuse are justly condemned (John 3:16–18).

Because God is holy, we who are unholy cannot possibly approach him. Sin separates us from God (Isa 59:2). Recognizing this should make us humble when we come before him, like Isaiah who said, "I am a man of unclean lips" (Isa 6:5). The only one who can cleanse us so that we can approach God is God himself. He did this through Jesus Christ, who died to make us holy. In gratitude for what he has done, we need to live holy lives, offering ourselves to God (Rom 12:1).

The Spirit World

Africans Traditional Religion asserts that the world is permeated with divinities and spirits who can have positive or negative effects on every aspect of life. It is believed that bad spirits inflict injury and cause accidents and suffering. Spirits are also said to possess and influence human beings for their own purposes. These beliefs still exert a powerful influence today. In fact, strong belief in the spirit world and morbid fear have led many African Christians and churches into unbiblical doctrines and practices.

The preoccupation with the occult, spiritism and witchcraft in many quarters is a clear indication that this subject needs urgent attention. Christians need to base their thinking about the spirit world on the Bible, rather than on traditions. But that does not mean that we have to reject everything in African Traditional Religion. The Bible agrees with it that there are different categories of spirits, and that some are good while others are evil. The good spirits are known as angels; the evil as demons.

Good spirits: Angels

The nature of angels

Like humans, angels were created by God (Col 1:16–17). They were probably the first beings to be created, since they rejoiced over creation (Job 38:4–7). However, unlike us; they are entirely spiritual. Yet they can assume human bodies (Gen 19:1–2; 32:23–32; Judg 13:16) and carry out human activities such as accepting hospitality (Heb 13:2) and opening prison doors (Acts 5:19; 12:7). They can see God (Matt 18:10). They are not omniscient (all-knowing) and do not have full knowledge of the future, but they do have great knowledge (Judg 13:18; Mark 13:32). They are powerful (2 Thess 1:7; 2 Pet 2:11; Rev 5:2; 10:1; 18:21), full of glory (Acts 6:15), and those who did not fall with Satan (see below) are morally pure (1 Sam 29:9; 2 Sam 14:17; 14:20).

We know the names of two angels, who appear to have high positions. One is Michael (Rev 12:7), whose name means "Who is like God?" This name suggests that no one – not even one of the greatest angels – is comparable to God.[16] Michael is referred to as a prince (Dan 10:13; 12:1) and is the only angel to be referred to as "the archangel" (Jude 9; 1 Thess

---

[16] C. Fred Dickason, *Angels: Elect and Evil* (Chicago: Moody, 1975), 67.

4:16). The other angel whose name we know is Gabriel, whose name means "The strength of God" (Dan 8:16–27; 9:21; Luke 1:19, 26–35).

There also appear to be different categories of angels: seraphim (a name that means "burning ones" – Isa 6:2–6); cherubim (Exod 25:18–20; Ezek 1:5–18; 10:12); morning stars (Job 38:4, 7); messengers (Dan 4:13, 23); and principalities and powers (Eph 1:20–21; Col 1:16).

The functions of angels

The Bible tells us more about the functions and duties of angels than it does about their nature. In fact their very name is a reflection of their function, for in both Greek and Hebrew the word translated "angel" means "messenger". They are messengers who carry out God's decrees. In Scripture, they perform the following roles:

a) *Serving believers.* Angels are "ministering spirits" sent to serve believers (Heb 1:14). In this capacity they intervened to prevent Abraham from sacrificing Isaac (Gen 22:11–18), guided Eliezer, Abraham's servant, in his search for a wife for Isaac (Gen 24:7), guided Jacob (Gen 31:11, 13; 32:1), encouraged Joshua (Josh 5:13–14), commissioned Gideon and Isaiah (Judg 2:1–4; Isa 6:1–4) and instructed Manoah on how to raise his son, Samson (Judg 13:15–18). Jesus himself was ministered to by angels (Matt 4:11).

b) *Protecting believers.* Lot was delivered by an angel (Gen 19:15–16). Elijah was encouraged and taken to heaven by angels (1 Kgs 19:4–7; 2 Kgs 1:3, 15; 2:17; 6:17). Angelic beings defended Elisha (2 Kgs 6:16–17) in a literal fulfilment of the promise in Psalms that "the angel of the LORD encamps around those who fear him" (Ps 34:7; see also Ps 91:11).

c) *Acting as intermediaries between the unseen world of the divine presence and the human world.* (Job 1; Heb 2:22; Rev 1:1). Moses was given the law by angels (Acts 7:35, 38, 53; Heb 2:2). An angel gave illumination to Zechariah (Zech 1:14–16). Gabriel announced the birth of Jesus to Mary (Matt 1), and Joseph was encouraged by an angel to take Mary as his wife (Matt 1:20).

d) *Supervising believers.* They supervise individual believers (Matt 18:10) and communities of believers (Dan 10:13, 20; 12:1; Rev 2:1, 8, 12, 18; 3:1, 7, 14).

e) *Destroying.* Angels carry out destruction when ordered to do so by God: "And God sent an angel to destroy Jerusalem … the angel who was destroying the people" (1 Chr 21:15). An angel destroyed the Assyrian army (2 Kgs 19:15, 35). An angel slew Herod for not giving praise to God (Acts 12:23). Angels will play a prominent role in the future destruction of the world and its inhabitants (Rev 12:7–9; 14:14–20).

f) *Worshipping.* Angels worship God for eternity (Rev 7:11).

Evil spirits: Demons

God created everything good (Gen 1:9, 18, 21, 25, 31). Since angelic beings are creatures of God, they were also originally created good and holy. However, as creatures they were not infallible. Some fell into sin and rebelled against God (2 Pet 2:4; Jude 6).

Satan

The leader of the rebellious angels is referred to by many names that describe not only his nature but also his activities.

- *Satan* means "the one who resists" or "the adversary" (1 Chr 21:1; Job 1:6; Zech 3:1; 2 Cor 11:14; 1 Pet 5:8).
- *Lucifer* means "day-star", "bright one" or "shining one" (Isa 14:12). It refers to the glorious position Satan originally held and to his ability to deceive by appearing to be "an angel of light".
- *Abaddon* or *Apollyon* means "destroyer" and is used of the angel of the Abyss and king of demons (Rev 9:11).
- *The dragon*, sometimes referred to as the "old serpent", indicates his ferocity and murderous power (Rev 12:3, 4, 7, 9; 13:2; 20:2) and his nature as the destroyer (Rev 9:11).
- *The serpent*, "the gleaming one", suggests subtlety and guile (Gen 3:1; 2 Cor 11:3; Rev 12:9; 20:2). The sound of the name in Hebrew reflects the hissing sound made by snakes.
- *The devil* means "accuser" or "slanderer" (Jas 4:7; Rev 12:9–10). The dramatic story of Job depicts Satan accusing Job before God (Job 1–2).
- *The tempter* (Matt 4:3; 1 Thess 3:5) indicates Satan's primary purpose of luring us to do evil.
- *Beelzebul/Beelzebub* was a pun on the name of a Philistine deity. It means "Lord of flies" or "Lord of filth" (dung). He was regarded as the prince of demons (Matt 12:24–27; Mark 3:22; Luke 11:15–19).

- *The god of this world* (2 Cor 4:4), the prince of this world (John 12:31; 14:30; 16:11) and the prince of the power of the air (Eph 2:22) all indicate his sphere of influence.
- *The evil one* (Matt 13:19; Eph 6:16; 1 John 5:18–19), referring to his malignant nature.
- *An enemy* (Matt 13:28).

Ezekiel 28 and Isaiah 14 are two passages that are widely, although not unanimously, regarded as referring to Satan. From them we can deduce that Satan was created perfect and beautiful, along with all other creatures (Ezek 28:13, 15; Ps 148:2–5; Col 1:16). He occupied a very important position in the angelic hierarchy (Ezek 28:4; see also Jude 8–9), but fell through pride and was cast down, along with other angels who joined his conspiracy (Rev 12:10). He is now the archenemy of God, the head of all evil forces (Mark 3:22–26). He and his cohorts oppose God and seek to prevent fallen humanity from seeing the truth (2 Cor 4:4). But the death of Christ brought about his judgement, which will be finally implemented at the end of the age when Satan will be sentenced to eternal doom (Rev 20:5).

Other evil spirits

The other evil spirits or demons were also originally created holy (Gen 1:31) but followed Satan in his rebellion against God (Matt 12:24–27; 2 Pet 2:4; Rev 12:7–10). They are unclean, unholy, violent and fierce (Matt 10:1; 8:28) and have the power to work miracles (Rev 13:12–15; 16:14). They are numerous and can seem to be all-knowing and all-powerful (Eph 6:11–12; Rev 12:7–12). However, only God is all-powerful, and he has complete authority over evil spirits. At the end of the age, he will send them to eternal condemnation.

The activities of evil spirits include the following:

a) *Opposing believers* in their lives and ministries (Rom 8:38–39; Eph 6:12).

b) *Encouraging the worship of idols*, which leads people away from God and the truth (2 Kgs 17:7–6; 1 Cor 10:20).

c) *Teaching false doctrines* to lure believers from the truth (1 Tim 4:1; see also 2 Tim 4:4).

d) *Enslaving the weak and vulnerable* and keeping them under Satan's grip through superstitions, false tales and myths.

e) *Causing disease*, both physical and mental (Matt 9:32–33; 2 Cor 12:7).

There is debate about whether these evil spirits are bound or free. The debate centres around Revelation 12:7–9, which speaks of Satan being defeated and hurled from heaven, and 2 Peter 2:4, which says that "God did not spare angels when they sinned, but sent them to hell, putting them in chains of darkness to be held for judgement".

Lockyer represents one position when he argues that the angels referred to in these verses are a specific subset of the fallen angels:

> These angels are not to be confused with those who are free to roam and act at the bidding of their satanic lord. Originally they were one with the rebellious hosts; but somewhere, somehow, these angels, presently in captivity, became separated from the rest and were thrust by God into darkness. These are fallen angels who left their first estate and are reserved until the final judgement. Their revolt must have been more deeply and more heinously criminal, to have deserved the immediate loss of their freedom and millennia of severe bondage. The liberty they had after their expulsion from heaven was taken from them.[17]

However, the general teaching of Scripture suggests that rather than these being a subgroup of angels who committed some specific sin, we should see these passages as referring to the general sin that resulted in Satan and his angels being cast out from the presence of God. Their condemnation is final and cannot be changed, which is consistent with Peter's description of them as being "in chains of darkness to be held for judgement". They are restricted because of their rebellion and will remain so until the final judgement. But in the meantime, they are free to roam and do the will of their master, Satan.

Evil spirits and disease

Africans tend to attribute diseases and mental ailments to Satan and evil spirits. While it is true that some diseases and mental states can be caused by demonic activity (Luke 13:32), this is not true in every case. In

---

[17] Herbert Lockyer, *All the Angels in the Bible: A Complete Exploration of the Nature and Ministry of Angels* (Peabody: Hendrickson, 1995), 53–54.

Matthew 4:24, for example, a distinction is drawn between epilepsy and demon possession, which can cause similar symptoms (see Matt 17:15–18). It is thus wrong to claim that all diseases are attributable to demons.

God has given human beings the ability and wisdom to find medical cures for diseases, and such cures should be accepted with thanksgiving. If a person is suffering from malaria and clearly needs anti-malarial treatment, he or she should be given the appropriate drugs. There is no need to ask for prayers of deliverance for a clearly physical problem that needs a physical solution. On the other hand, those sicknesses that are clearly caused by demonic activity do call for prayers for deliverance. There is thus a need for great discernment when dealing with disease.

Demon possession

Demons can and have possessed human beings (Luke 8:26–38; Acts 16:16–18), but it is unlikely that a Christian can be demon-possessed. The only passage that seems to suggest that this may be a possibility is Acts 5:3, where Peter asks Ananias, "How is it that Satan has so filled your heart that you have lied to the Holy Spirit and have kept for yourself some of the money you received for the land?" Is this "filling" of his heart equivalent to what Paul speaks of in Ephesians 5:18, when he tells Christians to be "filled with the Spirit"?

The answer to the question may be found by looking at the context of Peter's words in Acts. The believers were selling their property and sharing their possessions (Acts 4:36–37), and "Ananias, together with his wife Sapphira, also sold a piece of property" (Acts 5:1). Ananias and Sapphira were believers, but they allowed Satan to temporarily take over their hearts so that they "lied to the Holy Spirit", which was synonymous with lying to God (5:4). It seems that this was a temporary condition rather than a permanent state of demon possession.

While believers cannot be demon-possessed, they can be influenced by the devil or demons through suggestion, pressure and temptation. It is therefore vital that we heed the exhortation in Ephesians 5:1. Being constantly filled with the Holy Spirit will prevent the influence of the devil.

Evil spirits, sexual activity and procreation

In African folklore, spirits are able to marry, perform sexual activities and procreate. This belief has crept into the church, and so one hears stories of women who claim that they have had sexual intercourse with spiritual beings. One of my former students testified to having confronted a woman who was possessed by a demon who claimed that the woman was his wife and that she had become pregnant many times but had aborted the pregnancies. What does the Bible have to say about such things?

In Matthew 22:23–33 Jesus commented on the nature of angels. He was being asked a question about a widow who had lost many husbands in her lifetime. His interrogators wanted to know, "at the resurrection, whose wife will she be?" In response, he told them that at the resurrection we will all be like the angels in heaven, who do not marry. In other words, angels do not have sexual intercourse and procreate. However, Jesus was talking about angels, not about evil spirits. This passage does not rule out the possibility that spiritual beings who contradict and oppose God's original plan for them may be capable of marriage and procreation.

Genesis 6 tells of the "sons of God" intermarrying and procreating with the daughters of humans. Though the immediate context concerns the godly line marrying and procreating with the ungodly line, there remains the possibility of angelic cohabitation with human beings. If angels are able to take up human bodies and be entertained with food and drink, it is not impossible that they could take on human form to intermarry with human beings. But it is impossible to speak with certainty on this subject.

What about the children brought forth from such unions? The Igbo hold that evil spirits can plague a family in the form of *ogbanje* ("children who come and go", that is, children who are born only to die and be reborn and die several times over). The Yoruba have an equivalent term, *abiku* ("predestined to death"). But these beliefs (which are by no means universal) do not answer the question of whether children fathered by a demon would be redeemable, able to be saved.

These beliefs, however, are held only by particular communities and cannot be accepted as proof that spirit beings can procreate. All that can be said is speculative. Scripture is silent on this subject.

Christians and the spirit world

Fear of the spirit world has led many African Christians into syncretistic beliefs and practices. The African church is permeated with descriptions of demonic activities that are rooted in the pre-Christian world view and are not consistent with biblical revelation. The weak and vulnerable

– especially children and the elderly – are sometimes accused of involvement in witchcraft and abused. Angels like Gabriel and Michael have been given almost godlike status and offered worship.

These attitudes are not only found among lay people. There are church leaders who focus solely on deliverance ministries and neglect the preaching of the gospel of Jesus Christ. They adopt titles such as "man of God", "woman of God", "supersonic man of God" and "demon destroyer", which draw attention to themselves rather than to God. Their preaching is a mix of truths and untruth as they appeal to select Bible passages before making wild leaps into dramatic speculation. In many respects they resemble the magicians of old and traditional spiritists and diviners. They claim to be able to decree God to do something, command and bind Satan, cast him into the Abyss or the ocean, bind territorial spirits, bind the strong man, take dominion over an area in Jesus' name, and storm the gates of hell.

A major problem with such teaching is that it "gives unhealthy attention to the devil and demonic activity. It underemphasizes the finished work of the cross, as well as the work of the Holy Spirit and angels … it all has to do with giving direct attention to the devil and demons, which is something the Bible has not commanded us to do. In fact, it could be quite dangerous".[18] Nowhere does the Bible teach us to look out for demons or Satan. Our task is to preach the gospel and live our lives in the power of the Holy Spirit.

> We are to watch against Satan (1 Pet 5:8), to give no place to him (Eph 4:27), and to resist him (Jas 4:7). Our enemy is free on earth to the length of his chain, but no further (Job 2:5). He cannot go beyond God's permission nor injure God's elect. His freedom of range in the air and on earth is that of a chained prisoner under sentence. By faith we must appropriate the victory over all satanic powers Christ secured by His death and resurrection.[19]

The Bible teaches the following principles that should govern our response to the angelic and demonic presence in the world.

---

[18] Mike Wakely, "A Critical Look at a New Key to Evangelization", *Evangelical Missions Quarterly* 31:2 (1995), 161. Though this article deals mainly with territorial spirits, the point applies equally to the present preoccupation with satanic and demonic activities.

[19] Lockyer, *All the Angels in the Bible*, 63.

1. *God is sovereign over Satan and demonic spirits.* Preoccupation with the demonic world and spiritual warfare shows that we lack "a clear belief in the sovereignty and centrality of God ... [and in] the presence of the risen Christ with 'all authority in heaven and on earth'".[20]

2. *Good and bad (evil) spirits do exist and affect our human condition.* Scripture indicates that human beings are always battling with evil spirits, for our struggle is not against flesh and blood, but against principalities and powers (Eph 6:12). It is a real battle with real spirits who seek to influence people for evil and corrupt their understanding of Christian doctrine. They seek to bring about the conditions Paul described when he wrote, "The Spirit clearly says that in later times some will abandon the faith and follow deceiving spirits and things taught by demons" (1 Tim 4:1).

3. *The power of God in the believer is stronger than the demonic powers seeking to attack the believer.* Both the Old and New Testaments teach that God's power ensures total victory over physical and spiritual forces. When the Assyrian army posed a serious threat to Judah, King Hezekiah encouraged his subjects with these words: "Be strong and courageous. Do not be afraid or discouraged because of the king of Assyria and the vast army with him, for there is a greater power with us than with him. With him is only the arm of flesh, but with us is the LORD our God to help us and to fight our battles" (2 Chr 32:7–8). The Apostle John similarly wrote: "the one who is in you is greater than the one who is in the world" (1 John 4:4).

4. *God's presence protects the believer and gives a sense of security.* One of the most consistent teachings of Scripture is that God is with his people and with individual believers. During the exodus, God's constant presence was manifested by the pillar of fire and the cloud (Exod 13:21). God promised Joshua, "Have not I commanded you? Be strong and courageous. Do not be terrified; do not be discouraged, for the LORD your God will be with you wherever you go" (Josh 1:9). In the New Testament, Jesus teaches the same truth (Matt 28:19–20). God's presence overrules satanic and demonic fears and attacks.

5. *The binding of Satan and prayers of deliverance are based on the finished work of Christ on the cross* (Matt 12:25–46). Satan and all

---

[20] Wakely, "A Critical Look", 162.

supernatural powers are under the authority of the risen Christ. Paul declares that "having disarmed the powers and authorities, he made a public spectacle of them, triumphing over them by the cross" (Col 2:15). The deliverance and binding of the "strong man" (Satan) has been accomplished by the "stronger man", Jesus Christ (Matt 12:29). Technically, no preacher can deliver a person from the devil or demons; Christ has already done it. In many instances, the binding of Satan and prayers of deliverance give more credit to the might and power of the man or woman of God than to Jesus, whose name is used only as part of the final push for deliverance. Although in Christ Christians have power over Satan and all evil forces, they should be cautious of giving more prominence to this power than to Christ himself. The mission of the preacher and the believer is to preach about the one who is stronger than the "strong man". This is the good news.

6. *Angels also provide God's protection and security to believers.* The story of Elisha and the Aramean armies demonstrates that God sometimes sends angels to provide protection from enemies (2 Kgs 6:8–17). Angelic beings are also sometimes described as actively fighting on behalf of God's people: "The Lord sent an angel, who annihilated all the fighting men and the commanders and officers in the camp of the Assyrian king. So he withdrew to his own land in disgrace" (2 Chr 32:21). In the days of the early church, angelic beings personally delivered the disciples from prison; for example, in Acts 5:19, "an angel of the Lord opened the doors of the jail and brought them out" (see also Acts 12:7–10). Thus the writer to the Hebrews asks the rhetorical question, "Are not all angels ministering spirits sent to serve those who will inherit salvation?" (Heb 1:14). The history of the church includes numerous instances of angelic beings providing security and protecting believers from their enemies.

7. *Spirit beings are not to be worshipped or given undue attention.* Colossians 2:18 refers to the tendency among some believers to worship angels, which is wrong. The Apostle John was warned not to worship angelic messengers but to worship only God (Rev 19:10; 22:8–9). Angelic messengers lead us to God, not to themselves. Human beings and angels equally worship God; Revelation 7:11 states that the angels "fell down on their faces before the throne and worshipped God".

Christians should also not be disrespectful towards Satan and demons. The Bible presents Satan as shining and intelligent. Giving Satan respect does not mean honouring or glorifying him, but recognizing his place. Jude 8–9 is instructive in this regard: "In the very same way, on the strength of their dreams these ungodly people … heap abuse on celestial beings. But even the archangel Michael, when he was disputing with the devil about the body of Moses, did not himself dare to condemn him for slander but said, 'The Lord rebuke you!'" Cursing or abusing celestial beings such as Satan and evil beings is not our mandate.

8. *Believers belong to a different kingdom and king.* Colossians 1:13–14 states that God "has rescued us from the dominion of darkness and brought us into the kingdom of the Son he loves, in whom we have redemption, the forgiveness of sins." The kingdom of light belongs to our mighty God, who is able to save us completely (Heb 7:25). He has saved us not merely in the future but also from the hold, rule and captivity of the devil and evil forces in the present. They cannot break God's dominion and molest, harass or terrorize God's citizens.

Questions

1. What is the name of God in your community? How is God traditionally understood there?

2. Is the God of the Scriptures the same as the God of African Traditional Religion? Back up your answer from the Bible.

3. What is the biblical evidence for the doctrine of the Trinity? What biblical proof is there for the deity of the Son and the Holy Spirit?

4. What does your community believe about the nature and activities of evil forces (demons)? How do these views compare with what the Scriptures say about evil spirits?

5. How have angels sent by God ministered to you or other believers you know or have read about?

6. Can demons attack Christians? Back up your answer from the Bible.

7. What, according to the Bible, is the solution to the fear of demonic and spiritual attack?

8. Can a Christian be demon-possessed? How does the story of Ananias and Sapphira in Acts 5 shed light on this subject?

9. What beliefs are held in your church about occultism and witchcraft?

10. Why do you think God allows people to suffer? What practical lessons can we learn from the suffering of Job and of Paul in 2 Corinthians 12:7–10?

Further Reading

Donald G. Bloesch. *God, Authority & Salvation*. Vol. 1 of *The Essentials of Evangelical Theology*. San Francisco: Harper, 1982.

David Burnett. *Unearthly Powers: A Christian Perspective on Primal and Folk Religion*. Eastbourne: MARC, 1988.

C. Fred Dickason. *Angels: Elect and Evil*. Revised edition. Chicago: Moody, 1995.

Keith Ferdinando, *The Battle is God's: Reflecting on Spiritual Warfare for African Believers*. Bukuru: ACTS, 2012.

David Jeremiah. *What the Bible Says about* Angels. Sisters: Multnomah, 1996.

Byang H. Kato. *Theological Pitfalls in Africa*. Kisumu: Evangel, 1975.

J. N. D. Kelly. *Early Christian Doctrines*. Revised edition. London: HarperOne, 1978.

Martin Nkafu Nkemnkia. *African Vitalogy: A Step Forward in African Thinking*. Nairobi: Paulines Publications Africa, 1999.

Agrippa Goodman Khathide. *Hidden Powers: Spirits in the First-Century Jewish World, Luke–Acts and in the African Context: An Analysis*. Kempton Park: AcadSA Publishing, 2007.

Herbert Lockyer. *All the Angels in the Bible: A Complete Exploration of the Nature and Ministry of Angels*. Peabody: Hendrickson, 1995.

A. Scott Moreau. *The Word of the Spirits: A Biblical Study in the African Context*. Nairobi: Evangel, 1990.

Arthur W. Pink. *The Nature of God*. Chicago: Moody Press, 1999.

Yusufu Turaki. *Foundations of African Traditional Religion and Worldview*. Nairobi: WorldAlive, 2006.

4

CREATION AND THE FALL

Africans have always believed that God is not only the creator of humanity but the creator of the universe and all that is in it. John Mbiti notes, "Over the whole of Africa creation is the most widely acknowledged work of God."[1] Maurice M. Makumba states,

> The coming into existence of the universe is closely linked to the African conception of God as Supreme Being; and if Supreme then also in charge of the being and sustenance of the world. This quality of God as Creator is mainly expressed in the stories and myths of African communities, which were orally passed from one generation to the next.[2]

The African names for God and descriptions of him give evidence of this belief. The Akan of Ghana, for example, refer to God as the "Creator, Originator, Inventor, Architect".[3] The Hausa of Nigeria say, *Allah mai kome mai kowa*, which translates as "God is the owner and creator of everybody and everything in the universe". In this respect, the African understanding of creation is close to the biblical one. However, it is only in the Bible that we find a complete picture of God's act of creation.

The Creation of the Universe

The Bible clearly states God created the entire universe and all that is in it (Gen 1:1). Everything that exists, whether animate or inanimate, physical or spiritual, material or immaterial, was created by him. Nehemiah 9:6 states, "You alone are the LORD. You made the heavens,

---

[1] John Mbiti, *African Religions and Philosophy* (2nd. ed., Oxford: Heinemann, 1990), 39.

[2] Maurice M. Makumba, *Natural Theology with African Annotations* (Nairobi: Paulines Publications, 2006), 204.

[3] Mbiti, *African Religions and Philosophy*, 39.

even the highest heavens, and all their starry host, the earth and all that is on it, the seas and all that is in them. You give life to everything, and the multitudes of heaven worship you" (see also Ps 90:2; Isa 40:26; Matt 19:4; Rom 1:25; Col 1:16).

God created the universe out of nothing: he did not make use of any pre-existing material (Gen 1:1–2; John 1:3). Nor did he make it out of any part of himself. In other words, the universe is distinct from God, and is not simply an extension of him, as pantheists maintain. This point is important because it "has profound repercussions for our interpretations of evil, for if the world is an extension of God then either (a) evil and good are equally ultimate, or (b) there is no final distinction between good and evil: whatever is, is good".[4] However, not everything in creation was made out of nothing: humankind was made out of some of the materials that God had already created (Gen 2:7).

The universe that God created was good. This point is made repeatedly in the account of creation (Gen 1:10, 12, 21, 25, 31).

God still preserves and sustains the universe. He is not like a watchmaker who makes a watch and then withdraws, leaving it to function totally on its own. On the contrary, God is still actively involved in the universe he created. He is "sustaining all things by his powerful word" (Heb 1:3) and "in him all things hold together" (Col 1:17).

> If God were to withdraw his upholding word, then all being, spiritual and material, would instantly tumble back into nothing and cease to exist. The continuation of the universe from one moment to the next is therefore as great a miracle and as fully the work of God as is its coming into being at the beginning.[5]

The universe depends on God for its survival.

But if God is good and created and sustains a good universe, why is there so much evil, pain and suffering in the world? This is a serious question that will be dealt with later in this chapter. At this stage, it is enough to point out that sometimes suffering follows when people try to thwart the laws of nature that God established at creation. For example, the law of gravity states that any object that is dropped will fall.

---

[4] Bruce Milne, *Know the Truth: A Handbook of Christian Belief* (rev. ed.; Downers Grove: InterVarsity Press, 1998), 90.

[5] Ibid., 92.

We cannot defy this law and jump from a ten-storey building. If we do this, we fall to our death. Though God created the law of gravity, he did not cause the death of the one who jumped off a building.

The Creation of Humanity

Genesis 1:27 gives a summary statement that "God created mankind in his own image, ... male and female he created them". Genesis 2 provides more detail about the creation of human beings. These passages make it clear that there is only one human race. We are all descended from one set of parents – Adam and Eve. This is true regardless of whether we are Black, Caucasian, Chinese, African or Japanese.

. We are also told that all of humankind was created in the "image of God". At its most fundamental level this must mean that there is some resemblance between us and our creator. There is disagreement about what exactly the points of similarity are, but we can safely say that human beings are like God in the following respects:

- *Being intelligent.* Adam gave evidence of this when he named the animals (Gen 2:20).

- *Having emotions.* Adam's excitement can be felt as he looked at his wife and exclaimed, "This is now bone of my bones and flesh of my flesh" (Gen 2:23).

- *Being social.* In the account of creation, God is presented as saying "Let us make mankind" (Gen 1:26). The plural "us" indicates that God himself lives in community within the Trinity. The man God created was also a social being, leading God to say, "It is not good for the man to be alone. I will make a helper suitable for him" (Gen 2:18). John Stott states that a human being "is a body-soul-in-community. For that is how God has made us."[6]

- *Having a conscience.* Adam and Eve knew what was good and what was bad, and when they sinned, they hid from the presence of the Lord (Gen 3:8).

- *Having a spirit through which to relate to God.* This distinguishes human beings from other created beings.

---

[6] John Stott, *New Issues Facing Christians Today* (Grand Rapids: Zondervan, 1999), 23.

Another question that theologians have long debated relates to our human nature. What are we? Our consciousness tells us that we are not merely physical entities but that we have an immaterial aspect. But what is this immaterial aspect? There are two main schools of thought.

1. *Body and soul.* The dichotomous view says that we consist only of a material element (the body) and an immaterial element (the soul). In support of this view, scholars quote Genesis 2:7, which states that God made Adam from the soil (body) and made him a "living soul" (KJV). "Soul" and "spirit" can be understood as interchangeable terms (Gen 41:8; Ps 42:6; Matt 20:28; John 12:27; 13:21; Heb 12:23).

2. *Body, soul and spirit.* The trichotomous view asserts that we do not merely have a body and a soul, but also a spirit. Supporters of this view also quote Genesis 2:7, which says, "the Lord God formed a man from the dust of the ground and breathed into his nostrils the breath of life, and the man became a living being." This can be interpreted to include the giving of both a spirit ("the breath of life") and a soul (whence the KJV translation, "a living soul"). Supporters also cite Hebrews 4:12, which speaks of both the soul and the spirit, and Paul's prayer in 1 Thessalonians 5:23, "May your whole spirit, soul and body be kept blameless", which implies three constituents.

The Fall

Earlier I mentioned the problem of the existence of evil in a universe created and upheld by a good God. Some Eastern religions have responded to this dilemma by attempting to deny the existence of evil, arguing that everything around us is just an illusion. But the Bible does not support this view. Other religions have responded by arguing that the universe is governed by two powerful deities, one good and the other evil, who are locked in eternal conflict. Sometimes evil wins; sometimes good overcomes evil. But this view is incompatible with the Bible, which asserts that God has ultimate control. True, there are evil beings who oppose him, but they too are his creations, even if they have rebelled against him. For some reason he still permits them to exist. But we know that he has also defeated them though the death of Christ on the cross. Eventually God will judge them (Rev 20:10).

The African understanding of sin

African Traditional Religion has less to say about the origins of sin than the Bible does. However, there are myths that give glimpses of the separation of God from human beings. For example, it is said that at one time God was close to humans beings, but then humans did something that made God retreat into the skies. The exact nature of the offence varies. In one version, a woman was pounding grain with her pestle and accidentally hit God in the face as she raised it above her head. Another version claims that men set fire to grass, and the smoke irritated God so much that he was forced to retreat. Some of the myths present a version of events that is similar to that in Genesis:

> Many myths say that the separation came as a result of the first men breaking one of God's regulations. The regulation concerned varies from people to people. Some say that people were forbidden to eat eggs, to eat animals, to eat certain fruit or yam, or to fight with one another. On breaking this regulation, men were sent away or God withdrew from them, and they lost many of the original benefits that they once received from God. [7]

These myths contain the grain of truth that it was indeed an offence committed by human beings that led to God being distant from humankind. But none of them suggest that either God or human beings made any attempt to heal the separation and restore their previous intimacy. Nor do any of these stories explain how evil took root in the human heart.

Africans do have various explanations for our constant struggle with sin and evil. A South African man explained to me that the sin and temptation in his life comes from his ancestors. According to tradition, he has two ancestors who were brothers – one good and the other evil. Both ancestors try to influence his life. The good one motivates him to do good and avoid evil, while the evil one tempts him to do evil. Morality lies in listening to the voice of the good ancestor. Others believe that Satan, evil spirits, people possessed by evil spirits, and aggrieved ancestors are behind many of the ills afflicting society.

---

[7] John S. Mbiti, *Introduction to African Religion* (Oxford: Heinemann, 1975), 80–81.

Africans tend not to speak of evil and sin as abstract concepts but see them as realities that manifest themselves in concrete human situations involving offences, wrongdoing, and the breaking of taboos and traditions. Laurenti Magesa explains this:

> In African Religion, wrongdoing relates to the contravention of specific codes of community expectations, including taboos. Individuals and the whole community must observe these forms of behavior to preserve order and assure the continuation of life in its fullness. To threaten in any way to break any of the community codes of behavior, which are in fact moral codes, endangers life, it is bad, wrong or 'sinful'.[8]

The consequences of bad behaviour also manifest themselves in daily life. For example, disrespecting one's parents is believed to lead to a childless marriage. According to the Bajju of Nigeria, committing adultery with the wife of a relative results in the death of the husband of the adulteress and sometimes of the adulterer, unless a special cleansing ritual is followed. Wrongdoing will always bring negative consequences until atonement is made. Thus many of the sacrifices in African Traditional Religion are attempts to reconcile a wrongdoer or wrongdoers with the gods, ancestral spirits and other people in order to avert the consequences of wrongdoing.

The African understanding of wrongdoing and the need for atonement provides a bridge for presenting biblical teaching about sinful humanity and God's provision of atonement through Christ.

Biblical teaching on the fall

The Scriptures explicitly teach that all suffering can be traced back to the sin of Adam and Eve who disobeyed God by eating the forbidden fruit (Gen 3:1-6). Their fall from grace broke their spiritual relationship with God. That was why they then hid from God (Gen 3:8), and God sent them out of his garden (3:23). These actions illustrate the point Isaiah makes: "your iniquities have separated you from your God; your sins have hidden his face from you, so that he will not hear" (Isa 59:2). We all now endure separation from God, which represents spiritual death

---

[8] Laurenti Magesa, *African Religion: The Moral Traditions of Abundant Life* (New York: Orbis, 1998), 166.

(Rom 6:23; Eph 2:5). This is only one of the three forms of death that have become the lot of all humanity. The other two are physical death (Heb 9:27) and eternal death, the ultimate separation of evil men and women from the holy God (Rev 20:5).

Not only did the fall break our relationship with God, it also affected our relationships with one another. Marriage, which should be permanent, monogamous, heterosexual and loving, has been displaced by temporary, polygamous and homosexual unions. Couples hate one another. Instead of showing love and respect, men seek to dominate their wives. God's gift of sex within marriage has been abused in rape and assault. Unborn children, who should be considered gifts from God, are aborted. Government has been perverted: instead of ensuring justice for all, it is now exploitative. Coups d'état, dictatorship and autocracy have become the order of the day.

Nature itself has been corrupted. Romans 8:22 describes the groaning of nature as it looks forward to its ultimate redemption. Because of the fall, the soil is often infertile, work is difficult, and childbirth is painful (Gen 3:16–19). Natural disasters are common, and so are sickness and suffering. Human actions exacerbate problems, as is shown on a large scale by global climate change and on a small scale by the lung cancers that result from smoking.

Sin has affected every aspect of our being – our minds, hearts and bodies. Jeremiah 17:9 states that we are totally corrupt (see also Gen 6:5; Pss 14:1–3; 36:1–4; Rom 3:10; 23; 7:18; Eph 2:3; 4:18). Even our good actions are like "filthy rags" in God's sight (Isa 64:6). This corruption of all aspects of our lives is what theologians mean when they talk about "total depravity". They are not saying that we no longer have any goodness or freedom. Though we are tainted by sin, we are still capable of doing some good things. We do still bear the image of God.

There are some who hold that the image of God was lost at the fall. However, this view seems to fly in the face of Scripture. When Paul speaks of the need for us to "put on the new self, which is being renewed in knowledge in the image of its Creator" (Col 3:10), he implies that God's image is still present, although it is badly damaged and in need of renewal. So the question that needs to be debated is how badly this image was damaged. Is it so broken that we are incapable of any goodness (the Calvinist view) or are we wounded but not incapable of good (the Roman Catholic and Arminian position)?

The biblical evidence affirms that the image of God in us has been damaged but not destroyed by sin (Gen 9:6; 1 Cor 11:7; Col 3:10; Jas 3:9):

> The *imago dei* has been darkened but not destroyed. It is marred by sin, but it still exists. Man continues to reflect the glory of his Creator, even in his sin and defiance. Man, even in the state of sin, has natural talents, intelligence, and also a moral sense though because of sin it cannot be regarded as a safe or sure guide.[9]

To put this in other words, though the face of a king may be distorted on a coin, it still remains the image of the king.

This understanding of who we are helps us to understand why human beings are such a mix of good and bad. John Stott rightly describes us as "a strange, bewildering paradox, dust of earth and breath of God, shame and glory ... noble and ignoble, rational and irrational, loving and selfish, Godlike and bestial."[10]

Every man or woman, whether a believer or an unbeliever, has a conscience – the ability to know right and wrong (Rom 2:15). We also have a will that enables us to choose how to act. But the fall has radically affected our ability to choose to do what is right. In Romans 7, Paul argues that even when he wanted to do what was right, another power (sin) forced him to do evil. We need the Holy Spirit to enable us to act according to the will of God and not according to the sinful desires and intentions of the heart (Phil 2:13; John 7:17).

This truth of human incapacity is hinted at in the Hausa saying *mutum dan tare ne*, which can be translated as "humanity is only nine". No human being scores a perfect ten out of ten. None of us can attain perfection.

---

[9] Donald G. Bloesch, *God, Authority and Salvation* (vol. 1 of *Essentials of Evangelical Theology*, San Francisco: Harper, 1982), 91.

[10] Stott, *New Issues*, 44.

Sin and Adam's Descendants

Through the sin of one man and one woman, the entire human race became sinful. To put it in theological terms, we can say that the fall was total, comprehensive and universal. How and why did it happen this way? Why should Adam and Eve's sin affect all of humanity?

Before responding to this question, we need to think more about the nature of the human soul. God breathed a soul into Adam (Gen 2:7), but how did his descendants receive souls? Some argue that souls exist before bodies, and are simply assigned to babies as they develop in the womb. This idea can be traced back to the Greek philosopher Plato. But there is no biblical support for this view. Moreover, if this idea of pre-existent souls were correct, we could not really be held responsible for our actions; our souls would determine who we are and what we do.

Others argue that God creates a unique soul for every person at conception. Only the body is generated by the parents; the soul is added later in a baby's development. This is the Roman Catholic position. But while it is true that the Bible does speak of God creating the soul (Num 16:22; Eccl 12:7; 57:16; Zech 12:1; Heb 12:9), it also speaks of God as the creator of the body (Ps 139:13; Jer 1:5). A more serious problem with this creation theory is that it implies that God makes sinful souls, for we are all sinners. But God is good, and he can have nothing to do with sin.

The explanation that best fits the biblical data is known as the traducian theory. It holds that the whole human race was created by God in Adam as body, soul and spirit. Now God no longer creates people directly; he does so through the human process of procreation. Acts 17:26 is used to support this view: "From one man [Adam] he [God] made all the nations." Another passage that is cited is Hebrews 7:9, which indicates that the yet unborn Levi paid tithes when Abraham paid tithes, indicating that Levi was within Abraham.

These explanations regarding the transmission of the soul have implications for our understanding of how Adam's sinful nature was passed on to his descendants. This transmission has clearly happened, for the Bible makes a direct connection between the sin of one man (Adam) and the sin of all people: "sin entered the world through one man, and death through sin, and in this way death came to all people, because all sinned" (Rom 5:12). God's judgement against Adam also applies to every one of Adam's descendants, for "all have sinned and fall short of the glory of God" (Rom 3:23). How did this come about? Let us look at some of the theories that have been put forward. It is worth paying attention to these, because they have important implications for our understanding of how people can be saved from their sinful condition, as we will see in the next chapter.

1. *Pelagianism* was developed in the fourth century by a British monk named Pelagius. He agreed with the creation theory of souls, and so believed that every soul was directly created by God. Because God cannot create evil, every soul must thus be innocent. So Pelagius argued that Adam's sin affected only himself and was not passed on to his descendants. When we sin, it is not because we have a sinful nature but because we are following Adam's bad example. Our wills are completely free, and we have the capacity to do what is good. Many preachers today seem to adopt this position (whether consciously or not) when they speak as if we have total freedom to choose to obey God. But this is contrary to Scripture, which says that our hearts are "deceitful above all things and beyond cure" (Jer 17:9). It also undermines Paul's teaching about the unmerited grace of God. Pelagianism is thus widely regarded as heretical, but it has influenced the theology of Unitarianism and liberal Protestantism.

2. *Augustinianism* is based on the thinking of Augustine, who was the bishop of Hippo in North Africa in the fourth century. He upheld the doctrine of original sin, which states that when Adam sinned, his nature was corrupted. He then passed on this corrupted nature to his descendants, with the result that they too have a sinful nature (Gen 1:26–27; 5:2; Rom 7:1). This is why the psalmist says, "Surely I was sinful at birth, sinful from the time my mother conceived me" (Ps 51:5). He was sinful not just because of his own conscious deeds but because sinfulness was an inherent part of his nature. Other Bible passages also indicate that our sinful nature was inherited by natural generation (Job 14:4; 15:14; Ps 58:3; Eph 2:3).

3. *The federal theory.* Some argue that we are sinners not because we inherited a sinful nature from Adam, but because he was the head of the human race. As such, whatever he did was equivalent to the action of the entire human race. Thus we are all sinners because he sinned (Rom 5:12). This position is very similar to that known as the

realistic theory or *natural headship*, which says that because we were all within Adam (as his future descendants) when he sinned, we are all co-sinners with him.[11]

4. The *corporate personality theory*. Some argue that there is a close association between each individual and the group of which he or she is part. Thus when Achan sinned, the nation suffered defeat and his own family shared his punishment (Josh 7; see also 1 Sam 24:21). On the same basis, when Adam sinned, the rest of humanity shared his guilt.

While there may be disagreement about the details of how it comes about, the key biblical and theological truth to be remembered is that in Adam all humanity is guilty of sin before God. We have all "sinned and come short of the glory of God" (Rom 3:23). All of us stand in need of salvation.

Questions

1. What are the traditional beliefs in your community about how the world and people were created? In what respects are these similar to the Christian view, and in what ways are they different?

2. What does your community believe about how sin or evil came into the world? How does this affect your community's understanding of human nature and of how best to deal with sin?

3. What are the key scriptural passages concerning original sin?

4. What is the meaning of "total depravity"? What is the scriptural evidence for this doctrine?

5. Does the Augustinian theory, the federal headship theory or the corporate personality theory better reflect the teaching of Scripture?

Further Reading

Donald G. Bloesch. *God, Authority & Salvation.* Vol. 1 of *The Essentials of Evangelical Theology.* San Francisco: Harper, 1982.

---

[11] Henry C. Thiessen, *Lectures in Systematic Theology* (rev. by Vernon D. Doerksen; Grand Rapids: Eerdmans, 1979), 188–189.

Anthony A. Hoekema. *Created in God's Image*. Grand Rapids: Eerdmans, 1986.

Maurice M. Makumba. *Natural Theology with African Annotations*. Nairobi: Paulines Publications, 2006.

Bruce Milne. *Know the Truth: A Handbook of Christian Belief*. Revised edition. Downers Grove: InterVarsity Press, 1998.

Yusufu Turaki. *The Trinity of Sin*. Jos, Nairobi and Accra: HippoBooks / Grand Rapids: Zondervan, 2012.

5

CHRIST AND SALVATION

The doctrine of salvation is the centrepiece of Christian theology. Without it, the whole Christian religion disintegrates. It is what distinguishes Christianity from all other religions. But before we begin to study the doctrine of salvation, it is important to remind ourselves of the scope of our need for salvation. As seen in the previous chapter, humanity and all creation are mired in sin from which we cannot escape. Sin has separated us from God for all eternity. It has also brought physical and emotional suffering into our world. So what is needed is salvation on all these levels: spiritual, physical and emotional. Thus any teaching about salvation that deals only with our spiritual well-being and ignores other aspects of life is distorted and does not reflect the teaching of the Bible. Christ came so that we could have life "to the full" (John 10:10). This also includes our social life. Although we come to salvation individually, we then immediately become part of the community of God. We are reborn into the family of God just as we were originally born into our human families.

At the heart of the doctrine of salvation is the person and work of Jesus Christ. Scripture clearly identifies him as "the pioneer and perfecter of our faith" (Heb 12:2). It also insists that salvation is for those who confess their faith in Jesus Christ on the basis of his death, burial and resurrection (Rom 10:9; Acts 16:31). There is no salvation outside of the person and work of Christ (Acts 4:12). All those who are without him are lost.

As the Swiss theologian Hans Küng reminds us, "Jesus Christ is neither an unhistorical myth nor a superhistorical idea, doctrine or world view. He is rather the historical Jesus of Nazareth, who according to the testimonies in the New Testament is the standard for believers of all times and all churches as the Anointed One of God."[1] Any life or

---

[1] Hans Küng, *Theology for the Third Millennium: The Ecumenical View* (trans. Peter Heinegg; New York: Doubleday, 1988), 156.

philosophy that detracts from this complete understanding of Christ will lead to a distorted view of Christianity.

Before we look at what the Bible has to say about who Christ is and what he has done, we will look at some of the ways contemporary African theologians have understood him.[2]

Christ in Contemporary African Theologies

Western theologies have often ignored the African context, and so African theologians have felt the need to express the Christian faith in a way that is deeply rooted in their own cultures and expressed in their own language. Thus Efoe Julien Penoukou seeks to root it in the cultural context of his own Ewe-Mina ethnic group in Togo and Benin. They conceive of reality "as a continuous passage from life to death and from death to life", and so Penoukou's Christology focuses on the death and resurrection of Jesus.[3] So does that of Kwesi Dickson of Ghana. Charles Nyaminti, a Tanzanian, similarly roots his Christology in the African world view, but he chooses to focus on the African understanding of what it means to be human, and so focuses on the incarnation as the highest expression of this.

Other theologians identify Christ's role in terms of familiar African roles. Thus Harry Sawyer of Sierra Leone presents Christ as being like the African Elder Brother. As such, he is the head of the great family, the church. J. S. Pobee from Ghana seeks to understand what it means for Christ to be truly God and truly man according to the Akan tradition and focuses on Christ as the Great Ancestor (*Nana* in the Akan language) who supersedes all spiritual beings and ancestors among the Akan. A. T. Sanon from Burkina Faso presents Jesus as the Head and Master of Initiation and interprets the various stages of Jesus' life in light of the African understanding of initiation. Cécé Kolié sees Jesus' role as Healer as the most meaningful to Christianity in North Africa. (British missiologist Aylward Shorter, too, focuses on healing in his Christology.) Bénézet Bujo focuses on the concept of Jesus as the proto-ancestor: "the unique ancestor, the source of life and highest model of ancestorship".[4]

---

[2] Robert J. Schreiter, *Faces of Jesus in Africa* (Maryknoll: Orbis, 2005) offers a good review and summary of these Christologies.

[3] Ibid., 27.

[4] Ibid., 10.

South Africa's struggle against apartheid led theologians such as Laurenti Magesa from East Africa to develop the theme of Christ as the liberator, under the influence of South American liberation theology.

There are several positive aspects to these presentations of Christ. It is good to use creativity when seeking to present Jesus in a way that makes sense to a particular community. It is also good to learn from anthropological studies that give us insight into the world views of those we hope to reach and provide relevant language in which to communicate theology. For example, words like ancestor, healer, diviner, elder brother, guest, and master initiator have profound meanings in Africa, and capturing these words for the Christian religion is very important for the establishment of Christianity on the continent. Translation of the biblical world view into an African Christian world view helps to make Christianity truly African. It also ensures that the questions that African Christians struggle with are seriously discussed.

But there are also problems with any study of theology that takes human culture rather than divine revelation as its starting point. A theology written "from below" tends to emphasize how we relate to God rather than how God relates to us. The result is that many African Christologies make no attempt to deal with who Christ is but instead focus only what he does for us. Even when they do address the bigger question, they often contain sweeping generalizations rooted in anthropology rather than in theology.

Fundamentally, theology is making sense of the word of God. The emphasis should be on understanding God from his perspective; thus his word should be the primary text of theology. However, many African theologies reflect the African world view in which humanity is at the centre of the universe. The source of theology therefore becomes human experience and beliefs, and the African world view is the basis from which to judge the meaning of Scripture. African experiences of God become equal in authority to the experiences of God's people in the Old and New Testaments. However, as discussed in chapter 2, while God is indeed the creator and father of all human races and has revealed himself to them all in history, nature and conscience, the special revelation of the Scriptures has a greater authority than human experiences or traditions. It is too optimistic to think that the perception and understanding of God in the African world view is exactly the same as the understanding we derive from the Bible.

Another major weakness in developing theology from an anthropological perspective is that it undermines exegesis, which is the study of a Bible passage in order to find its true meaning. Too often, an anthropological meaning is imposed on the Bible rather than allowing the text to speak for itself. But a balanced Christology must be truly biblical: it must understand the true meaning of the word of God while also speaking to the needs and aspirations of the people in the local context. Insights gained from anthropological study do not have the same revelatory status and authority as the truth of the inerrant word of God. Consequently, all insights obtained from such studies must be subjected to the scrutiny of the Scriptures. Our theology should be judged by the rigorous way in which we interact with the Scriptures and apply them to the local context. Note that the main issue here is not whether the questions being discussed arise from the biblical text or from the local context, but the source of final authority. The Scriptures must have the final and ultimate judgement.

A serious weakness of African Christology is that it tends to see Jesus Christ simply through the lens of human images. To describe him only as a healer, diviner and proto-ancestor is to honour his humanity but neglect his deity and divine attributes. Yes, he may be elevated to the status of a super-ancestral spirit who is always there to help in times of need, but those who ascribe him such a status fail to recognize that he is truly and fully God (Col 2:9). A view of Christ which emphasizes his humanity without at the same time emphasizing his deity distorts the Bible's teaching.

Having said all this, it is time to turn to the Scriptures and see what the Bible itself teaches about Christ.

Who Christ Is

In the discussion of the Trinity in chapter 3, we pointed out that the Bible teaches that Jesus Christ, the Second Person of the Trinity, is truly God and truly man. This claim can be supported from both the Old and New Testaments

Fully God

1. In Genesis 1, God refers to himself in the plural: "Let us make mankind in our image" (Gen 1:26–27; see also Gen 11:7, where he

says, "Let us go down and confuse their language"). In the context, and taken with the rest of the teaching of Scripture, this statement clearly indicates a plurality of persons within the Godhead.

2. Christ existed before creation and was its creator (John 1:1–3; Col 1:16; Heb 1:10).

3. The deity of Christ is explicitly stated (John 1:1–2, 18; 20:28; Rom 9:5; Heb 1:8; Titus 2:13; 1 John 5:20).

4. Jesus is frequently identified as Lord and God (John 20:28; Acts 2:34–36; Rom 9:5; 10:9; 1 Cor 12:3; Phil 2:11), both titles that assert his divinity.

5. Jesus is offered the same worship offered to God (2 Tim 4:18; 2 Pet 3:8; Rev 1:5–8). This is particularly striking in light of the fact that his first followers were Jews who accepted the Old Testament, with its insistence that there is only one God and that he alone is to be worshipped (Exod 20:3–6; Deut 6:4).

6. Jesus possesses the attributes of deity: he is eternal (John 1:1, 15; 8:58; 17:5, 24), omnipresent (Matt 18:20; 28:20; John 3:13; Eph 1:23), omniscient (John 2:24–25; Col 2:3), omnipotent (Isa 9:6; John 5:19; Heb 1:3; Rev 1:8) and immutable (Heb 1:12; 13:8).

8. Jesus does things that that only God can do: he forgives sins (Matt 9:2, 6; Luke 7:47–49); he rose from the dead (John 10:17–18); he raised others from the dead (Luke 7:12–16; Mark 5:35–43; John 11:38–44); and he will judge the world (John 5:22).

Fully human

Christ's full humanity is rarely debated. It is easier for us to understand than his divinity, and is explicitly taught by numerous Scriptures which show that he experienced the complete human life cycle: conception, birth, life, suffering and death.

1. He was born like every other human being (except Adam and Eve). Thus, he was born by a woman (Gal 4:4; Matt 1:18–21; Luke 1:30–31). True, his conception was miraculous, being brought about by the Holy Spirit rather than a man, so that Mary conceived despite being a virgin (Matt 1:18–20). Yet because of his birth from a human parent, Jesus has genuine human parentage (Matt 1:1–17). He

can be said to be descended from the royal line of King David, in accordance with Old Testament prophecy (Luke 1:26–33).

2. He grew up like any other normal human being, needing food, water, drink, clothing and shelter (Matt 4:2; 8:24; 21:18). He was thus familiar with the human experiences of hunger, thirst, happiness and sadness (Matt 26:38; Mark 8:12; John 4:6). He could sense danger and seek to escape it, which also speaks of a very real humanity (John 12:27; see also Heb 4:15).

3. He experienced suffering and death like a normal human being (Mark 15:37; Heb 2:18). If he were merely a disguised spirit being, like an angel, he would not have died.

The mystery of the divine and human in Christ

There is a great mystery in the incarnation, the event in which the pre-existent Christ took on human form and came to live among us on earth (John 1:1, 14; Phil 2:5–11). "How could that one life be both completely human and completely divine?"[5] As people have wrestled with understanding this truth, some explanations have been offered that the church has rejected as untrue to Scripture. Some lay too much stress on his divinity; others on his humanity. People still fall into these heresies today, often without even knowing it, and so it is worth knowing a little bit about them in order to avoid them:

• *Gnosticism* was a heresy that arose from dualistic thinking that saw good and evil, spirit and matter, God and a demiurge as in perpetual conflict. Gnostics associated matter with the demiurge (a god of evil, opposed to the holy God). They therefore insisted that Jesus could not have been human because being human requires a human body, and a body is composed of matter, which is inherently evil. So Jesus must only have appeared to be a human being while he was in actual fact a spirit. Gnosticism was condemned by the early church.

• *Docetism* drew heavily from Gnosticism and also held that Jesus was fully God, but not human. He only appeared to be human and to have a human body. (The name of this heresy comes from the Greek word *dokew*, which means to "appear" or "seem").

---

[5] D. M. Baillie, *God was in Christ: An Essay on Incarnation and Atonement* (London: Faber & Faber, 1963), 106.

- *Ebionism* gets its name from a Jewish Christian sect who argued that Jesus was merely the human son of Mary and Joseph, but became divine when God adopted him at his baptism.

- *Arianism* was taught by Arius, an early Christian who argued that Jesus was a created being and was therefore not fully God. It was in response to Arius' teaching that the Nicene Creed of AD 325 was drawn up. It insists that Jesus is "very God" and "very man" (see chapter 3).

- *Nestorianism* denied that Christ's nature was a union of both his divine and human natures. It maintained that Jesus had two personalities, one human and one divine. The Council of Ephesus of AD 431 condemned this teaching as heretical.

- *Apollinarianism* attempted to honour the divine nature of Christ by argued that although Jesus had a human body, he did not have a human mind. His mind and spirit were purely divine. This position, too, was condemned at the Council of Constantinople in AD 381.

- *Eutychianism* attempted to refute the Nestorian view that Christ had two distinct natures by arguing that his divine and human natures were fused into a third nature, which was neither divine nor human. The Council of Chalcedon in AD 451 condemned this teaching and confirmed the two natures of Christ united in the one person of Christ.

The reason the church rejected all of the positions above was that they did not agree with the Scriptures. The Gospels clearly show that Jesus was conscious of his existence as one person, pre-existent yet incarnate in human nature. He was conscious of his pre-existence with the Father (John 3:31; 8:58) and told the Pharisees, "Before Abraham was born, I am!" (John 8:58). They understood this to be a clear claim that he was equal with God, and so sought to stone him for blasphemy (8:59). He was conscious of being the Son of God (Matt 4:3, 6). At both his baptism and his temptation, the Father announced from heaven that Jesus was his Son. Jesus was also conscious of being fully human. He often referred to himself as "the Son of Man" (Matt 9:6; 12:40; Mark 8:31; Luke 19:10; John 3:13–14).

Other inspired writers of the Scriptures also asserted that Jesus was the eternal God and yet fully human (John 1:1, 14, 18; Col 2:9).

Hebrews 1:3 asserts that "the Son is the radiance of God's glory and the exact representation of his being." Colossians 2:9 has the same force and clarity: "For in Christ all the fullness of the Deity lives in bodily form."

Christ's equality with God is also emphasized in the great hymn in Philippians 2:6–11. However, the reference in 2:7 to Christ making himself nothing, or emptying himself, has led to debate about the extent to which he did this. Did he give up his divinity when he became human? The answer would appear to be No, which is why the NIV does not translate 2:7 as "emptied". What the hymn is saying is that Christ gave up the privileges of being God when he accepted human nature. It does not say that he ceased to be God. This interpretation is consistent with other scriptural statements about Jesus becoming "flesh" and making "his dwelling among us" (John 1:14, 18). A view that interprets Christ's emptying of himself as reducing his divinity does damage to the Bible's teaching that Jesus was fully God (Col 2:9).

The unity of the two natures in Christ is something that we cannot fully explain; yet to deny it is unbiblical. In the same way, there is much about God that baffles our minds. Yet the Scriptures state that Christ revealed the true God to us, and we must therefore focus more on the incarnation if we are to have a true picture of God. It will help us to get rid of some of the preconceived notions of God that often cloud our understanding of the true God revealed in Christ.

> It is astonishing how lightly many people assume that they know what the word "God" means. But it is still more astonishing that even when we profess Christian belief and set out to try to understand the mystery of God becoming man, we are apt to start with some concept of God, picked up we know not where, an idol of the cave or of the market-place, and then to attempt the impossible task of understanding how such a God could be incarnate in Jesus. If the Incarnation has supremely revealed God, shown Him to us in a new and illuminating light, put a fresh meaning into the very word that is his name, *that* is the meaning that we must use in facing the problem of the Incarnation, because that is what God really is. It is only as Christians that we can hope to understand the Incarnation.[6]

---

[6] Ibid., 118–9.

What Christ Has Done

Why did Christ come to this earth as a divine and human person? Or in other words, what was the work he came to do? The answer is that he came to perform three types of work, namely a prophetic ministry, a priestly ministry and a kingly ministry.

1. *Prophetic ministry.* A prophet is one who "reveals God to us and speaks to us the words of God".[7] The Old Testament predicts Christ's ministry as prophet (Deut 18:15–18). The New Testament records Jesus being called a prophet during his earthly ministry (Matt 16:14; Luke 7:16; John 4:19; 6:14; 7:40). "Christ is of course truly and fully a prophet. In fact, he is the one whom all the Old Testament prophets prefigured in their speech and in their actions."[8]

2. *Priestly ministry.* A priest is a "God-appointed mediator between God and man through whose intercession, by the offering of blood, atonement is made and justification obtained for the guilty sinner (Lev. 4:16–18)".[9] In the Old Testament, Jesus Christ is predicted to be a priest (Ps 110:4; see also Heb 5:6; 6:20; 7:21). As a priest, Jesus acted on behalf of people before God (Mic 6:6–7; Heb 10:4–7; 7:26–27). The sacrifice he offered was perfect, final and permanent (Heb 9:11–14; 10:12–14). He now intercedes for us as priest (Heb 7:25; Rom 8:34; John 17:1–26).

3. *Kingly ministry.* In the Old Testament, the king had complete authority over his subjects, whom he was to rule with justice and righteousness. The Old Testament predicted that Christ would be a king, and he was recognized as such in the New Testament (2 Sam 7:16; Ps 45:6–7; Isa 9:7; Dan 7:13–14; Matt 4:17; Luke 1:32–33; 17:21; Rev 19:16). Christ's absolute rule will be demonstrated visibly when he sits on the glorious throne in heaven (Matt 13:41; 25:31; Heb 12:2).

Not only did Christ fulfil the offices of king, prophet and priest, but he also accomplished something that only he was qualified to do. Being fully God and fully human, and without sin (Heb 2:17; 1 John 3:5), Jesus offered himself as a substitute for us. He died in our place, bearing

---

[7] Wayne Grudem, *Systematic Theology* (Grand Rapids: Zondervan, 1994), 624.

[8] Ibid., 625.

[9] Emery H. Bancroft, *Christian Theology: Systematic and Biblical* (2d ed.; Grand Rapids: Zondervan, 1976), 111.

God's punishment for sin on our behalf (2 Cor 5:21; Gal 1:14; Eph 5:2; Heb 9:28). Christ's sacrificial death provided salvation for sinful humanity. This aspect of Christ's work is known as his atonement.

Another way of describing what Christ did for us is to say that he paid our *ransom*. As sinners, we were all held captive by the devil. So Jesus came "to give his life as a ransom for many" (Mark 10:45; see also Eph 1:7; Heb 9:12; 1 Tim 2:6; 1 Pet 1:18). This metaphor should not be pushed to the point where we say that God "paid" Satan to set us free. The Bible teaches that the sacrifice of Jesus satisfied God's wrath against sin and reconciled sinners to God. In doing this, it also set us free from our captivity to Satan.

When we focus on God's anger against sin, we can also describe Christ's death as an *expiation* (Matt 16:22; Luke 18:1; Heb 2:17) that appeased God's wrath and reconciled sinners to God (Rom 5:1, 10–11; Eph 1:16; Col 1:19–20).

We could sum up Christ's work by saying that "the reason the Son of God appeared was to destroy the devil's work" (1 John 3:8). The writer to Hebrews makes the same point: "Since the children have flesh and blood, he too shared in their humanity so that by his death he might break the power of him who holds the power of death – that is, the devil – and free those who all their lives were held in slavery by their fear of death" (Heb 2:14–15) His work on the cross defeated Satan (John 12:31; 14:30), who will ultimately be cast into the lake of fire (Rev 20:10).

Because of what Christ has done, he is also the founder and head of the church, "which he bought with his own blood" (Acts 20:28).

The Extent of Christ's Atonement

Two important questions have been raised about the work of Christ: 1) Did he die for all people or only for the elect? 2) Is it a case of "once saved, always saved" or can one lose one's salvation? In other words, what happens to Christians who have backslidden or who die without repenting of their sins? The answers we give to these questions have important implications for how we go about evangelism and for how we live as Christians. Thus these are far more than merely matters of intellectual curiosity.

Did Christ die for all?

John 3:16 says that "God so loved the world that he gave his one and only Son". This implies that Christ loved and died for the whole world. But we also know that not everyone will be saved. Thus some of those for whom Christ died will not be saved. How is this possible? In wrestling with this problem, theologians tend to fall into one of two camps, influenced by their understanding of who God is in relation to sinners.

The Arminian position

Unlike the Pelagians who deny that the fall directly affected all of Adam's descendants, Arminians acknowledge that we are deeply affected by sin in every part of our being and are unable of ourselves to reach out to God. However, they argue that through his prevenient grace, God gives everyone a free will that enables them to choose to respond to God, repent of their sins and come to salvation. God foreknows who will do this, and this is what the Bible means when it speaks of God electing or "choosing" some people. Because people have free will, they can also choose to reject God's gracious offer of salvation, which is offered to all, regardless of merit. One of the most influential preachers to hold the Arminian position was John Wesley (1703–1791), the English evangelist and founder of Methodism.

The Calvinist position

Calvinism was strongly influenced by Augustine of Hippo (AD 354–430) who stressed that we completely lost our free will when Adam and Eve sinned. Unlike the Arminians, Calvinists insist that this free will has never been restored.

The Calvinist position is often summmarized using the mnemonic TULIP:

- **Total depravity**: all men and women are affected by sin in every part of their being and are incapable of doing anything good in God's sight.
- **Unconditional election**: God unconditionally and sovereignly elects those who will experience his salvation. This choice is not based on a human response to him, but purely on God's love before those whom he chooses are even born and able to make a response.

- Limited redemption: Christ has secured the redemption only of those who are his, the elect.
- Irresistible grace: all those who have been elected will come to salvation. They cannot resist this grace extended to them by God.
- Perseverance of the saints (believers): those who are so chosen and redeemed will persevere in the faith and will not backslide or fall from grace because God will keep them from doing so.

Discussion

Both the Arminian and the Calvinist positions can claim biblical support. My own position is that the Calvinist position is closer to the Bible's teaching as a whole. However, I also think that the traditional Calvinist position as described above needs to be modified because its stress on limited redemption does not do justice to the many passages in the Bible that say that Christ died for the whole world. Besides John 3:16, these include:

- John 1:29: "the Lamb of God who takes the sins of the world".
- 1 Timothy 2:5–6: "Christ Jesus, who gave himself as a ransom for all people".
- Titus 2:11: "For the grace of God has appeared that offers salvation to all people".
- Hebrews 2:9: Christ came so that "he might taste death for everyone" (see also 2 Pet 3:9; 1 John 2:2).

On the other hand, several passages teach that Christ died to secure the salvation of a particular group:

- John 17:9: "I pray for them. I am not praying for the world, but for those you have given me, for they are yours".
- Ephesians 5:25: "Christ loved the church and gave himself up for her".

On balance, it seems that the Bible teaches that Christ's atonement was intended for the whole world, but that only those who are called are ultimately saved. Scripture clearly teaches that some will perish even though Christ died for them: "there were also false prophets among the people, just as there will be false teachers among you. They will secretly introduce destructive heresies, even denying the sovereign Lord *who bought them* – bringing swift destruction on themselves" (2 Pet

2:1, emphasis added). A revised Calvinistic scheme would thus read as follows: Total depravity, unconditional election, unlimited atonement–limited redemption, irresistible grace, and perseverance of the saints.

This position does give rise to many questions about the relationship between the justice of God and predestination, election and foreknowledge. Nevertheless, it is clear that predestination (God's selection of who will believe) is explicitly taught in Scripture (Rom 8:28–29; Eph 1:11). However, when speaking about predestination, we must never treat it in isolation from God's entire plan of salvation. All have sinned and all are destined for eternal damnation. In his infinite love, God has provided salvation in Jesus for those who confess their sin and believe in the grace of God (2 Cor 5:18–20). Outside of this provision of God, nobody can be saved (Acts 4:12). It is the grace of God that draws sinners to God for his own glory. Predestination is not based on God's prior knowledge of who will believe in him, but is a purposeful, loving setting apart for himself before creation of all those whom he chooses to come to a saving knowledge of Jesus Christ.

Can one lose one's salvation?

Arminians would argue that given our free will, we can indeed choose to turn away from God and lose our salvation (Heb 3:7–19; 6:4; 10:26–27). They say that the Calvinist doctrine of the perseverance of the saints (or the eternal security of the believer) allows those who have come to conversion to live carelessly and irresponsibly. Calvinists would dispute this. They argue that a redeemed life results in responsible behaviour. If a person lives irresponsibly, it may indicate that he or she was never saved. It is not that believers will achieve total perfection or sinlessness in this life, for the Bible calls us to ongoing repentance and changed lives. But the doctrine of perseverance gives those who have been redeemed confidence that they will not backslide or fall from grace because God will keep them from falling.

Questions

1. The Arminian and Calvinist views of human nature and free will affect our understanding of salvation. Which view best fits the biblical evidence? How does the position you support affect your preaching and evangelism?

2. How would you respond to someone who insisted that Jesus was only an ordinary man and not fully God?

3. What does the priestly ministry of Christ mean according to Romans 8:34, and how does that help you in your Christian life? What other biblical passages teach about Christ's intercession for believers?

4. What does the kingly ministry of Christ mean to you as regards your approach to spiritual warfare, witchcraft, the occult and secret societies? (Consider passages such as Matt 28:18; 1 Cor 15:25; Eph 1:20–22).

5. What does Ephesians 2:6 mean when it speaks of God raising us up with Christ and seating us "with him in the heavenly realms in Christ Jesus"?

6. What does the Bible teach about the assurance of salvation?

7. How would you advise Christians who have doubts about whether they are going to heaven after death?

8. What does conversion mean (Acts 2:38)? Please share the testimony of your conversion.

9. How can you know that one can be born again? (John 1:13; 3:3-8; Titus 3:5; 1 Peter 1:3).

Further Reading

James Montgomery Boice and Philip Graham Ryken. *The Doctrine of Grace: Rediscovering the Evangelical Gospel*. Wheaton: Crossway, 2002.

Anthony A. Hoekema. *Saved By Grace*. Grand Rapids: Eerdmans, 1989.

Leon Morris. *The Atonement: Its Meaning and Significance*. Downers Grove: InterVarsity Press, 1983.

Earl D. Radmacher. *Salvation*. Nashville: Thomas Nelson, 2000.

Robert J. Schreiter, ed. *Faces of Jesus in Africa*. Maryknoll: Orbis, 2005.

John R. W. Stott. *The Cross of Christ*. Downers Grove: InterVarsity Press, 2006.

6

THE HOLY SPIRIT AND SALVATION

In the past, the Holy Spirit was often neglected in Christian thinking, but Pentecostalism has awakened the church to the reality of the Spirit's role in our salvation and in our Christian life.

Who the Holy Spirit Is

The Holy Spirit is not a thing or an inanimate object. He is a full person with all the traits of a person. This is clear from John 14:16–18, where Jesus referred to the Holy Spirit as "*another* advocate", indicating that the Spirit is a person with the same nature as Jesus, but distinct from Jesus (see also John 15:26). There are also other indicators in Scripture that the Holy Spirit is a person:

1. The Holy Spirit was involved in the creation of the universe (Gen 1:2). As such, he must be included in the "let us" statements in Genesis 1:26 and 11:7, which indicates that he is fully God. Like God, he is the giver of life (Job 33:4).

2. He is often referred to in parallel with the Father and the Son (Matt 28:19; Acts 5:3–4; 2 Cor 13:14; 1 Pet 1:2, 20–21). It does violence to Scripture to try to interpret these texts as implying that the Spirit has a lower status than the Father and the Son. Moreover, he is explicitly equated with God in Acts 5:3–4.

3. When Jesus speaks about sinning against the Holy Spirit (Matt 12:31–32) he must be referring to a person, for one cannot sin against an inanimate object.

4. The Spirit has divine qualities, such as holiness, omnipotence (Luke 1:35), omniscience (John 16:12–13; 1 Cor 2:10–11) and omnipresence (Ps 139:7–10).

What the Holy Spirit Does

The Holy Spirit does what God does, including creating and sustaining the universe, inspiring Scripture (2 Pet 1:20–21) and raising Christ from the dead (Rom 8:11). He is still active in the world today as he and the two other members of the Trinity, God the Father and God the Son, work together to accomplish our salvation. We see a clear example of their cooperation in the description of Jesus' baptism: The Son is baptized, the Father speaks from heaven, and the Holy Spirit descends as a dove (Luke 3:22).

To be able to understand the roles of the different members of the Trinity, we need to understand that there is more than one process involved in our salvation. These processes are not necessarily sequential – they can overlap or occur simultaneously. But it is useful to distinguish them in order to develop a fuller understanding of what salvation involves.

However, before looking at these in detail we need to remind ourselves that salvation is entirely the result of what God has done (Rom 3:21–23; Eph 2:8–9). This belief is referred to by theologians as monergism (a word that combines two Greek words meaning "sole" and "work"). It is contrasted with *synergism* (a word that comes from Greek words meaning "together" and "work"), which refers to the teaching that people cooperate with God in achieving salvation. The reason we cannot contribute anything to our salvation will become evident as we look at what salvation involves.

Regeneration

Because of Adam's sin (see chapter 4) we who are Adam's descendants are sinful in our thoughts and desires ourselves (Rom 3:10–20). The Bible describes us as "dead in ... transgressions and sins" (Eph 2:1–2; see also Rom 5:12). Those who are dead are incapable of saving themselves. The Spirit is the one who regenerates people, bringing them to life. He does this by convicting unbelievers of sin and of who Christ is (John

15:26; 16:8) and making it possible for them to be reborn spiritually (John 3:2–15; Titus 3:5). This rebirth makes them "children of God" (John 1:12–13). In other words, it brings them into union with God and establishes them as members of the body of Christ of which he is the head (1 Cor 12:13).

Justification

When people are moved by the Spirit to turn to him, God declares them righteous on the basis of Christ's death and resurrection (Rom 3:21–26; 8:1; 2 Cor 5:19–21; Eph 2:8–10). This is a legal declaration of their new status, a status they have neither earned nor deserved. "God has pronounced the eschatological verdict of acquittal over the man of faith in the present, in advance of the final judgement".[1]

Conversion (repentance and faith)

The Spirit moves people to repent, and God is eager to justify the repentant. But sinners must convert, or in other words, they must turn away from sin (repentance) and turn to God (faith). This is what Peter urged the people of Jerusalem to do (Acts 2:38). This conversion may take the form of a dramatic change, or it may be a process in which the person gradually comes to faith. But however it happens, the Bible uses powerful images to describe it, including deliverance from darkness to light (Col 1:13) and turning away from idols to serve the living God (1 Thess 1:9).

However, it is important to note that conversion is not something that earns or merits salvation. We do not deserve to be forgiven just because we repent. Salvation is by grace alone: "For it is by grace you have been saved, through faith – and this is not from yourselves, it is the gift of God – not by works, so that no one can boast (Eph 2:8–9). Even this faith is a work of God (John 6:29). God alone is the cause of salvation (John 1:12; 2 Cor 4:6; Col 2:12–13). By grace we are called (Gal 1:15), justified (Rom 3:24) and sanctified (Rom 6:12). By grace we have access into God's presence (Rom 5:2), an eternal inheritance and a good hope (2 Thess 2:16), and the strength to endure (2 Tim 2:1). Salvation is by grace alone from start to finish (2 Cor 6:1).

---

[1] George Ladd, *A Theology of the New Testament* (Grand Rapids: Eerdmans, 1974), 446.

Indwelling

The Holy Spirit dwells within every believer (John 14:16–17; 1 Cor 6:19). Where he is absent, that person is not saved (Rom 8:9; Jude 19). His indwelling is proof of the continuing presence of Jesus in the believer's life. The Scriptures teach that this is not an experience but a fact, and that it begins at conversion. This means that believers do not have to "prove" that they have the Holy Spirit – the only proof that is required is the growth of the fruit of the Spirit in their lives (Gal 5:22-23).

Sanctification

The repentant sinner who has come to conversion still struggles with the old self and needs the help of the Holy Spirit to live a life pleasing to God (Rom 6–8). The constant reminders in the Bible to repent of sin, to confess sins and believe in God (Heb 11:6; 1 John 1:6–9) clearly show that as long as we live in this world, we will be undergoing sanctification, the process of being made holy. This involves a separation to God, an imputation of Christ as our holiness, purification from moral evil, and conformation to the image of Christ.[2] It can thus be said that we have been sanctified, we are being sanctified, and we will be sanctified.

- *We have been sanctified.* The moment we become believers in Christ, we are sanctified. That is why Paul can say that the Corinthians "were sanctified" (1 Cor 6:11) and can call them "saints" (1 Cor 1:2; see also Eph 1:1; Col 1:2; Heb 10:10; Jude 3). This is sometimes referred to as "positional sanctification". It is the truth expressed in the words, "if anyone is in Christ, the new creation has come" (2 Cor 5:17).

- *We are being sanctified.* In 2 Thessalonians 2:13 Paul indicates that those to whom he is writing have already been sanctified; nevertheless, he still prays for their sanctification (1 Thess 5:23). He accuses those whom he addresses as "saints" of still being worldly (1 Cor 1:2; 3:3) and commands them to walk as is proper for saints (Eph 1:1; 5:3). He knew that becoming sanctified is a lifelong process in which we

---

[2] Henry C. Thiessen, *Lectures in Systematic Theology* (rev. Vernon D. Doerksen; Grand Rapids: Eerdmans, 1979), 288–289.

learn to "put off" our old lives and "put on" our new life in Christ (Col 3:8–13; see also Rom 6:13; 12:1–2). Paul says he himself is constantly striving to improve and is "pressing on towards the goal" (Phil 3:12). The Apostle John, too, speaks of the presence of sin in a believer's life and the need to repent (1 John 1:6–7).

- *We will be sanctified.* There will come a time when believers will be totally glorified with resurrection bodies. The mortal will put on immortality and sin will no longer have any hold on them (1 Cor 13:10; 1 Thess 3:13; Heb 9:28; 12:23; 1 John 3:2).

As part of his work of bringing salvation and sanctification, the Holy Spirit convicts us of sin and points to Jesus (John 15:26; 16:8). He interprets Scripture (John 16:13–14). He illuminates the mind (Job 32:8; 1 Cor 2:6–16; 2 Cor 3:14–17; 1 John 5:7, 11). He incorporates those who believe into the body of Christ (1 Cor 12:13). He seals them (Eph 1:13; 4:34). He guides (Rom 8:14; Gal 5:16, 25), empowers (Gal 5:17, 22; Eph 5:9) and teaches (John 14:26; 16:13; 1 Cor 2:14; 1 John 2:20, 27).

The Holy Spirit also distributes spiritual gifts (Rom 12:3–8; 1 Cor 12:1–14:40; Eph 4:7–16; 1 Pet 4:10–11). These gifts are intended for the good of the church (1 Cor 10:33; 12:7) and are diverse in "distribution, function and enablement (1 Cor 12:4–6)".[3] Given that not all believers have the same gifts (1 Cor 12:29–30), having or not having a particular spiritual gift is not a measure of spirituality (see chapter 9 for a fuller discussion of the gifts of the Spirit).

The Baptism and Filling of the Holy Spirit

The rise of Pentecostalism has led to much debate within the church about the difference between the baptism of the Spirit, the indwelling of the Spirit and the filling of the Spirit. Many Pentecostals insist that Spirit baptism is a unique experience that occurs some time after Christian conversion and is evidenced by speaking in tongues and special anointing. It is important to see what Scripture has to say on this topic.

Writing to the church in Corinth, Paul says "we were *all* baptized by one Spirit so as to form one body" (1 Cor 12:13; see also Eph 4:4–5).

---

[3] W. Robert Cook, *Systematic Theology in Outline Form* (Portland: Western Conservative Baptist Seminary, 1970), 151.

The word "all" makes it clear that all believers have received the baptism of the Holy Spirit, and that this is what brings them together in the body of Christ. This baptism of the Holy Spirit was first experienced on the day of Pentecost (Acts 1:5; 2:38), which marks the day the church was launched. As an inaugural event, it was accompanied by unusual experiences including tongues of fire and speaking in tongues (Acts 2:1–4). However, there is no evidence that every one of the 3,000 people converted on that momentous day had exceptional experiences involving a rushing wind, tongues of fire, and speaking in tongues (Acts 2:41). So it is wrong to assert that a believer who does not speak in tongues has not received the baptism of the Spirit. We could equally well insist that because tongues of fire settled on believers on the day of Pentecost, every believer today must also experience tongues of fire. To say this is not to deny that the gift of tongues was also given to believers elsewhere in Acts; it is simply asserting that we cannot require every believer to speak in tongues or to have other unusual experiences. The baptism of the Holy Spirit is a fact, not an experience. In this, it resembles regeneration and justification, both of which are things that God has done regardless of whether the believer feels reborn or justified at a particular moment.

What believers do experience is the *filling* of the Holy Spirit. Filling is something that we experience and can be commanded to experience. When Paul tells the Ephesians to "be filled with the Spirit" (Eph 5:18) he is saying that they should allow the Holy Spirit to have absolute control of every aspect of their lives. Not to be filled is a sin. In the same vein, Paul warns believers not to "grieve" or "quench" the Holy Spirit (Eph 4:30; 1 Thess 5:19). A Spirit-controlled life is clear evidence of a Spirit-filled life (Gal 5:16–17; Eph 5:19–21).

John Stott clarifies the difference between baptism and fullness in these words:

> When we speak of the baptism of the Spirit we are referring to a once-for-all gift; when we speak of the fullness of the Spirit we are acknowledging that this gift needs to be continuously and increasingly appropriated. ... Thus, the fullness of the Spirit was the consequence of the baptism of the Spirit. The baptism is what Jesus did (pouring out the Spirit from heaven); the fullness is what they received. The baptism was a

unique initiatory experience; the fullness was intended to be continuing, the permanent result, the norm. As an initiatory event the baptism is not repeatable and cannot be lost, but the filling can be repeated and in any case needs to be maintained. If it is not maintained, it is lost. If it is lost, it can be recovered.[4]

The Anointing of the Spirit

In the early 1990s I had the privilege of giving several lectures at a theological seminary in Nigeria. One of the students kindly invited me to a lunch at a nearby restaurant. During the meal he told me how much he appreciated my lectures, but suggested that I should consider a special anointing to increase their power (probably implying that he found my lectures boring!). I asked him why he thought so since he had said that I had the gift of teaching. Why would I need a special anointing if God had already given me this gift?

In the years since that lunch the topic of anointing has come up again and again in various contexts. I see billboards in African megacities inviting people to come and receive a "special anointing" or a "Holy Ghost anointing", or to come and hear some "anointed man of God". Radio and television advertisements broadcast a similar message. I hear Christians praying for a "special anointing". Many believe that anointing offers divine protection against enemies and opposition. A prominent Nigerian politician was recently quoted as saying, "I use holy water to bath every day. I drink holy water and use anointing oil to shield myself from attacks." Oil blessed and sanctified by a priest, pastor, or man or woman of God is recommended for use to bring blessing, protection and spiritual gifts such as speaking in tongues. Christians buy these oils and keep them at hand. For many African Christians, anointing is associated with the baptism of the Spirit, the filling of the Holy Spirit and miraculous gifts, especially the gifts of healing and speaking in tongues. A preacher or believer who does not heal or speak in tongues is regarded as lacking anointing and therefore not being a real Christian.

---

[4] John Stott and Michael Horton, *Baptism and Fullness: The Work of the Holy Spirit Today* (Leicester: InterVarsity Press, 2007), 47, 49.

The meaning of anointing

"Anointing" is the practice of rubbing oil, perfume, water or some other substance onto the body. It has long been practised in traditional Africa as part of religious ceremonies confirming someone's spiritual authority, or as a cleansing ritual when commissioning someone for an assignment, or simply as a medicinal ritual. It is thus not an exclusively Christian practice. Here, however, we will focus solely on its biblical and Christian usage.

Anointing in the Bible

Anointing is mentioned in both the Old and New Testaments in the following contexts:

Personal grooming. Anointing one's body was a common part of personal care in Old Testament times (Ruth 3:3; 2 Sam 12:20; Amos 6:6; Dan 10:3). This was still the case in New Testament times, which is why Jesus commanded that we should continue to anoint our bodies when we fast (Matt 6:16–18). Jesus himself received anointing when Mary poured perfume on his feet (Mark 14:8; John 12:3). The dead body of a loved one might also be anointed with perfume (Luke 23:56). Objects that required special care might also be anointed. Thus warriors anointed their shields both for protection and to keep the leather strong and supple in preparation for battle (2 Sam 1:21; Isa 21:5).

Setting apart. Both people and objects could be anointed to set them apart as holy. Thus Jacob anointed a stone at the site of his dream (Gen 28:18). The tabernacle and all its furnishings and equipment were anointed with a special oil (Exod 30:22–29; 40:9–10; Lev 8:11; Num 7:1). So were all the priests who served there (Exod 28:41; 29:7; 40:12–15).

Coronation. A person could be anointed in order to give them authority to rule. Saul and David were both anointed king by Samuel (1 Sam 10:1; 16:13) and their successors were also anointed (1 Kgs 1:39; 19:15–16). Kings were thus referred to as "the Lord's anointed" and as such they should not be harmed (1 Sam 12:3, 5; 24:10). Psalm 45:7 explains that this anointing signified God's gift of authority, strength and honour.

Healing. Anointing was used for medicinal purposes (Isa 1:6; Luke 10:34; Rev 3:18). Jesus may have had this practice in mind when he anointed the eyes of a blind man with mud (John 9:11). However, it appears that in this context and in the healings reported in Mark 6:13, the use of mud and of oil was more "a symbol of miraculous cure than a medicine".[5] The same is true of the anointing for healing that was done in the early church, which took place in the context of prayer (Jas 5:14-15). Clearly, the healing power did not lie in the oil, but in the application of the oil combined with prayer and pronouncing the name of Jesus.[6] Those who did the anointing were the elders in this church, and thus some churches, especially Orthodox churches and the Roman Catholic Church, have adopted anointing as a priestly ritual. Catholicism also promotes extreme unction, a final anointing performed when someone is gravely ill or at the point of death. A priest anoints the eyes, ears, nose, hands and feet of the dying person with oil and offers a prayer to cancel the sins of the patient and offer strength at such a difficult time. However, James does not seem to be commanding the use of holy oil as a religious rite; he is simply acknowledging the existence of the practice of anointing in the early church. Nor do these verses imply that only the elders can pray effectively for healing. In fact, just one verse later James says that "the prayer of a righteous person is powerful and effective" (Jas 5:16). An ordinary believer who exercises faith through prayer can heal the sick in the name of Christ. It is not the official status of the one anointing that cures, nor the sacredness of the anointing oil; it is the prayers of righteous men and women.

The Saviour's name. The Greek word "Christ" and the Hebrew word "Messiah" are both titles for someone who has been anointed. Thus when we speak of Jesus Christ, we are literally speaking of Jesus the Anointed One.

> "Anointing" came to be associated especially with Jesus (Acts 3:20) and the gift of the Spirit whereby he was appointed/ affirmed for the role as Messiah (Christ). He therefore was the "Anointed One" in a unique sense, so that in time the title

---

[5] Charles C. Ryrie, *The Holy Spirit* (rev. and expanded; Chicago: Moody, 1965), 177.
[6] Martin Dibelius, *James: A Commentary on the Epistle of James* (trans. Michael A. Williams; Philadelphia: Fortress, 1976), 252.

became part of the name by which he was known in the early church ("Jesus the Christ" came to be simply "Jesus Christ").[7]

The coming of the Anointed One was prophesied in Isaiah 61:1. Jesus announced the fulfilment of this prophecy in Luke 4:17–18 (see also Acts 4:27; 10:38; Heb 1:9). As the Anointed One *par excellence*, Jesus holds a permanent position as our priest, king and prophet.

The giving of the Holy Spirit. At Jesus' baptism, the Holy Spirit descended on Jesus and the voice of God declared that Jesus was his own Son (Luke 3:21–22). This may be the anointing that Jesus refers to shortly afterwards when he announces, "The Spirit of the Lord is on me, because he has anointed me" (Luke 4:18). Baptism and the gift of the Holy Spirit are also closely linked in Acts, where Peter tells the crowd to "repent and be baptized, every one of you, in the name of the Jesus for the forgiveness of sins. And you will receive the gift of the Holy Spirit" (Acts 2:38). Paul also speaks of believers as being "in Christ", which Gordon Fee explains as meaning that "in putting us into Christ, God christed [anointed] us, which means something like 'make us Christ's people'".[8] The meaning is similar to Paul's other saying that God has set his seal of ownership on believers, marking them as his children (Eph 1:13; 4:30; see also 2 Cor 1:21–22; 1 John 2:20, 27). It is the Holy Spirit who both seals and anoints believers.

In 1 John 2:27 the Apostle John encourages believers by reminding them that they have received an anointing that "teaches you about all things". The words clearly reflect Christ's promise to send believers the Holy Spirit as a reliable guide (John 16:8–10, 13) and indicate that anointing by the Spirit is key to the relationship between the Son and his children. He is the Anointed One, and he passes this anointing on to his offspring. This understanding of the giving of the Spirit as an anointing was powerfully symbolized in the early church where "the general procedure was that, on coming up from the baptismal water, the newly baptized Christian was anointed with scented oil, at the same time receiving the laying on of hands".[9] This practice is evidence that the

---

[7] Gordon Fee, *God's Empowering Presence: The Holy Spirit in the Letters of Paul* (Peabody: Hendrickson, 1994), 291–292.

[8] Ibid.

[9] J. N. D. Kelly, *Early Christian Doctrines* (5th ed.; London: A & C. Black, 1985), 432. Kelly goes on to explain: "According to Cyril of Jerusalem, just as Christ after His baptism received the Spirit

"ancient Church bore witness to the belief that every Christian receives from the Head of the Church the same Divine Unction that descended on the Christ".[10]

Several church fathers believed that the anointing and laying on of hands at the time of baptism actually conferred the Holy Spirit on the baptized.[11] A similar idea is still found in some churches where anointing with oil is associated with the gift of the Holy Spirit. Within the Roman Catholic, Anglican and Methodist churches, the concept of an anointing as a means by which power is transmitted from the priest to the believer has been further developed, especially in the rite of confirmation in which the bishop anoints the head of the one to be confirmed and says, "I sign thee with the Sign of the Cross, and I confirm thee with the chrism of salvation in the name of the Father, and of the Son, and of the Holy Ghost."

Summary

The above survey of the biblical texts on anointing shows that it is a mistake to assume that "anointing" refers exclusively to a spectacular spiritual experience that is different from the filling of the Holy Spirit (Eph 5:18). Rather, the New Testament teaches that anointing is the universal experience of all believers (1 John 2:20, 27) which is given by God at baptism when the believer is incorporated into the body of Christ. In purely biblical terms, the believer is exhorted to be filled, not anointed, with the Holy Spirit.

While it is true that that in the Old Testament in particular anointing was used to consecrate religious objects and commission and empower priests, prophets and kings, this was only one of its functions. In the New Testament, and especially for believers, anointing is linked to Jesus Christ who is the Anointed One of God. He is the one from whom

---

in the form of a dove, so the oil with which the newly baptized Christian is anointed symbolizes the Spirit Who sanctifies him. Through the words of blessing it has become the 'chrism of Christ, capable of producing the Holy through the presence of His divinity'" (432). Several other church fathers, including Cyril of Alexandria, Ambrose, and Augustine, also saw a link between the anointing at baptism and the Holy Spirit.

[10] Henry Barclay Swete, *The Holy Spirit in the Ancient Church* (Grand Rapids: Baker, 1976), 49.

[11] Wolfhart Pannenberg, *Systematic Theology* (Grand Rapids: Eerdmans, 1993), 3:268. Though there were variations between the West and the East, "the general theory was that through chrismation, with or without the laying on hands, the Holy Spirit was bestowed" (Kelly, *Early Christian Doctrines*, 432).

Christians get their anointing. Other uses of anointing that detract from this basic meaning often reflect traditional beliefs and practices rather than biblical teaching.

It is important to stress yet again that anointing is the universal experience of those who have been baptized or incorporated into the body of Christ (John 2:20, 27; 2 Cor 1:21–22). Just as Christ was anointed at baptism, so all believers have received anointing and cannot lose this anointing. There is no indication that some believers are without this anointing, and no suggestion that some believers need another special anointing. We cannot use the example of King Saul in the Old Testament to argue that anointing can be lost, for there is no New Testament example of a believer losing his or her anointing and being filled with an evil spirit, as Saul was.[12] At best, what the story of Saul teaches the church is that believers who becomes careless about how they live and disobey God will grieve and quench the Holy Spirit and thereby lose the power to serve God (Eph 4:30; 1 Thess 5:19).

If all believers have been anointed, this means that all believers have been set apart for service and dedication to God, just as the anointed priests were in the Old Testament. Philip Graham Ryken notes the implication of this truth:

> Now we belong entirely to the Lord. After all, we were bought with a price; so we no longer belong to ourselves but to God. This has staggering implications for everything we do and everything we have. It means that our possessions no longer belong to us; they belong to God and are to be used for his service. … What service have you been anointed to perform? There is not one single part of who we are or what we have that belongs to us. In the same way that the whole tabernacle was anointed with holy oil, we too have been set apart for God, body and soul.[13]

We need to stress that anointing "is not just a historical fact or a fact realized once in life; the Unction abides and continues to inspire as

---

[12] Some may suggest that this is true of Judas Iscariot, but Scripture never refers to his having been anointed.

[13] Philip Graham Ryken, *Exodus: Saved for God's Glory* (Preaching the Word series; Wheaton, Ill: Crossway, 2005), 942.

it inspired at the first".[14] Every believer is anointed and continues or should continue to demonstrate the impact of his or her anointing in life. However, it is not inappropriate to pray for a further anointing in the sense of a filling and empowering by the Holy Spirit to do God's service with boldness and power. When used in this sense, anointing is equivalent to – but not better or more powerful than – the filling of the Holy Spirit. Such anointing does not require a demonstration of spectacular signs such as speaking in tongues, visions, laughter, or being slain by the Spirit. It remains the prerogative of the Holy Spirit to decide how his anointing or filling will be demonstrated in a believer.

In conclusion, anointing is a clearly a biblical and theological truth as well as a traditional belief and practice in Africa. But as believers, all our beliefs should be subject to the final authority of Scripture. We need to know how anointing is spoken of in both the Old and New Testaments. We also need to be very cautious when any teaching on dogma is based on just one verse from the Bible, taken out of context. A basic hermeneutical principle is that a text without a context is a pretext – and this has been the tragedy of many biblical interpretations, including many of those relating to anointing.

Questions

1. Define regeneration, justification and conversion. Which Scriptures teach these doctrines?

2. Define monergism and synergism. Which view, in your own opinion, best reflects the Bible's teaching?

3. How would you respond to someone who insists that Spirit baptism must be followed by speaking in tongues?

4. Is the indwelling of the Holy Spirit different from the anointing of the Spirit? Give a biblical justification for your answer.

Further Reading

Craig Keener. *Gift & Giver: The Holy Spirit for Today*. Grand Rapids: Baker, 2001.

---

[14] Swete, *The Holy Spirit*, 385.

Ivan Satyavrata. *The Holy Spirit: Lord and Lifegiver*. Carlisle: Global Christian Library, 2012.

John Stott and Michael Horton. *Baptism and Fullness: The Work of the Holy Spirit Today*. Leicester: InterVarsity Press, 2007.

7
SALVATION AND THE CHRISTIAN LIFE

The fundamental biblical truths we have studied in the preceding chapters have important implications for how we live as Christians. We should be living out what we claim to believe. But all too often we fail to do so, either because we misinterpret Scripture or because syncretism creeps in as we allow our traditional beliefs and practices to negate or at least compromise these truths of Christianity. It is thus vital that we examine how we live in light of the basic truths of the Christian faith. We must also examine these beliefs to make sure that they are firmly rooted in the Bible.

The most important point of all when it comes to Christian living is that Jesus Christ is the basis of the Christian life. He is its "pioneer and perfecter" (Heb 12:2) who "according to the testimonies in the New Testament is the standard for believers of all times and all churches".[1] Thus, we need to make sure that nothing about the way we live is at odds with who Christ is and what he has done.

Secondly, we need to remember that our salvation is holistic, and thus applies to every area of our lives. We should not restrict our Christian living only to the "spiritual" dimension. Jesus certainly did not do so. He introduced his own ministry in the following terms: "The Spirit of the Lord is on me, because he has anointed me to proclaim good news to the poor. He has sent me to proclaim freedom for the prisoners and recovery of sight for the blind, to set the oppressed free, to proclaim the year of the Lord's favour" (Luke 4:18–19). His actions matched his words. He provided not only spiritual salvation, but also physical and emotional

---

[1] Hans Küng, *Theology for the Third Millennium: The Ecumenical View* (trans. Peter Heinegg; New York: Doubleday, 1988), 156.

healing. Thus, for example, when he met with a paralyzed man he not only forgave the man's sin but also healed him (Luke 5:17–25).

A critical aspect of Christ's work was his confrontation with the devil and demonic activity. He healed many people of demon possession, stating that "Now is the time for judgement on this world; now the prince of this world (i.e. the devil – 2 Cor 4:4) will be driven out" (John 12:31). He also said, "if it is by the Spirit of God that I drive out demons, then the kingdom of God has come upon you" (Matt 12:28). These passages demonstrate that salvation relates not only to delivery from sin, but also to delivery from the devil and spiritual attacks. Salvation relates to the total well-being of the individual. We should never reduce the salvation provided by Jesus to only deliverance from sin.

In our Christian living, we also need to remember that our salvation is past, present and future. Our past sins have been forgiven and we no longer need to live in bondage to them. As explained in the previous chapter, we have been justified, or in other words, declared righteous by God. In the future, we will be glorified, and thus we can look forward to complete and final salvation at the return of our blessed Lord and Saviour, Jesus Christ. But in the present, we are being sanctified, that is, we are undergoing the process of being conformed to the image of Christ (Rom 8:29). We do not have a choice about this: We are commanded "just as he who called you is holy, so be holy in all you do; for it is written: 'Be holy, because I am holy'" (1 Pet 1:15; compare Lev 19:2). This is not an easy and automatic process, and so the writer of the letter to the Hebrews urges his readers to "make every effort to live in peace with everyone and to be holy; without holiness no one will see the Lord" (Heb 12:14). We have been saved from our sins, but we still struggle with our sinful nature and still need to confess our sins daily before God.

We also still struggle with trials and tribulations. Being saved does not provide immunity from sickness or other physical and emotional needs. This was true even for the great Apostle Paul: "We are hard pressed on every side, but not crushed; perplexed, but not in despair; persecuted, but not abandoned; struck down, but not destroyed. We always carry around in our body the death of Christ, so that the life of Jesus may also be revealed in our body" (2 Cor 4:8–10). Paul experienced physical hardships, sleepless nights, hunger, poverty and having nothing (2 Cor 6:4–10). He had health problems, such as "the thorn in my flesh" (2

Cor 12:7). Those he loved battled illness, so much so that he feared that his close friend Epaphroditus was going to die (Phil 2:26–27). He sent his spiritual son, Timothy, practical advice about how to deal with a stomach complaint (1 Tim 5:23). Though the believer is promised victory, it is delusional to think that all our earthly problems are removed as the result of being saved. The consuming desire for prosperity in terms of health and wealth has blinded many to the reality of sin and its consequences for humankind and our environment. We will only experience full salvation from sin, evil, sickness, suffering and poverty at Christ's return (1 Thess 3:13; Heb 9:28; 12:23; 1 John 3:2).

But in the midst of these troubles, we who have believed in Jesus Christ can enjoy full assurance of salvation. No matter how guilty we may feel, our guilt has been blotted out. We no longer stand condemned before God (Rom 8:1), but have been declared righteous (Gen 15:6; Rom 3:12–17); we are children of God (John 1:12) and have eternal life (John 3:16; Rom 6:23). This assurance is not rooted in our personal faithfulness or strength, but in the sovereign will of God who preserves those who are his and keeps them from falling (Jude 24). Though there may be times when believers – especially new believers – face questions and doubts, God reassures them of their status as his children (John 1:12). As such, they can be confident of ultimate victory. They do not need to fear the daily struggle against sin and evil because they are sustained by the power of God (Rom 8:30–31; 1 John 4:4).

Moreover, they do not have to face the battle alone. All who confess the Lordship of Christ are incorporated into the body of Christ, the church. Every believer is a member of this community of God (1 Cor 12:13) and God requires that his children work together.

Finally, we need to remember that any view of salvation that focuses only on this life is distorted and unbiblical. The Bible clearly warns us that "If only for this life we have hope in Christ, we are of all people most to be pitied" (1 Cor 15:19). The hope of a believer should not be set on this world but on the life to come. The resurrection and the future should be dominant in our thoughts. We look towards the day when sin, temptation, evil and the devil will be judged (Rev 20:10; 21:8) and when God "will wipe every tear away from [our] eyes. There will be no more death or mourning or crying or pain, for the old order of things has passed away" (Rev 21:4). Then, and only then, sin and its effects will be totally and for ever removed from afflicting humanity.

Having said all this, and outlined the great truths of our faith, how do we actually apply these principles to the issues and problems of daily life? How do we live the abundant life that Christ wants us have? To help model how this can be done, we can look at some issues that are of particular concern to African believers.

Blessings and Curses

In ancient times, people attached great importance to the spoken word, considering it

> the medium of powers which effectively influence events. This is not, of course, true of simply any word, but it certainly applies to words spoken with great emphasis and firm intention, of which the supreme examples are the curse and the blessing. … Naturally, too, the invocation of the deity imbues the word with special efficacy, and the curse and the blessing thus become weapons in the hand of the poor and helpless before which even the strongest may quail. In popular belief such words have what is virtually a life of their own; they are like independent beings waiting their opportunity to invade reality. And even when this is denied them they remain dangerous for a long time, like a long-forgotten mine in the sea, or a grenade buried in a ploughed field.[2]

African Traditional Religion also holds that "the spoken word has intrinsic power which is released by the act of utterance and is independent of it".[3] Thus Africans do not come to the issue of blessings and curses with a neutral mind. Many believe that gods, priests, diviners, chiefs, parents and all those invested with authority have the power to bless and to curse. Fathers sometimes curse rebellious sons so that they will never be able to have children. Mothers aggrieved by the bad behaviour of their daughters curse them so that they will suffer the same emotional trauma

---

[2] Walther Eichrodt, *Theology of the Old Testament* (trans. J. A. Baker; Philadelphia: Westminster, 1967), 2:69.

[3] W. Mundle, "Curse", in *Dictionary of New Testament Theology* (Grand Rapids: Paternoster, 1975), 1:416.

in the future. Diviners and witch doctors curse worshippers who break taboos or refuse to make certain ritual sacrifices.

The all-important question of whether blessings and curses are or are not effective is very difficult to answer. All that can be offered as evidence are anecdotes. For example, I have been told about a man who was dating the elder of two sisters, but changed his mind and married the younger sister. Embittered by her rejection, the elder sister pronounced a curse upon her younger sister and her new husband, declaring that they would have children but never enjoy them, and would experience great suffering. In time, the couple had three sons. Two were paralyzed from the waist down, and the third became a drug addict. This caused the couple much emotional strain, which took its toll on the wife, who died a few years after becoming a Christian. To the villagers, this was a bulletproof case showing that the sister's curse had worked.

It is also believed that unless the power of the word is broken, a person who has been cursed will remain under the curse forever. Rituals are thus important as a means of removing curses or rendering them impotent.

Many elements of these beliefs have been transferred into Christian faith and practice in Africa, with serious repercussions. There are now many preachers, churches and ministries dedicated to delivering those who are perceived to be under a curse, whether imposed on them as an individual or as a generational curse inherited from their ancestors. So the questions raised in relation to blessing and cursing are real and deserve a biblical and theological response. We will begin by looking at instances of blessing and cursing in the Bible to see what we can learn from them.

Blessing and cursing in Scripture

It should be noted that blessings have always been part of God's relationship with humankind. We bless God by giving him thanksgiving, praise and adoration (Ps 103). God blesses us with spiritual and physical well-being (Ps 5:12–13; Matt 6:33; 7:9–11).

In the Old Testament we often read of one person blessing another or a group of people. Moses blessed the people on several occasions (Exod 29:43; Deut 33). Eli the priest blessed Elkanah and his wife Hannah (1 Sam 2:20). Boaz's workers responded to his greeting by saying, "The

LORD bless you" (Ruth 2:4). Samuel blessed sacrifices before the people partook of them (1 Sam 9:13). Aaron is said to have "lifted his hands toward the people and blessed them" (Lev 9:22). We learn something of the content of priestly blessings in Numbers 6:24–27: "The LORD bless you and keep you; the LORD make his face shine upon you and be gracious to you; the LORD turn his face toward you and give you peace."

The writers of the New Testament similarly blessed the recipients of their letters with a benediction (Rom 16:25-27; 2 Cor 13:14; Jude 24–25). There are thus good grounds for our continuing the wonderful biblical practice of blessing church members. The benedictions recommended in many ministerial manuals are not merely reflections of an ancient tradition but also enjoy strong scriptural support.

The opposite of blessing is cursing, and this is something that Jesus and the New Testament writers urged Christians not to do, saying "bless those who persecute you; bless and do not curse" (Matt 5:44; Rom 12:14). A curse can be defined as

> an invocation (a calling down) of harm or injury upon a person or people, either immediately or contingent upon particular circumstances. It is an utterance of a deity or a person invoking a deity consigning person(s) or thing(s) to destruction or divine vengeance. It is a malediction – the opposite of a benediction – or imprecation: an evil inflicted on another.[4]

There are numerous examples of cursing in the Old Testament. The first comes immediately after the fall:

> God said to the serpent, "Because you have done this [tempted Eve], cursed are you above all livestock and all wild animals! You will crawl on your belly and you will eat dust all the days of your life." ... To the woman he said, "I will make your pains in childbearing very severe; with painful labour you will give birth to children. Your desire will be for your husband, and he will rule over you." To Adam he said, "Because you listened to your wife and ate fruit from the tree about which I commanded you, 'You must not eat from it,' cursed is the

---

[4] Tokunboh Adeyemo, *Is Africa Cursed? A Vision for the Radical Transformation of an Ailing Continent* (rev. and updated; Nairobi: WordAlive, 2009), 11.

ground because of you; through painful toil you will eat food
from it all the days of your life." (Gen 3:14, 16–17)

These curses were a direct response to the sin of Adam and Eve, and
extend to all their descendants (Gal 3:10–12).

The next reference to a curse in Scripture follows very soon after the
fall, and is associated with the first murder, when "Cain attacked his
brother Abel and killed him" (4:8). In response

The Lord said, "What have you done? Listen! Your brother's
blood cries out to me from the ground. Now you are under a
curse and driven from the ground, which opened its mouth to
receive your brother's blood from your hand. When you work
the ground, it will no longer yield its crops for you. You will be
a restless wanderer on the earth." (Gen 4:10–12)

As with Adam and Eve, there was a cause-and-effect relationship between
Cain's actions and God's judgement (or curse).

The same cause-and-effect relationship applies in Genesis 12:3, where
God promises, "I will bless those who bless you [Abraham], and whoever
curses you I will curse." Blessing Abraham will bring divine blessing;
maltreating Abraham will result in curses or calamity. Many years later,
Isaac pronounces a similar blessing on Jacob, saying, "May those who
curse you be cursed and those who bless you be blessed" (Gen 27:29).
He believed that his blessing upon Jacob was effective and irrevocable: "I
blessed him – and indeed he will be blessed!" (Gen 27:33).

Blessing and cursing are also contrasted in Deuteronomy 11:26–
28, where Moses, speaking on behalf of God, says, "See, I am setting
before you today a blessing and a curse – the blessing if you obey the
commands of the Lord your God that I am giving you today; the curse
if you disobey the commands of the Lord your God and turn from the
way that I command you today by following other gods, which you have
not known." Blessings again come as a result of obedience, and curses
as a result of disobedience.

It is interesting to contrast Moses and Balaam, whose story is told
in Numbers 22–23. Balaam is presented as "the diviner with the most
remarkable reputation of the day",[5] and as someone who had the power

---

[5] Ronald B. Allen, "Numbers" in *Numbers–Ruth* (vol. 2 of *Expositor's Bible Commentary*, Grand
Rapids: Zondervan, 1981), 887. Allen notes, "Balaam was an internationally known prophet,

to bless or curse. Yet though he was hired to curse God's people, he was not able to do so; he could only bless them, as directed by God who told him, "You must not put a curse on those people, because they are blessed" (Num 22:12). This episode reveals much about the beliefs regarding blessings and curses in the ancient world. It shows that the king had no doubt of Balaam's ability to bring blessing or calamity on other nations or peoples: "For I know that those you bless are blessed, and those you curse are cursed" (Num 22:6). We get some idea of the type of curse Balak wanted from Balaam from an example of a curse in an ancient Akkadian text: "May the great gods of heaven and nether world curse him, his descendants, his land, his soldiers, his people and his army with a baleful curse; may Enlil with his unalterable utterance curse him with these curses so that they speedily affect him."[6]

It appears that Balaam's power to bless and curse was effective when it came to unbelieving nations but was restricted when it came to God's chosen people. Thus we see that an unbeliever's power to bless or curse a believer is restricted by God. This is because God is sovereign over all other gods and beings, and also because he has blessed believers, declaring them to be righteous and holy, so that they need not fear an evil curse. Balaam asked the rhetorical question, "How can I curse those whom God has not cursed? How can I denounce those whom the LORD has not denounced?" (Num 23:8).

It should, however, be noted that believers who are rebellious and disobey God remove themselves from his protection (1 Cor 5:5). Such believers will be vulnerable to the attacks of the evil one, who at times works through curses.

Balaam did not manage to utter any curse, but the Bible shows that even when curses were uttered, they were not always effective. Goliath "cursed David by his gods" but was still defeated by him (1 Sam 17:43–50). Another example of curses being ineffective is found in 2 Samuel 16:5–8, which tells of how Shimei son of Gera, a member

---

a diviner expert in examining the entrails of animals and observing natural phenomena to determine the will of the gods." K. F. Keil and F. Delitzsch say that Balaam, "being endowed with a predisposition to divination and prophecy, ... practiced soothsaying and divination as a trade; and for the purpose of bringing this art to the greatest possible perfection, brought not only the traditions of the different nations, but all the phenomena of his own times, within the range of his observations." *The Pentateuch* (vol. 3 of *Biblical Commentary on the Old Testament*; trans. James Martin; Grand Rapids: Eerdmans, 1966), 161.

[6] Quoted in Allen, "Numbers", 887.

of King Saul's family, threw stones at King David and cursed him. That cursing was not effective, for David was restored to the throne. But the cursing was not taken lightly, and on his deathbed David urged his son Solomon to punish Shimei for it (1 Kgs 2:8–9). Careless words, even if they do not actually come to pass, are still wrong and can have negative consequences. Eichrodt offers the following interpretation of David's action:

> The curse of Shimei hangs like a threatening thunder-cloud over the head of the king, and its deadly lightning, if it does not strike him in his lifetime, may still harm his descendants. It may also, however, recoil on the head of the man who uttered it, and thus be rendered harmless; the mine is so to speak, exploded, even though it has not injured the man for whom it was intended. This explains the point of David's infamous testament to Solomon.[7]

Jehu's reference to Jezebel as "that cursed woman" (2 Kgs 9:34) might suggest that his curse was effective, for he killed her. But it was actually her own wickedness that brought her under divine judgement, which could not be revoked.

Although curses were generally uttered, they could also be written down. Thus Zechariah 5:1–3 mentions a "flying scroll" on which was written "the curse that is going out over the whole land; for according to what it says on one side, every thief will be banished, and according to what it says on the other, everyone who swears falsely will be banished. For everyone who steals shall be cleaned out according to what is on one side and everyone who swears falsely shall be cleaned out according to what is written on the other side" (Zech 5:3). This passage shows that curses on evil or wicked people were believed to be effective.

Cursing is not common in the New Testament, but there is one example that very clearly demonstrates that a divine curse signals destruction:

> When [Jesus] reached [the fig tree], he found nothing but leaves, because it was not the season for figs. Then he said to the tree, "May no one ever eat fruit from you again." And his disciples heard him say it. ... In the morning, as they went

---

[7] Eichrodt, *Theology of the Old Testament*, 69–70.

along, they saw the fig tree withered from the roots. Peter remembered and said to Jesus, "Rabbi, look! The fig tree you cursed has withered!" (Mark 11:12–14, 20–25)

This passage is consistent with other passages on the subject: curses are pronounced because of a lack of obedience. In this case, the fig tree was expected to bear fruit, but when it did not, it was cursed. It was not the words of Jesus that led to the tree's destruction; it was the tree's lack of fruit.

The only other, and very significant, context in which cursing is spoken of in the New Testament is in relation to the curse of the law and redemption in Christ (Gal 3:10–13). The curse of the law is the judgement and wrath of God that come upon those who do not obey his law (Rom 1:18; 2:5). All those who do not obey the law are under its curse (Gal 3:10). Christ, however, has set us free from this curse (Rom 3:25; 2 Cor 5:21).

Curses and individual believers

Derek Prince asserts, "A curse could be likened to a long, evil arm stretched out from the past. It rests upon people with a dark, oppressive force that inhibits the full expression of their personalities. It is an invisible barrier to receiving the blessings of the Christian life."[8] Evangelist Todd Bentley similarly holds that "A curse is evident in a person's life by continued defeats, unseen resistance that seems to hinder your every decision and there is no obvious reason why. Patterns of struggle evident in your family whether it is inherited sickness or financial lack."[9] However, these views are inconsistent with the teaching of the Bible, as we shall see. Sadly, many preachers make their living on this distorted understanding of curses. Believers are deceived and live under the constant fear of curses on their lives. So it is important to summarize the implications of the Scripture passages we have just looked at if we are to be able to answer questions like this: Does one person have the power to effectively curse another? What is the condition of believers who feel that they are under a curse?

The following important principles emerge:

[8] Derek Prince, *Blessings and Curses* (Grand Rapids: Chosen Books, 1994), 8.

[9] Todd Bentley, *Breaking Generational Curses – Part 1 & 2.* www.wherepeacefulwaters.com/articles/breaking_generational_curses 1.htm.

1. *A curse that is not backed by a just cause is ineffective.* Proverbs 26:2 states, "Like a fluttering sparrow or a darting swallow, an undeserved curse does not come to rest." It has no effect on the present or future welfare of the recipient. We know that Goliath's cursing of David did not have the intended effect (1 Sam 17:43). It was Goliath who was killed. Likewise, Shimei cursed David without effect (2 Sam 16:5; 1 Kgs 2:44–46). The same principle holds true today. Many early African converts were cursed by their parents for converting to Christianity yet received abundant blessing from God. Many of these converts were called "worthless", "useless" and "unprofitable", but later became salt and light in their communities. To give a specific example, a friend of mine who became a Christian was cursed and told that he would get no employment until he renounced Christianity and returned to the worship of the water spirit that possessed his mother. Nevertheless he continued in his Christian faith. When he graduated from high school he was the first among his friends to find employment (in fact, he had two job offers while his friends had none).

2. *Jesus endured the curse for us.* We need to remember that as sinners we have all been cursed for our failure to keep God's laws, but Christ has removed that curse from us by bearing it himself (Gal 3:10–14). All believers have been freed from the curse of the law (sin). Because of this, we are "a new creation": "The old has gone, the new is here!" (2 Cor 5:17). Thus even in cases where someone is affected by a curse, that curse is broken when the person decisively turns away from sin and finds salvation in Christ.

   As new creations, our past sins are forgiven. But sometimes the devil seeks to prevent us from enjoying the blessings that result from sins confessed and forgiven (Prov 28:13; 1 John 1:9). He rouses nagging fear and a sense of guilt that can hamper our lives and lead to suffering such as unemployment, lack of marriage, lack of promotion or lack of other progress in life. Believers who are in such circumstances or who fear that they are under a curse should undergo biblical counselling, focusing on Bible study, intercession and fellowship with other believers.

3. *Christians should renounce their evil activities of the past.* Converts should renounce sin when they turn to Christ. Those who come

from idolatrous and demonic contexts should also renounce all the works of the devil. For example, they should burn cultural items used in demonic worship, renounce any bonds or covenants made with the spirit world and make a complete break with all activities that promote Satan and his work. This is consistent with the response of the new converts in Ephesus: "Many of those who believed now came and openly confessed what they had done. A number who had practised sorcery brought their scrolls together and burned them publicly" (Acts 19:18–19). Believers who retain demonic practices or items connected with demonic activities are in danger of maintaining contact with and even being vulnerable to the attacks of the devil or the spirit world because, as the Bajju of Nigeria say, "an uncovered wound attracts flies". Destroying every remnant of demonic practices is also consistent with the Bible's teaching that the believer's body is the temple of God (2 Cor 6:14–18). Thus holding onto any kind of relic that belongs to the devil, spirits or the occult pollutes the holy temple of God. Getting rid of them ensures that the Spirit of God takes total possession of the believer, thereby preventing demonic spirits from attacking or terrorizing them. Believers are indwelt by the Holy Spirit (Rom 8:1–17) and should constantly seek the filling of the Holy Spirit (Eph 5:18).

4. *God has veto power over celebrated soothsayers and diviners.* Just as Balaam was known and feared as a soothsayer and diviner, so diviners and witch doctors are feared in African communities today. Even some Christians stand in awe and fear their supernatural power and apparent ability to curse people. However, Balaam's confession of his inability to curse God's people because of God's absolute power over evil (Num 23:8) should provide comfort and strength to those who fear being cursed.

5. *Scripture provides us with an armoury of weapons that can be used to divert, restrict or render impotent any evil desire or curse directed at believers.* Scripture insists that believers are no longer subject to the power of the devil. They are able to "escape from the trap of the devil, who has taken them captive to do his will" (2 Tim 2:26). They have been turned "from darkness to light and from the power of Satan to God" (Acts 26:18). They are described as God's "treasured possession" (Mal 3:17), "a people that are his very own" (Titus 2:14),

"the apple of his eye" (Deut 32:10; Zech 2:8), "a royal priesthood" (1 Pet 2:9) and "children of God " (John 1:12). On the basis of their position in Christ, they are promised victory: "Who will bring any charge against those whom God has chosen? It is God who justifies" (Rom 8:33); "neither death nor life, neither angels nor demons, ... nor any powers, neither height nor depth, nor anything else in all creation, will be able to separate us from the love of God that is in Christ Jesus our Lord" (Rom 8:38–39). When confronted by evil, we need to remember that "he who is in us is greater than he who is in the world" (1 John 4:4) and that "it is God who works in you to will and to act in order to fulfil his good purpose" (Phil 2:13).

6. *Believers should not attribute suffering to a curse that has been placed on them.* Suffering in a believer's life is part of God's special providence. The calamities that came upon Job did not result from the devil's curse but were allowed by God (Job 1–2). Paul, though blessed with many spiritual gifts, was afflicted by a "thorn in my flesh, a messenger of Satan" (2 Cor 12:7). Though he pleaded with the Lord to remove it, the Lord said to him, "My grace is sufficient for you, for my power is made perfect in weakness" (2 Cor 12:9). Note that Paul prayed for the removal of this problem three times and no more. He did not name it and claim healing for it. There are other instances in Scripture when Paul struggled with sickness without claiming healing. Because of Trophimus' sickness he left him behind in Miletus (2 Tim 4:20); his dear friend Epaphroditus was very ill and nearly died (Phil 2:25–30). Timothy, his son in the faith, had a stomach disorder for which Paul did not claim healing but recommended taking some wine (1 Tim 5:23). These incidents teach us an important lesson: "If you have prayed for healing and not received it, take heart – you are in good company."[10]

7. *Believers should be careful in their own speech.* Our words can either build or destroy. As Proverbs 12:18 states, "The words of the reckless pierce like swords, but the tongue of the wise brings healing" (see also Prov 18:21). We should thus take to heart James' warning: "no human being can tame the tongue: It is a restless evil, full of deadly poison. With the tongue we praise our Lord and Father, and with it we curse human beings, who have been made in God's likeness. Out of the same mouth come praise and cursing. My brothers and sisters,

---

[10] Randy Alcorn, *Money, Possessions and Eternity* (Wheaton: Tyndale House, 1989), 110.

this should not be" (Jas 3:8–10). As believers we should bless others, not curse them – even when they are persecuting us (Rom 12:14). We would be wise to learn from the scholars of the Talmudic period, who wrote: "Let yourself be cursed, rather than curse".[11] Not only is cursing morally wrong for believers, but like all wrong use of the tongue it can also have very undesirable consequences. For Shimei, his cursing of David led to his execution (2 Sam 16:5–9; 2 Kgs 2:9). And it is not only explicit cursing that is wrong. Negative words on their own can act like a poison and destroy someone emotionally and physically. For example, children who are called "stupid", "useless", "hopeless" or "worthless" by their parents often grow up feeling that they are unworthy and live stunted lives. We should be building others up, not tearing them down (Rom 15:2).

Generational curses

These days, there is much talk of generational curses in the church: evangelists refer to them, pastors preach on them, authors write about them and many believers think that such curses explain certain failures or misfortune in their lives. There is even discussion of whether the continent as a whole is cursed. William Mpofu sums up the paradox of Africa in the following paragraph:

> Africa is arguably the richest continent in natural resources. Some of the world's best minerals lie below the feet of the Africans. Africa is rich in fertile lands, wildlife, forests, water, sunshine, culture, philosophy, art and human beauty.
>
> In spite of all these abundant and rich endowments, the people of Africa remain poor, dogged by famine, disease, ignorance, violent crime, civil war, tyranny, fear, guilt and a debilitating inferiority complex and colonial hangover. The calamity of climate change and increasing global warming seems also to be weighing very heavily on Africa.[12]

---

[11] *Sanh.* 49a. The Talmud, a word that literally means "instruction, learning or studying", is the compilation of rabbinic scholarly oral teaching pertaining to the Torah (Law) that was passed on from generation to generation before eventually being written down. The Talmudic period stretches from the time of Ezra to the middle of the sixth century AD. The Talmud is highly esteemed in Judaism, second only to the Hebrew Scriptures.

[12] William Mpofu, "African Intellectuals: Suspects or Assets?" *The Thinker* 33 (Nov 2011): 48.

To some, the only explanation for such suffering in the midst of plenty is that Africa as a whole is under a curse. Others argue that curses are passed on with families, from one generation to the next:

> The proponents of generational curses postulate that when multiple cases of the same problem happen in a family line, it is a generational curse. Therefore, if a family has multiple cases of things like diabetes, alcoholism, divorce, stroke, heart disease, accidents, fornication, adultery, physical, mental or sexual abuse, anger, depression, suicide, idolatry or witchcraft, then that family is suffering from a generational curse. Some even attribute recurring, persistent sin, and even poverty, to a generational curse.[13]

Evangelist Todd Bentley writes,

> I have a friend that has always been plagued with poverty regardless of bettering himself in school, computer training, and hard work ethics. He has done everything within his own strength, fasting, tithing, devotion to God, faithfulness, you name it. He has never prospered, though he had the most giving heart of many I have met. I believe it is a curse of poverty which has been passed down and is now resisting, restricting and choking out the blessing that should be in his life.[14]

Derek Prince likewise identifies the following problems occurring over generations as indications of a generational curse: mental and emotional breakdown, repeated or chronic illness, barrenness, repeated miscarriages and related gynaecological problems, marriage breakdown and alienation within families, continuing financial or material insufficiency, being accident prone, and having a history of suicides or unnatural deaths.[15] He believes that there is a close correspondence between his list and the list of curses in Deuteronomy 28.

Those who promote the concept of generational curses argue that the best way to break a generational curse is to confess not only personal

---

[13] Musa Asake, "Generational Curses". Sermon delivered at ECWA Gospel Church, Tudun Wada, Jos, Plateau State, Nigeria, September 15, 2010.

[14] Todd Bentley, *Breaking Generational Curses*, www.upstreamca.org/curses.html.

[15] Prince, *Blessings and Curses*, 23–27.

sin but also the sins of one's ancestors. But what do the Scriptures have to say on this subject?

Generational curses in Scripture

The Scriptures do contain examples of curses being passed down from one generation to the next. The first is the curse on Adam and Eve at the fall, and the next is Noah's curse on his grandson Canaan: "Cursed be Canaan! The lowest of slaves will he be to his brothers. ... Praise be to the LORD, the God of Shem! May Canaan be the slave of Shem. May God extend Japheth's territory; may Japheth live in the tents of Shem, and may Canaan be the slave of Japheth" (Gen 9:25–26). These words of blessing and cursing are believed to have sealed the destiny of Noah's sons. Some Christians, particularly in the West, have mistakenly identified all black nations with Canaan, and thus claim that the lack of development in Africa and all the corruption and evil in black nations can be attributed to this curse. But this argument does not stand up, as there is no reason why Canaan should be taken to be black.

Genesis 27 records how Isaac blessed Jacob but predicted trouble, including slavery, bondage and suffering, for Esau. These words of blessing and cursing are matched by the fate of their descendants. However, it can be argued that it was Jacob and Esau's own actions, rather than the words of their father, that decided their future well-being. This is true, up to a point. But it is also true that their futures were predetermined by God even before they had a chance to do right or to do evil (Gen 25:23; Rom 9:13). Does this mean that we can dismiss the role of Isaac, who actually pronounced the blessing and curse on his children? This passage raises many questions about God's role and ours when it comes to blessings and curses.

Another curse is recorded in the book of Joshua. God had declared that the city of Jericho was to be considered a "devoted thing" and was to be destroyed totally – human beings, animals and buildings. In effect, the city was cursed. But interestingly, Rahab was not destroyed by God and Joshua. She actually became an ancestor of the Saviour (Josh 6:2–25; Matt 1:5) and was commended for her faith (Heb 11:31; Jas 2:25).

After the city had been destroyed, Joshua pronounced this curse, "Cursed before the LORD is the one who undertakes to rebuild this city, Jericho: At the cost of his firstborn son he will lay its foundations; at the cost of his youngest he will set up its gates" (Josh 6:2). Hiel of

Bethel attempted to rebuild Jericho. It did indeed cost him the lives of his firstborn son, Abiram, and his youngest son, Segub (1 Kgs 16:34). He incurred the curse of Joshua because he acted in direct contradiction to the divine prohibition on rebuilding the city. Achan was similarly punished with his entire family because he took that which God had explicitly commanded should not be taken or stolen (Josh 7). It is always dangerous to rebuild what God has declared should not be built again (Mal 1:4).

Since that time, Jericho has been rebuilt many times, and there is no evidence that the curse of Joshua is still in effect. In fact two of Israel's prominent prophets, Elijah and Elisha, were residents of Jericho. Jesus himself carried out ministry in Jericho (Luke 18:35; 19:1; Matt 20:29).

The supreme example of a generational curse is Deuteronomy 5:9, where God forbids the worship of other gods: "You shall not bow down to them [other gods] or worship them; for I, the LORD your God, am a jealous God, punishing the children for the sin of the parents to the third and fourth generation of those who hate me" (see also Exod 20:5; Num 20:5; 14:18). These verses are probably the most commonly used in support of generational curses. But we need to look at these verses in their context. The context is that God's curse is on those who hate him (by worshipping other gods) and not on those who love him. God will forgive those who love and obey him, but those who are idolatrous will incur his wrath (curse). This verse therefore should not be taken as teaching generational curses. Rather, the teaching is that God will forgive those who love and obey him and that those who are idolatrous will incur his wrath or curse. But when idolaters repent and turn back to God, they will experience God's love and compassion.

The idea of God visiting the sins of parents on their children to the third and fourth generation is consistent with other Bible teaching that if generation after generation continues in the evils and idol worship of their forebears, the consequences (punishment) will also continue. However, God's mercy will be upon the generation that turns away from such evil, and the curse will be terminated. For example, Jonah was told to prophesy that God would destroy the entire city of Nineveh for its evil ways. Yet the people of Nineveh repented, and "when God saw what they did and how they turned from their evil ways, he relented and did not bring on them the destruction he had threatened" (Jonah

3:10). The books of Kings and Chronicles also provide several examples of kings of Judah who had evil fathers but departed from their fathers' ways and knew God's blessing, rather than being punished for their fathers' sins. These kings include Asa, the son of Abijam (1 Kgs 15:9–11); Hezekiah, the son of Ahaz (2 Kgs 18); and Josiah, the son of Amon (2 Kgs 22).

Conversely, God punished the sons of wicked kings who did follow in their fathers' footsteps, as well as the sons of good kings who forsook the righteous ways of their fathers. God punished those kings not for their fathers' sins, but for their own sins of idolatry, wickedness and evil. Examples include Ahab, the son of Omri (1 Kgs 16:28–30); Jehoshaphat, the son of Asa (1 Kgs 22:41–43); Ahaziah, the son of Ahab (1 Kgs 22:51–52); Manasseh, the son of Hezekiah (2 Kgs 21); and Amon, the son of Manasseh (2 Kgs 21:18–23).

Thus the Scriptures do not teach that we will suffer simply because the sins of our ancestors were cursed. Each generation and each person who participates in evil receives a punishment or curse because of their own guilt. Each generation and each person who obeys God and does what is right receives blessings from the Lord.

We see the same principle applied at the human level in Deuteronomy 24:16. King Amaziah applied this law when he executed the murderers of his father but spared their sons because "parents are not to be put to death for their children, nor children put to death for their parents; each will die for their own sin" (2 Kgs 14:6). Ezekiel too preaches personal responsibility saying "the one who sins is the one who will die" (18:4). He insists that God does not punish children for their parents' sins, and vice versa. Ezekiel 18:20 continues with this idea: "the son shall not suffer for the iniquity of the father, nor the father for the iniquity of the son; the righteousness of the righteous shall be upon himself, and the wickedness of the wicked shall be upon himself."

God does not curse one generation for the sins of another, but if a generation continues to sin, influenced by the bad example of previous generations, the consequences of that sin will surely follow. God punishes each generation for its own sins.

Generational curses and believers

Earlier, I quoted the statement that "if a family has multiple cases of things like diabetes, alcoholism, divorce, stroke, heart disease, accidents, fornication, adultery, physical, mental or sexual abuse, anger, depression, suicide, idolatry or witchcraft, then that family is suffering from a generational curse."[16] However, the New Testament clearly teaches that we cannot simply lump the many different types of diseases and misfortunes that afflict human beings together and attribute them to a curse. It is wrong for African pastors and church ministries to lump sicknesses together, claiming that they are all caused by evil forces and curses so that the person suffering from them requires deliverance from Satan. To do so is to disregard Jesus' own ministry. The people who were brought to him for healing included those "who were ill with various diseases, those suffering severe pain, the demon-possessed, those having seizures, and the paralyzed" (Matt 4:24). He responded by treating some of them for physical illnesses, which he healed by laying on hands, speaking a word of command, or using natural elements such as dirt, saliva and water (Mark 7:31–35; 8:22–25; Luke 8:40–49.). In other cases, he recognized that there was a need for supernatural deliverance from demonic influences (Mark 7:24–29; Luke 9:37–43). In still other cases, he indicated that a misfortune was caused by human sin (John 5:14; see also 1 Cor 11:29–30), but he also made it clear that this was not always the case (Luke 13:4; John 9:2–3). Victims of calamities or recurring sicknesses are not necessarily more sinful than others, and it is therefore critical not to jump to conclusions about the causes of misfortunes. We should be like Jesus who called all his followers to repentance (Luke 13:5).

Jesus' teaching is borne out by modern medicine. Genetic research has revealed that many so-called generational curses are actually genetic diseases that are passed on from generation to generation. These include sickle cell anaemia, certain forms of cancer, mental disability, mood disorders, infertility, high blood pressure and diabetes. It is important for the African church to realize that these are physical conditions that can be diagnosed and even treated. Ignorance and superstitious beliefs have caused much havoc. Atrocities have been committed against victims of genetic misfortunes in the belief that they are suffering from "curses" from which they need deliverance. Preachers and ministries have enriched themselves by playing on people's fears in this area. Genetic health problems should be acknowledged as such and be given

---

[16] Musa Asake, "Generational Curses".

proper attention. Prayers and medical attention are necessary. Medical science is not opposed to God if practised in accordance with his will.[17]

Conversely, physical or spiritual problems that are caused by demonic forces must be fought and conquered accordingly. In these situations, prayers for deliverance are biblical (Acts 16:16–18). However, to become preoccupied with issues of demonic deliverance is unscriptural. The priority is the preaching of the good news of the deliverance that Christ has brought.

The Blood of Jesus

Linked to the belief in the power of spoken words to bring a blessing or a curse on someone is the idea that invoking the name of a god will bring about a desired outcome. Before their conversion, many Africans were accustomed to invoking the names of deities and ancestral spirits to resolve particular problems. Once converted, they tend to carry on the practice, simply substituting concepts like "the blood of Jesus" and "the name of Jesus":

> Repeating the phrase "blood of Jesus" (almost like a mantra), some advocate "sprinkling the blood" by their verbal repetitions over one's paycheck in order to get an increase in salary, "sprinkling the blood" over one's automobile so it will run perfectly, "sprinkling the blood" over the airplane so you will be assured of a safe trip.[18]

A respected Christian leader in Nigeria once told me that he invoked the blood of Jesus and believed that it saved him from a potential car crash. He was driving on one of Nigeria's major roads, when he noticed that every car ahead of him (eight cars in a row) suddenly developed a flat tyre at a particular point in the road. He knew that his car would be no

---

[17] For more on this and related topics, see my book, *African Christian Ethics* (Jos, Nairobi and Accra: HippoBooks / Grand Rapids: Zondervan, 2008), 204–214. See also George H. Kieffer, *Bioethics: A Textbook of Issues* (Reading, Mass.; Addison-Wesley, 1979); John F. Kilner, Rebecca D. Pentz and Frank E. Young, eds., *Genetic Ethics: Do the Ends Justify the Genes?* (Grand Rapids: Eerdmans, 1997); John Feinberg and Paul Feinberg, *Ethics for a Brave New World* (Wheaton: Crossway, 1993); Anderson J. Kirby, *Genetic Engineering* (Grand Rapids: Zondervan, 1982); Timothy J. Denny and Gary P. Stewart, eds., *Genetic Engineering: A Christian Response. Crucial Considerations for Shaping Life* (Grand Rapids: Kregel, 1999).

[18] James A. Fowler, "The Blood of Christ" (1999), 5. Available at www.christinyou.net/pages/bloodchrst.html.

different, so he invoked the blood of Jesus. His car tyres did not go flat. Stories like this abound.

The use of blood in rituals is common in many religions, dating back to the days before Moses. In African Traditional Religion it is used for ritual purposes such as cleansing, purification, atonement, initiation and protection. Sins such as adultery, fornication, revealing the secrets of the gods or insulting parents require blood sacrifices to appease the gods. Diviners and native doctors also use blood to protect their patients against evil spirits. Thus, when Africans are converted to Christianity, they come prepared to read a certain set of meanings into "the blood of Jesus", seeing it as a potent weapon in their new-found faith. Fowler writes,

> People have a tendency to take a truth (particularly a 'religious' truth which accumulates superstitious significance), and let their imaginations run wild with it. The original truth soon develops many hypothetical accretions which have no substantiation. People have a tendency to build traditions around their interpretations, and these sometimes become as important as, or more important than, the original scriptural truth itself.[19]

It is not a surprise, then, that "the blood of Jesus" is used in daily life by African Christians. But is this usage correct? What does the Bible say about blood? What does the New Testament teach about "the blood of Jesus"?

Blood in the Old Testament

1. At a fundamental level, blood signified the whole life of an animal or person. The ESV captures this in its translation of Genesis 9:4 "But you shall not eat flesh with its life, that is, its blood". The NIV reads, "You must not eat meat that has its lifeblood still in it. And for your lifeblood I will surely demand an accounting. I will demand an accounting from every animal. And from each human being, too, I will demand an accounting for the life of another human being. 'Whoever sheds human blood, by humans shall their blood be shed; for in the image of God has God made mankind'" (Gen 9:4–6).

---

[19] Ibid., 1.

2. Blood was an important element in many sacrifices, such as those for atonement, forgiveness of sins, cleansing, and purification (Exod 23:18; 24:8; 29:20; Lev 1:5; 4:17, 34; 12:13; 14:4–7; see also Mark 14:24; Heb 9:22). The blood offered signified the "presentation to God of life, the life of the victim".[20] Leviticus 17:11 reads, "For the life of a creature is in the blood, and I have given it to you to make atonement for yourselves on the altar; it is the blood that makes atonement for one's life." Though it is not explicitly mentioned, blood must have been spilled to provide the skins that God used to cover the nakedness of Adam and Eve after they sinned (Gen 3:21). This prefigures the violent death of Christ and the shedding of his blood as a sacrifice for the sins of his people.

3. At the time of the exodus, God commanded the Israelites to put the blood of lambs on their door posts. Exodus 12:13 states, "The blood will be a sign for you on the houses where you are, and when I see the blood, I will pass over you. No destructive plague will touch you when I strike Egypt." The blood was to protect the firstborn sons of Israel from destruction by the angel of God.

Was it the blood itself that protected the firstborn children? No; the blood of the animal had no inherent protective power. It was God who saved them, through their obedience. It was he who gave the Israelites the command to sacrifice the lambs that would stand in their place (substitution).

> Deliverance was through the obedience of faith. For the Israelite, it was a new and hitherto unheard-of thing, that the destroying angel was to come, and that the blood on the door would deliver him. But he believed God's word, and in that belief he did what he had been commanded.[21]

Similarly, when the Israelites were dying of snake bites, God told Moses to set up a bronze snake so that anyone who looked at it would not die.

---

[20] Leon Morris, *The Cross in the New Testament* (Grand Rapids: Eerdmans, 1965), 219. Morris also suggests that the blood "could mean that what is ritually presented to God is the evidence that death has taken place in accordance with His judgment on sin. For blood in separation from the flesh is not life but death." I do not see why the two meanings cannot be joined together: the ritual presented the life of the victim to God and was evidence that death had taken place to indicate judgement on sin.

[21] Andrew Murray, *The Blood of the Cross: Christ's Blood Can Protect and Empower You* (1935; repr. New Kensington: Whitaker House, 1984), 96.

Numbers 21:9 reads, "So Moses made a bronze serpent and put it up on a pole. Then when anyone was bitten by a snake and looked at the bronze snake, they lived." It was not the snake that made people live, it was their obedience to God shown by looking up at the snake he had provided.

The "blood of Christ" in the New Testament

The Old Testament sacrifice of the Passover lambs foreshadowed the death of Christ on the cross as the ultimate Passover Lamb, sacrificed as a ransom for the sins for the whole world (John 1:29). Thus it is not surprising that the New Testament attaches great importance to the blood of Christ, variously referred to as the blood of Jesus (Heb 10:19; 1 John 1:7), the blood of Christ (1 Cor 10:16; Eph 2:13; Heb 9:14), the blood of Lord (1 Cor 11:27) and the blood of the Lamb (Rev 7:14; 12:11). Paul even refers to the service of Communion (the Eucharist) as a "participation in the blood of Christ" (1 Cor 10:16; see also 1 Cor 11:25). The overwhelming thrust of all these references is to build on the Old Testament connection between blood and sacrifice to bring out the sacrificial element in Christ's life and death. The stress is never on Christ's actual physical blood – in fact the New Testament does not state that he actually shed a lot of blood.[22]

Romans 3:25 explains that God sent Christ "as a sacrifice of atonement, through the shedding of his blood – to be received by faith". In Romans 5:9 we read that we are "justified by his blood". Ephesians 1:7 states that "It is through his blood that we have redemption". Colossians 1:20 shows that God's purpose was "through him to reconcile to himself all things ... by making peace through his blood, shed on the cross" (see also Eph 2:13). Revelation 5:9 also emphasizes the redemptive function of Christ's blood: "You are worthy to take the scroll and to open its seals, because you were slain, and with your blood you purchased for God persons from every tribe and language and people and nation."

The most detailed treatment of the blood of Jesus is given in the book of Hebrews, where the main message is that the blood of

---

[22] George Ladd points out, "The idea of shed blood refers to the slaughter of the sacrificial lamb whose throat was cut and whose blood gushed forth. Nothing like this happened to Jesus. The blood and water (John 19:34) that came from Jesus' side did so after he had expired. In the New Testament, blood means life violently taken away, life offered in sacrifice." *A Theology of the New Testament* (Grand Rapids, Eerdmans, 1974), 426.

Jesus was given as an atonement and provided for a permanent and complete redemption of humankind from sin. Referring back to the Old Testament, it asserts that "without the shedding of blood there is no remission of sins" (Heb 9:22). On this verse, F. Laubach notes,

> Surrender of life is the essential prerequisite for the granting of forgiveness. The Old Testament gave typographical expression to the power of the blood to remove sin and save, making it a fundamental element of every cultic sacrifice for atonement. The New Testament sees in the death of Christ the ultimate significance and fulfilment of this idea.[23]

The New Testament repeatedly stresses that Christ's work was voluntary. He said that he laid down his own life (John 10:17–18; 1 John 3:16) and John records that he "gave up his spirit" (John 19:30). Here and elsewhere, the laying down of his life and the offering of his blood refers to the whole of his life and ministry, not just to his hours on the cross. The blood must never be separated from the high priest!

To summarize what has been said: "blood" is used in Scripture primarily to signify the sacrificial death of Christ for the whole world. It has "a supernatural, heavenly, divine power to cover and blot out sin before God immediately and forever. Accept this as God's truth and rest upon it."[24]

The idea that the blood of Christ is protective derives more from an African approach to blood sacrifices than it does from the Scriptures:

> Such false ideas entrap innocent and gullible Christian people into false faith, into the deification of the blood of Christ, into occultic forms of magical fetishes such as "pleading the blood" or "sprinkling the blood" by repeating verbal mantras. Such concepts and procedures relegate important biblical truth to the realm of "hocus-pocus" and constitute what Paul would call "a gospel other than the one we preached to you" which is not gospel at all (Gal 1:8)![25]

Some may argue that there are verses in Scripture that support the idea that Christ's blood is protective. The first verse they quote is 1 Peter

---

[23] F. Laubach, "Blood", in *New Dictionary of New Testament Theology* (ed. Colin Brown; Grand Rapids, Zondervan, 1967), 1:223.

[24] Murray, *The Blood of the Cross*, 96.

[25] Fowler, "The Blood of Christ", 11.

2:24: "by his wounds you have been healed"; but it is important to look at this verse in its whole context. Here is the full verse: "'He himself bore our sins' in his body on the cross, so that we might die to sins and live for righteousness; 'by his wounds you have been healed'". Peter is quoting Isaiah 53:5: "But he was pierced for our transgressions, he was crushed for our iniquities; the punishment that brought us peace was on him, and by his wounds we are healed." This prophecy concerns Christ's substitutionary atonement: his taking our place and bearing our sins and their punishment on the cross. While we can appeal to the death of Christ when praying for help with dealing with our physical problems, that is not the primary meaning of this verse. Peter is teaching that we are redeemed through Christ's death.

The second verse that is often quoted by those who claim that Christ's blood can be used to ward off demonic attacks is Revelation 12:11: "They triumphed over him by the blood of the Lamb." Though we do not debate the potency of Christ's work that destroyed the works of the devil (1 John 3:8), we doubt that the thrust of the passage in Revelation is to teach that the blood is an agent of protection against the assaults of the devil. In context this verse deals with future events, specifically the final judgement of the devil. How can something that will take place in the future become a present practice? Even if one interprets the passage in Revelation as referring to the present time, the interpretation that stresses "the blood" being used to conquer satanic power and demonic attacks is very narrow in the light of the rest of Scripture, which teaches that it was by virtue of the whole life of Christ that Satan has been defeated for all time. Christ gives us power over Satan and his hosts. We have no right to extract "the blood of Christ" in order to use it for our little battles here on earth.

> We must beware of fanciful, speculative "spiritualizing". We must beware of mystifying, superstitious fantasies about the blood of Jesus. This has often been a result of taking Old Testament "types" and pushing them beyond their pictorial pre-figuring and thus developing one's theology around vague conjectures. Types are valid. They are pictures. The sacrificial types of the Old Testament are fulfilled in Jesus Christ. But we cannot take the pictures and superimpose them on the New Testament to create spiritual concepts that are never noted by

the inspired Scripture of God! Many Christians have done so and are guilty of regarding the blood of Jesus as having more significance than Scripture indicates.[26]

The Name of Jesus

The use of the words "in the name of Jesus" is biblical and expresses important theological truths. But as with the "blood of Jesus", this phrase is now being used in unexpected ways. It has gained currency, especially among Christians in Africa, as a formula to be used in mystical and superstitious ways in prayers for deliverance from demonic and occultic practices. Its frequent use during public prayers and on public occasions in Muslim-dominated areas such as Northern Nigeria has possibly been encouraged by the Muslim habit of constantly saying *bismillahi ar rahmani* ("in the Name of Allah, the Most Gracious, the Most Merciful").

The name of God in Scripture

In the ancient world, it was believed that to know a person's name or a deity's name was to know something about him or her and that to invoke the name of a person was to assert authority based on that name. We see this in the Old Testament, which treats the name of the Lord as "such a powerful expression of His personal rule and activity that it can be used as an alternative way of speaking of Yahweh himself (Lev 18:21; Ps 7:17; Amos 2:7; Mic 5:4)".[27] Thus the name of Yahweh should be "hallowed" or "kept holy" (Isa 29:23; see also Matt 6:9).

The name of Yahweh was used in blessings (Num 6:24–27; Deut 10:8; 2 Sam 6:18), in curses (2 Kgs 2:24), and when swearing oaths (Deut 5:11). It was never to be misused (Exod 20:7) or brought into disrepute (Lev 19:12; 20:3; 21:6). This means, in part, that "the holy name had in all circumstances to be safeguarded against improper use, ... it was used by Israel at sacrifice, in prayer, in blessing and cursing,

---

[26] Ibid., 5.
[27] Hans Bietenhard, "Name", in *New International Dictionary of New Testament Theology* (Grand Rapids: Zondervan, 1976), 2:649–650.

and also in the holy war (Ps 20:7), and it had been given her for this purpose."[28]

God's name was also invoked when appealing to him to fulfil his promise that "wherever I cause my name to be honoured, I will come to you and bless you" (Exod 20:24).

The same pattern of usage recurs in the New Testament, where the names and titles associated with Christ testify to who he is and what he does. Jesus means "Saviour" (Matt 1:21), Emmanuel means "God with us" (Matt 1:23), Christ means Messiah (John 1:41). Christ is also spoken of as the Word of God (John 1:1; Rev 19:13) and as Lord (Phil 2:9–11). Sometimes it is enough simply to refer to "the Name" (Acts 5:41; 3 John 7). Saving truth is found only in his name (Acts 4:12; 1 Cor 6:11). The apostles preached that belief in his name will bring forgiveness of sins (Acts 10:43; 1 John 1:2:12) and escape from judgement (John 3:18). God gives the Holy Spirit in the name of Jesus (John 14:26). Thanks are given in his name (Eph 5:20). People are baptized in the name of Jesus (Matt 28:19–20; Acts 2:38; 8:16; 10:48; 1 Cor 1:13). Failing to show respect to someone who belongs to Christ is equivalent to showing disrespect for the "noble name" of Christ (Jas 2:7). Persecuting Christians is synonymous with persecuting Jesus (Acts 9:4–5).

Power is associated with the name of Jesus (Acts 4:7; 16:18). Miracles are performed in his name (Mark 9:38–40; Luke 10:17) and the sick are healed (Acts 3:6; 14:10). Unbelievers are punished when they attempt to use his name for their own glory (Acts 19:13–16). Paul used the name of Jesus to admonish (2 Thess 3:6) and give judgement (1 Cor 5:3; 2 Thess 3:6).

One day, everyone "in heaven and on earth and under the earth" will bow at the name of Jesus (Phil 2:10–11). By using the phrase "heaven and earth", Paul indicates that all beings (angelic and human) will submit to Christ's lordship. This includes even Michael and Gabriel – the two angelic beings with the highest status – for Christ's name is superior to theirs (Heb 1:4).

We become believers by calling on Christ's name, an act by which we acknowledge that Christ is Lord and give him the right to control our lives. This requires fidelity to Christ and entering into a relationship with him, which is signified by baptism (1 John 3:23; 5:13). It is only

---

[28] Eichrodt, *Theology of the Old Testament*, 183.

through Christ's name that forgiveness of sins is obtained (Acts 4:12; 10:43). For Luke and Peter, salvation is summed up in the name of Jesus (Acts 3:6; 8:12).

To pray in the name of Jesus is to pray according to his will in the fulfilment of the mission he gave to the disciples (John 14:13; 15:16; 16:23, 26). Such prayer is an expression of the belief that Jesus came from God, that he is God's Son, and that the Father will respond to such belief by hearing the prayer that is offered. As believers in Jesus, the disciples can act in his name, that is, on his commission and in his power. "Jesus called his twelve disciples to him and gave them authority to drive out impure spirits and to heal every disease and sickness" (Matt 10:1; see also Mark 6:7–13; Luke 9:1). "They [the disciples] drove out many demons and anointed many sick people with oil and healed them" (Mark 6:13). On the return of the seventy-two followers whom Jesus commissioned, they reported with joy, "Lord, even the demons submit to us in your name" (Luke 10:17). Peter, after Pentecost, used the same formula to heal the crippled man at the gate when he said to him, "In the name of Jesus Christ of Nazareth, walk" (Acts 3:6).

The passages cited above clearly indicate that believers can have the power to heal and to drive out demons. However, these gifts of healing and exorcism seem to be special gifts given only to some believers (1 Cor 12:28-30). But the broader point is that the disciples believed that the name of Jesus was powerful, and they practised this belief by calling on his name. Christians today should also believe that the name of Jesus has power to accomplish the things they desire in accordance with the will of God (Matt 28:19–20; Acts 1:8).

However, simply invoking the name of Jesus does not automatically bring salvation, healing or power. His name is not a magical formula that can be used to manipulate supernatural forces. Invoking the name of the Lord always implies believing in him and having a relationship with him. This is what is happening when church elders anoint a sick person with oil in the name of the Lord (Jas 5:14). We need to recognize that we can ask God to heal in the name of Jesus, but it remains his prerogative whether to do so. Praying in the name of Jesus is not about forcing God to do something; rather, it is bending our human will to God's will. Unbelievers try to manipulate God in their prayers. Believers know that they cannot force God to do what they want.

Using the name of Jesus

In New Testament times it was common for people to use the names of gods and spiritual powers to cast out demons (Luke 11:14).[29] Some non-Christian Jews attempted to do the same with the names of God and Jesus. However, Jesus condemned such tactics when there was no faith to back them up (Luke 11:24–26). The apostles also encountered people who saw the power of Jesus as a way to make money, and things ended badly for those who misused Christ's name (Acts 8:18; 19:11–20).

The use of the name of Jesus does not always guarantee a positive response. The man possessed by evil spirits who called on Jesus not to torment him did not have his request granted. Instead, Jesus commanded the evil spirits to come out of him (Mark 5:6–8). On the day of judgement, entry into heaven will be denied to people who used the name of Jesus for their own selfish purposes without having a personal relationship with him (Luke 7:21).

The right use of the name of Jesus involves recognizing that the name represents all of who he is and what he has done for humanity. It is the presence and power of Jesus Christ that brings about complete healing, as evidenced by the healing of Aeneas at Lydda (Acts 9:34). It is also true that presentation of the gospel of salvation in Jesus Christ is more important than all other personal needs. Thus in Acts 3:6 Peter healed the lame beggar by offering him Jesus Christ, in whose name he was healed. Salvation in Jesus is the context of all healing.

African Christians need to remember that casting out demons or evil spirits in the name of Jesus is not the central purpose of preaching or living the Christian life. This is vividly illustrated in Paul and Silas' encounter with a girl who had a spirit of fortune-telling (Acts 16:16–18). She followed them around for days until "finally Paul became so annoyed that he turned around and said to the spirit, 'In the name of Jesus Christ I command you to come out of her!' At that moment the spirit left her" (16:18). Paul had not been looking for an opportunity to cast out demons, and Christians should not make casting out demons their priority. That place belongs to the preaching of the gospel of Jesus Christ. As Twelftree says: "The contemporary church would do well to follow the example of the early church, not to ignore the demonic, but

---

[29] Graham H. Twelftree, *In the Name of Jesus: Exorcism among Early Christians* (Grand Rapids: Baker Academic, 2007), 52.

to focus attention on Jesus, who defeats the demonic. Undue concern and involvement with the demonic has often been seen as opening oneself up to its influence."[30]

The New Testament knows nothing about forcing or commanding God or Jesus to do anything. Jesus is Lord and stands above all magical compulsion. The New Testament equally says nothing about using the name of Jesus as a talisman. The use of the name of Christ may bring healing (Jas 5:14), but such healing does not come through pronouncing a set formula but through the Lord's response to a prayer made in faith and obedience to him.

Prayer

If our salvation in Christ is holistic, intended not only to redeem our souls but also to bless us with fullness of life in the present, this has implications for our prayer life. How should we be praying in the midst of life's spiritual, economic and political struggles? What does it mean to say that the fullness of life affects every aspect of life – physical, spiritual and emotional?

The first thing to recognize is that we cannot expect our prayers to solve all the problems we face in the present. As pointed out earlier, our salvation is past, present and future. Total salvation, which will remove all physical problems, temptations and evil, will only be realized in heaven.

Nor should our prayers be focused solely on this life. As 1 Corinthians 15:19 states, "If only for this life we have hope in Christ, we are of all people most to be pitied." A view of salvation that focuses only on this life is distorted and unbiblical. So when we think about our circumstances, we should be fully aware of our future hope of resurrection with Christ.

But none of this means that we are not to pray. In fact, in both the Old and New Testaments we are commanded to pray. For example, in 2 Chronicles 7:14 God said, "If my people, who are called by my name, will humble themselves and pray and seek my face and turn from their wicked ways, then I will hear from heaven, and I will forgive their sin and will heal their land." Prayer and confession of sin are prerequisites for forgiveness and healing. Similarly Jeremiah 33:3 says, "Call to me

---

[30] Ibid., 294.

and I will answer you and tell you great and unsearchable things you do not know."

Jesus himself prayed, and he taught his disciples to pray (Matt 6:5–13). In the hour of crisis, he told them to "watch and pray so that you will not fall into temptation. The spirit is willing, but the flesh is weak" (Matt 26:41).

In his letters, Paul frequently urged believers to pray: "Devote yourselves to prayer, being watchful and thankful" (Col 4:2); "Pray continually" (1 Thess 5:17); "Brothers and sisters, pray for us" (1 Thess 5:25). Prayer makes it possible for God to grant our requests for such things as healing (Jas 516). Through prayer, impossible things can become possible.

As noted above, prayer in the name of Jesus is not magical or some kind of amulet or talisman that can be used to force God's hand. As Randy Alcorn says, we must not use prayer and faith as

> a crowbar to break down the door of God's reluctance, rather
> than a humble attempt to lay hold of his willingness. When we
> claim the blood of Christ, believing that God must take away
> this illness or handicap or financial hardship, are we asking him
> to remove the very things he has put into our lives to make us
> more Christlike?[31]

Prayer should always be made in obedience to God and in submission to his will. For example, if we pray that a person will not die, our prayer may be contrary to God's will and the prayer will not be answered in the way we want.

Reverence for Ancestors

One of the most persistent religious beliefs in Africa is that ancestral spirits have power to influence our daily lives. This belief continues to exert a profound influence on Christian life and practice. Yusufu Turaki writes, "Belief in and reverence for the ancestors is fundamental to traditional African thinking. It is believed that those who die at a mature age do not cease to be members of their community but continue to play an active

---

[31] Randy Alcorn, *Money, Possessions and Eternity* (rev. ed.; Carol Stream: Tyndale House, 2003), 87.

role in the lives of their descendants."[32] In moments of crisis, African Christians sometimes turn to their ancestors to solve their problems. The result is syncretism, a mixture of Christian and traditional beliefs. Yet clearly many Christians seem to have no difficulty in embracing conflicting belief systems, as long as their problems are solved.

What exactly is reverence for ancestors? Some erroneously think that it is worship of ancestors in the place of God. This could not be further from the truth. In the African world view, God is sovereign and has no equal. Spirits, including ancestral spirits, are not equal to God and cannot be worshipped. Simply put, ancestral spirits are merely mediators for their descendants. Though the ancestors are dead, their spirits are constantly watching and guiding their descendants through life.

This belief is linked to the belief that when people die, they do not cease to exist but continue to live meaningful lives. As the "living dead" they are custodians, protectors and guides of their descendants, who will one day join them. They communicate with the living through visions and dreams, as well as through revelations to diviners and sangomas. Because the ancestors live through the memories of their descendants, it is important that they not be forgotten. If this happens, they will become the "dead dead".

The existence of these ancestors is very real to those who venerate them, and so is the belief that the ancestral spirits are able to help their descendants in times of crisis and need. It is at this point that many African Christians stumble in their faith, for these spirits may require sacrifices, ritual purifications, prayers and rites for dealing with certain issues or events.

To illustrate how this works, let me recount the story of a taxi driver whom I know (whom I will here call Jabu). He was a Seventh-Day Adventist. We often talked about issues such as religion, sport, politics and economics. In 2010, I asked him about his family and his wife, Simphiwe, and whether she was a Christian. Jabu told me that she had started out as a Christian but was now training as a sangoma, a religious diviner who is believed to be able to communicate with the ancestral spirits and to provide spiritual healing for problems such as disease or fear of the spirit world. I asked Jabu how his wife had come to take this step.

---

[32] Yusufu Turaki, "The Role of Ancestors", in *Africa Bible Commentary* (ed. Tokunboh Adeyemo; Nairobi: WordAlive, 2006), 480.

He explained me that in life there are times when crises force one to re-evaluate one's beliefs. This had happened for them when they had found themselves unable to have a second child. They had one child, and had consulted many doctors, none of whom could explain why Simphiwe could not conceive again. Then a few people had told them that the ancestral spirits were angry with Simphiwe and that she needed to make sacrifices to the spirits if she wanted to become pregnant. Initially Jabu and Simphiwe resisted this advice. Yet, since they desperately wanted to have another child, they eventually yielded and made sacrifices to the ancestral spirits. Simphiwe did indeed become pregnant, and she bore a healthy son. In response she became committed to the ancestral spirits, making sacrifices to them as required. As far as Jabu was concerned, the ancestral spirits had met their needs and deserved to be listened to for guidance in life. This did not mean that, for them, God had been replaced by the ancestral spirits – God was still God – but the ancestral spirits had their own role to play.

If the church is to win the war against the practice of ancestral veneration and the strong temptation for believers to revert back to it, it must begin by acknowledging the following points on which we all agree.

- There is a sovereign God who is separate from all other spirits including ancestral spirits.
- There is indeed life after death. Death is not the cessation of personal existence.
- We all have real needs and all need a religion that is relevant to our daily life. God must be able to provide protection, security and guidance during times of crises.
- We all need some form of mediator between us and the spiritual world.

This final point is the one where we can present Christ as the ultimate mediator. Through his life, death and resurrection, he reconciled sinful human beings to God (Rom 5:1). He fulfilled the law (Matt 5:17) – and not only the Old Testament sacrifices and the priestly order, but also the laws of other religions, including those related to the veneration of ancestors. Although in Matthew Christ was speaking of the Mosaic law, passages such as Romans 1:19 and 2:14 suggest that God has revealed something of himself to all peoples, including Africans (see chapter 2). It is thus possible to understand ancestral belief and practice as predicting or foreshadowing the mediatorial role of Christ described in the book of Hebrews. As Turaki observes, the best approach to those who venerate their ancestors "may be modelled on the one taken in the book of Hebrews which was written against a religious background similar to that found in traditional religion. Taking this approach, it can be said that Jesus has come to fulfil our African ancestral cult and has taken the place of our ancestors, replacing them with himself."[33]

Because Christ fulfilled all laws, including those related to our ancestors, the rituals associated with veneration of our ancestors are now null and void. Christ has assumed all the functions our ancestors fulfilled in traditional beliefs. He is the only mediator between God and humanity (1 Tim 2:5) and he is able to sympathize with us and intercede on our behalf in all areas of life. As Hebrews 4:15–16 states,

> We do not have a high priest who is unable to empathize with our weaknesses, but we have one who has been tempted in every way, just as we are – yet he did not sin. Let us then approach God's throne of grace with confidence, so that we may receive mercy and find grace to help us in our time of need.

Indeed, Christ has promised to be with us at all times until the end of the age (Matt 28:18–20).

To those who assert that ancestor worship meets the real human needs of Africans, we can point out that the Bible is full of accounts telling how God met the real needs of his people, some of whom were in a very similar situation to that of Jabu and Simphiwe described above:

- Sarah could not have a child; at ninety she was "past the age of childbearing" (Gen 17:17; 18:11). Yet God promised Abraham that "Sarah will bear you a son" (17:19) and "Sarah became pregnant and bore a son to Abraham in his old age at the very time God had promised him" (21:2).

- The Lord closed Rachel's womb so that she could not have children (Gen 29:31), yet he later "listened to her and enabled her to conceive" (30:22).

---

[33] Ibid.

- The Lord closed Hannah's womb so that she could not have children (1 Sam 1:6). Yet after she prayed, the Lord gave her a son named Samuel (1 Sam 1:20).

- The Shunammite woman who could not have children was promised a child by Elisha, the man of God, and she became pregnant and gave birth to a son (2 Kgs 4:14–17).

- Zechariah and Elizabeth were God-fearing people but unable to have a child. Elizabeth was barren and advanced in years (Luke 1:7). Their prayers were answered, and an angel told them that they would have a son. It came to pass just as the angel had spoken (1:13).

- Jesus healed people with all kinds of needs and ailments: the demon-possessed, bleeding, bereaved (Mark 5; John 11); those who were deaf-mute (Mark 7); the hungry, those afflicted with leprosy, the paralyzed (Luke 5); and the blind (Luke 18:35–43).

God answers the prayers of his people when they pray in faith. All those who are burdened are invited to take their needs to Christ (Matt 11:28) because he cares deeply about the concerns of all his children (Ps 55:22; see also 1 Pet 5:8). Believers can have confidence that the Lord can provide more than they ask for (2 Chr 25:9). However, they must humbly remember that God may choose to answer their prayers by enabling them to bear their suffering or pain. When Paul prayed for the removal of his thorn in the flesh, the Lord did not remove it. His answer to Paul was, "My grace is sufficient for you, for my power is made perfect in weakness" (2 Cor 12:9). Through God's grace we too can bear our sufferings in this life and take hope in God's promise of a new life to come without pain and suffering (Rev 21:4).

People will always go where they believe their problems will be adequately addressed. Christianity is well able to handle such problems, and it remains for the church to provide these biblical perspectives. Failure to do so will lead to more believers becoming syncretistic or even returning to their old ways of life, which Christ has graciously discontinued. Christ has come to give full and abundant life to African Christians, even in the midst of their problems (John 10:10).

Questions

1. What do we mean when we say that salvation is "holistic"? How should this affect the presentation of the gospel of Christ in the world today?

2. What does your community believe about curses, including generational curses?

3. How would you counsel somebody who strongly believed that he or she was under a curse?

4. What is the biblical meaning of the phrases "the blood of Christ" and the "name of Jesus"? How should such phrases be used, and not used?

5. What authority is in the name of Jesus? Cite Scripture in support of your answer.

6. How would you counsel people who believe that they need to consult the ancestors for help with particular needs?

7. In what specific ways does the book of Hebrews speak to the issue of veneration of ancestors and the practices associated with it?

8. How would you help someone who has prayed for healing, or children, or employment, and has not received it?

9. Study Numbers 6:24–27 and Jude 24–25 and write down the lessons you have learnt from these passages.

Further Reading

George Ladd. *A Theology of the New Testament*. Revised and updated. Grand Rapids: Eerdmans, 1993.

Derek Prince. *Blessings and Curses*. Grand Rapids: Chosen Books, 1994.

Randy Alcorn. *Money, Possessions and Eternity*. Revised edition. Wheaton, Ill: Tyndale House, 2003/

James A. Fowler. "The Blood of Christ", 1999. <www.christinyou.net/pages/bloodchrst.html>.

Leon Morris. *Apostolic Preaching of the Cross*. Grand Rapids: Eerdmans, 1956.

_____. *The Cross in the New Testament*. Grand Rapids: Eerdmans, 1965.

Graham H. Twelftree. *In the Name of Jesus: Exorcism among Early Christians*. Grand Rapids: Baker Academic, 2007.

8

THE COMMUNITY OF GOD

African theologians have not given as much scholarly attention to the theology of the church as they have to the theology of Christ and salvation. Yet the church in Africa has been growing dramatically. In his book *The Next Christendom: The Coming of Global Christianity,* Philip Jenkins has documented how the centre of gravity of Christianity has shifted from the northern to the southern hemisphere – South America, Africa and Asia. In one of his other books, he states,

> By 2025, Africa and Latin America will vie for the title of the most Christian continent. ... The figures are startling. Between 1900 and 2000, the number of Christians in Africa grew from 10 million to over 360 million, from 10 percent of the population to 46 percent. If that is not, quantitatively, the largest religious change in human history in such a short period, I am at a loss to think of a rival. Today, the most vibrant centers of Christian growth are still in Africa itself.[1]

Churches planted in Africa have grown into megachurches and have reached out to other regions of the world. For example, the Evangelical Church Winning All (ECWA, formerly known as the Evangelical Church of West Africa) and the Church of Christ in Nigeria (COCIN) – both of which are offshoots of Serving in Mission (SIM, formerly known as Sudan Interior Mission) and Sudan United Mission (SUM) – have memberships of millions in Africa, Europe and the United States. Other churches that have grown rapidly and attract not only indigenous African peoples but people from around the world include the Winners'

---

[1] Philip Jenkins, *The New Faces of Christianity: Believing the Bible in the Global South* (New York: Oxford University Press, 2006), 9. Jenkins goes on to explain, "A map of the 'statistical center of gravity of global Christianity' shows that center moving steadily southward, from a point in northern Italy in 1800, to central Spain in 1900, to Morocco by 1970, and to a point near Timbuktu today" (9).

Chapel (Nigeria), the Redeemed Christian Church of God (Nigeria), Rhema Bible Ministries (South Africa), the Pentecost Church of Ghana, the International Pentecostal Holiness Church (IPHC) in Zuurbekom (South Africa), the Grace Bible Church (Soweto, South Africa), Jesus Celebration Centre (Mombasa, Kenya), Nairobi Pentecostal Church (Kenya), the Synagogue Church of the Nations (Nigeria) and the Zionist Christian Church (Southern Africa).

The churches listed above embrace many different models of mission, church government, leadership style, worship, liturgy and so on. Unfortunately, this is not the place to explore these issues. What we are setting out to do here is to articulate a broad theology of the church that is both biblical and relevant to the African situation.

Contemporary Models of the Church

The model, metaphor or image that we use when we speak about the church provides us with an insight into how the church sees itself and how it seeks to operate in society. So it is worth our while to spend some time looking at various models that have been put forward by scholars and theologians.

1. *An institution.* The institutional model defines the church in terms of its visible structures and the rights and powers of its officers.[2] Dulles argues that "throughout its history, from the very earliest years, Christianity has always had an institutional side. It has had recognized ministers, accepted confessional formulas, and prescribed forms of public worship. All this is fitting and proper."[3] There is nothing wrong with this. However, there is a problem when the church veers into institutionalism and places too high a value on visible structures and powers. This attitude represents "the deformation of the true nature of the church – a deformation that has unfortunately affected the church at certain periods of its history, and one that remains in every age a real danger to the institutional church. A Christian believer may energetically oppose institutionalism and still be very much committed to the church as institution."[4]

---

[2] Avery Dulles, *Models of the Church* (New York: Doubleday, 1978), 34.
[3] Ibid., 32.
[4] Ibid.

2. *A mystical communion.* Those who regard the church as a mystical communion think of it as consisting of all people of faith, living and dead, who are united in communion with one another in God's Spirit through Christ. This view emphasizes the fellowship of believers in a loving community centred on God, but it also opens the door to prayers to and for the dead.

3. *A sacrament.* A sacrament is defined in the Book of Common Prayer as "an outward and visible sign of God's inward grace". Those who see the church as a sacrament regard it "in the first instance as a sign. It must signify in a historically tangible form the redeeming grace of Christ. It signifies that grace as relevantly given to men of every age, race and condition. Hence the church must incarnate itself in every human culture."[5]

4. *A herald.* If the church's main task is to be God's herald in the world, then the proclamation of the faith has to be given higher priority than interpersonal relations and mystical communion.[6]

5. *A servant.* Those who adopt a servant model see the church as part of the total human family, sharing the same concerns as the rest of humankind.[7] They emphasize the church's responsibility to serve others rather than its own interests.

6. *A lecture hall.* At times the church is seen as a place where people simply gather to listen to the word of God being spoken to them. Though this model encourages great biblical exposition by the ministers of the church, it fosters passivity in the congregation.[8]

7. *A theatre.* In this model, "the priest appears, the choir sings, the congregation responds; all attention is centred around the drama which is about to be re-enacted on the altar. The bell tinkles, responses are given and the sacramental moment is reached."[9]

---

[5] Ibid., 63.

[6] Ibid., 76.

[7] Ibid., 91.

[8] This and the following three models are drawn from Peter Savage's chapter, "The Church and Evangelism", in *New Faces of Evangelism: An International Symposium on the Lausanne Covenant* (ed. C. Rene Padilla; Downers Grove: InterVarsity Press, 1976), 106–109.

[9] Savage, "The Church and Evangelism", 107.

8. A corporation. Some see the church as in the "business of retailing religion, much as any other commodity is marketed. Its goal is to make the goods and services of religion available to the people."[10]

9. A social club. Some portray the church as if it is a club, with potential members identifying themselves "with the social interests it represents and the services it provides". As with social clubs, people only qualify for membership if they satisfy certain conditions.[11]

10. A religious shopping mall. The church is sometimes regarded as a place people can go to find what they want and reject what is not needed.[12] In the USA, one sometimes hears believers say that they are "shopping" for a church – meaning that they are looking for a church that matches their idea or understanding of church.

11. A community of disciples. In the 1978 revision of his book *Models of the Church*, Dulles added this model as the one which best fits the biblical data.[13] This was the position taken by Vatican II (1962–1965),[14] which resolved to move radically away from an understanding of the church as an ecclesiastical hierarchy to a more biblical and ecumenical view of the church as a body of people, with the laity having an important role. The Lausanne Covenant of 1974 (which was agreed upon by 2,300 participants representing 150 countries and a broad spectrum of Protestant denominations and which is acknowledged as one of the key ecumenical documents in the history of the church) also agreed with this model. It stated, "The church is at the very centre of God's cosmic purpose and is his appointed means of spreading the gospel. [It] is the community of God's people rather than an institution."[15]

Savage agrees: "the church is the community of God's people and must be characterized by both comprehensiveness and cohesiveness, that is, it must extend itself to include all kinds of people while at the same time maintaining a strong bond of unity."[16] Howard Snyder

---

[10] Ibid., 107.
[11] Ibid., 108.
[12] Howard A. Snyder, *The Community of the King* (Downers Grove: InterVarsity Press, 1977), 34.
[13] Dulles, *Models of the Church*, 2–3.
[14] Ibid., 27.
[15] Point 6 of the Lausanne Covenant, www.lausanne.org/covenant.
[16] Savage, "The Church and Evangelism", 109.

claims that "a properly biblical understanding of the Kingdom of God is possible only if the church is understood – predominantly, if not exclusively – as a charismatic community and God's pilgrim people, his kingdom of priests ... the messianic community, the community of the King."[17]

As we shall see, it is the model of "the community of God" that best describes the church and fits the biblical data.[18]

The Church as the Community of God

The idea of the church as a community resonates very well with Africans. Although we are all born as individuals, we grow up and live within communities. None live entirely by themselves. For Africans, one could even say that existence is meaningless without the concept of community, as is highlighted by the common sayings "I am because we are, and since we are, therefore I am"[19] and "I am because we are related".

> The community is where you get your values and beliefs and your early training in life. It is the community where you establish the deepest and most enduring relationships of life. It is the group of people from which you derive your name and your identity as a person. It is the community in which you find a sense of purpose in life because you help to make it what it is. Likewise, the church is the community where you are to get your values and beliefs and your early training in the Christian life. It is the community where you will establish the deepest and most enduring relationships in life. It is the group

---

[17] Snyder, *The Community of the King*, 40.

[18] See also Samuel Waje Kunhiyop, "Towards a Christian Communal Ethics: The African Contribution", *Cultural Encounters*, 6:2 (2010). This article was first presented at the Evangelical Theological Society, New Orleans, November 2009. It is notable that many books on the theology of the church (ecclesiology) now use the term "community" to describe the church. These books include Mark Husbands and Daniel J. Treier, eds., *The Community of the Word: Toward an Evangelical Ecclesiology* (Downers Grove: InterVarsity Press, 2005); Howard A. Snyder, *The Community of the King* (Downers Grove: InterVarsity Press, 1977). Stanley J. Grenz's monumental treatise on theology is appropriately titled *Theology for the Community of God* (Nashville: Broadman & Holman, 1994).

[19] John Mbiti, *African Religions and Philosophy* (2nd ed.; Oxford: Heinemann, 1990), 113.

of people from which you derive your name as a Christian and your identity as a child of God.[20]

The concept of the church as a community also resonates with Africans because of the scope of this community. It includes all believers worldwide and each local community (church) and is also connected to the past (believers who have died) and to the future (those who have yet to be born spiritually). This way of seeing the church acknowledges the role of our spiritual ancestors. These ancestors are the believing dead (Hebrew and Christian) who are interested in our lives and exert influence over them, serving as examples and encouragements for us. Hebrews 12:1 talks of them when it speaks of the "witnesses that surround us", referring to the heroes of the faith whose names are listed in Hebrews 11).

Our ancestors include not only the heroes of the faith such as Abraham, Isaac, Jacob, David, Jeremiah and the Apostle Paul, but also local heroes of faith who have exemplified Christian character and virtues. African Christians can look to African Christian heroes. We can remember their names and achievements by talking, singing and writing about them, or as part of the rich African tradition of funeral rites, naming ceremonies and annual festivals. The conversions of individuals or communities, baptisms and the celebration of the Lord's Supper can also be used as occasions to tell of our heroes in song and dance.

How does one join this community? One does it in the same way as a child joins a community, that is, by being born into it. That is why every person must be born again to become part of this redeemed community (John 3:3, 5; Titus 3:5). Although believers receive spiritual birth individually, they grow and live within a community of God's people: "The individual act of faith by which we are born anew takes place in the context of the church, which proclaims the gospel, nurtures the converts, and shares the eternal blessings for which it was chosen by God."[21]

---

[20] Wilbur O'Donovan, *Biblical Christianity in African Perspective* (Carlisle: Paternoster, 2000), 155–156.

[21] Stephen Charles Mott, *Biblical Ethics and Social Change* (New York: Oxford University Press, 1982), 129. He goes on to observe, "Since the Bible shows our basic need for and dependence on community, it is not surprising that God's salvation calls us into a community."

Personal conversion, ethical responsibility and accountability are vital, but they cannot be lived out in isolation from the rest of God's people. This truth is evident in both the Old and New Testaments.

The community of God in the Old Testament

Community is not a human invention. It finds its true and original meaning in God, who is one but exists in plurality as the Father, Son and Holy Spirit. This means that there is relationship (a community) within the Godhead. Thus it is logical to conclude that when God said, "Let us make mankind in our image, in our likeness" (Gen 1:26), part of what was meant was that men and women are also relational and exist in community. This God-given need for relationships is also manifest in the creation of Eve from Adam (Gen 2:18–24).

In the Old Testament, the nation of Israel was the community of God's people. The faith of Abraham, so great that God "credited it to him as righteousness" (Gen 15:6), can only be fully appreciated in the context of what God did through that faith – bringing into existence the nation of Israel (Gen 12:3). A great community came out of this one man.

While it is true that certain individuals such as Jacob, Deborah, David, Elijah, Ezekiel, Jeremiah and Daniel stand out because of their great personal faith and relationship with God, they all operated within the community that belonged to God and which he had founded. This was the community to which God said, "I will ... be your God, and you will be my people" (Exod 6:7; 19:5; Lev 26:12; Jer 30:22; Ezek 36:28; Hos 2:23). That is why the community is called the community *of God*. God called the nation of Israel his own people, his anointed people, his possession, "the apple of his eye" (Deut 32:10).

Because the Israelites were the people of God, God's word was the community's ultimate source of guidance in matters of life and faith. Obedience to God's law (the Torah) was an essential aspect of belonging to the community. All the Israelites, including their leaders, were to read and obey the teachings of the law of God, and their kings were to rule in accordance with it (Josh 1:6–8). God also provided officers such as the priests and Levites to guide the community in their understanding of the law and in their worship, which was to be carried out according to his word, particularly as set out in the books of Leviticus and Deuteronomy (see Neh 8).

This Old Testament community of God foreshadowed the new community that God was going to create for himself in the New Testament (Jer 33). Paul explicitly teaches that the New Testament community, the church, is in some sense the new Israel (Rom 9–11; Gal 6:16). While there is a basic distinction between the church and Israel, the general features of God's dealings with his people as a community in the Old Testament offer parallels for our study of the community of God in the New Testament.[22]

The community of God in the New Testament

The concept of the church pervades the New Testament. Rudolf Schnackenburg observes, "The church is everywhere present in the New Testament even where it is not manifest in concepts and imagery. ... Not a single New Testament author wrote as a mere private individual, but all took up their pens only as members and for the benefit of the society to which they professedly belonged and impelled by motives which concern all who believe in Christ."[23]

The New Testament basically continues the Old Testament concept of community, adding its own distinctive elements. Thus, like the Old Testament community, the New Testament community was bought and redeemed by God. So Paul echoes Psalm 74:2 ("Remember the nation you purchased long ago, the people of your inheritance, whom you redeemed") when he says that Jesus Christ "gave himself for us [the church] to redeem [purchase] us from all wickedness and to purify for himself a people that are his very own" (Titus 2:14). The whole purpose of Christ's mission as Messiah was to save his people from their sins (Matt 1:21). He is the founder and keeper of his church. He gave it life,

---

[22] Note that dispensational approaches often stress the distinction between the church and Israel, whereas non-dispensational systems ignore this distinction and emphasize the general features of God's dealings with his people throughout history. Charlies Ryrie, who is considered an authority on dispensationalism, defines it as follows: "Dispensationalism views the world as a household run by God. In His household-world God is dispensing or administering its affairs according to His own will and in various stages of revelation in the passage of time. These various stages mark off the distinguishably different economies in the outworking of His total purpose, and these different economies constitute the dispensations." *Dispensationalism Today* (Chicago: Moody, 1965), 29.

[23] Rudolf Schnackenburg, *The Church in the New Testament* (New York: Herder & Herder, 1965), 9.

and as the "the pioneer and perfecter of faith", he continues to maintain it (Heb 12:2).

However, unlike the Old Testament community, which was predominantly Jewish, the New Testament community includes people from all the nations of the earth (Matt 28:19–20). Jesus started by calling together a group of twelve disciples who formed his initial core group (Matt 16:18). This group then expanded dramatically at Pentecost, and continued to expand as Gentiles joined the church (Acts 2:44–47; 4:32–35; 5:12–16; 6:1–7; 11:26; 13:1; 14:23; 15:14).

Jesus explicitly stated that he would "build my church" (Matt 16:18). The Greek word translated "church" is *ekklesia*, a word that can refer to a spiritual or a non-spiritual gathering (local or universal), and can even signify a mob (Acts 19:32, 39, 41). It is the Greek equivalent of the Old Testament Hebrew word *qahal*, which is translated as "assembly" in Deuteronomy 9:10 (see also Deut 10:4; 18:16; Lev 10:17; Num 1:16; Judg 20:2; 1 Kgs 8:14) and as "congregation" in Psalm 22:22, 25. Both words mean "called out" and carry the idea of community. Stephen used the word *ekklesia* when he said that Moses "was in the *assembly* in the wilderness, with the angel who spoke to him on Mount Sinai, and with our ancestors; and he received living words to pass on to us" (Acts 7:38). In the biblical sense, God's community is not "called out" for its own sake but on God's initiative and for his purposes. As William Barclay states,

> The church ... is a body of people, not so much assembling because they have chosen to come together, but assembling because God has called them to himself; not so much assembling to share their own thoughts and opinions, but assembling to listen to the voice of God.[24]

In Acts and in Paul's writings, the word *ekklesia* is used to refer to local congregations of believers in specific geographic locations. Thus we read of the churches in Jerusalem, Thessalonica, Corinth, Colossae, Ephesus and Cenchreae (Acts 8:1; 11:22; 20:17; Rom 16:1; 1 Cor 1:2; 2 Cor 1:1; Col 1:2). But the word is also used in a wider sense to signify the universal congregation of the community of God's people

---

[24] William Barclay, *New Testament Words* (London: SCM, 1964), 70. The idea of gathering to listen to the voice of the Lord is caught by the English word "church", which comes from the Greek *kuriokos*, meaning "of the Lord".

in Christ (Matt 16:18; 1 Cor 10:32; 12:28; 15:9; Eph 5:25–30; Phil 3:6; Col 1:24). "In the universal sense the church consists of all those who, in this age, have been born of the Spirit of God and have by that same Spirit been baptized into the body of Christ (1 Cor 12:13; 1 Pet 1:3, 22–25)."[25] In both local and universal senses, the word refers to a single entity in which the emphasis is on community rather than on the individuality of each member.

When the church is thought of in the universal sense, a distinction is often drawn between the *church militant* and the *church triumphant*. The church militant are the believers who are still alive in the world, while the church triumphant are those who have died and now live in glory with Christ.

Biblical metaphors for the church

Earlier in this chapter, we looked at some models of the church. It is worth taking time to look at the many models (or metaphors) the New Testament uses when it speaks about the community of God:

> The Bible provides a rich kaleidoscope of imagery about the church composed of around one hundred metaphors and statements. The thread on which all other jewels are hung is the idea of the church as an *ekklesia* ("assembly", "gathering"). This word, taken from common usage where it applied to the "calling out" of citizens for a civic meeting or of soldiers for battle, is used exclusively throughout the Old and New Testaments to refer to the people of God.[26]

- *The people of God* (2 Cor 6:16; 1 Pet 2:9). This image emphasizes the people who make up the church. They are described as chosen, a royal priesthood, a holy nation, those who belong to God (1 Pet 2:9). Often in the church today, the emphasis falls on the organization, finances and structures, and the basic idea that the community is about people is missed.

---

[25] Henry C. Thiessen, *Lectures in Systematic Theology* (rev. Vernon D. Doerksen; Grand Rapids: Eerdmans, 1979), 311.

[26] P. S. Milner, "Church", in *Dictionary of Biblical Imagery* (eds. Leland Ryken, James C. Wilhoit and Tremper Longman III; Downers Grove: InterVarsity Press, 1998), 147.

- *The body of Christ* (1 Cor 12:27; Eph 1:22–23). The Swiss theologian Hans Küng connects the ideas of the church as the people of God and the body of Christ:

  It is fundamental from every point of view to see the Church as the people of God; this idea is found not only in Paul, but is the oldest term to describe the *ecclesia*, and it emphasizes the crucial continuity between the Church and Israel and the Old Testament. Only by seeing the Church as the people of God can we understand the idea of the Church as the body of Christ; then we shall see that the concept "body of Christ" describes very fittingly the new and unique nature of this new people of God. The Church is only the body of Christ insofar as it is the people of God; but by being the new people of God constituted by Christ it is truly the body of Christ. The two concepts of the Church are linked precisely through their Jewish roots.[27]

  The image of the church as the body of Christ emphasizes the church's place as "the focal point of Christ's activity now"[28] as well as the connectedness or community aspect of God's people (Gal 6:2; Eph 4:11–16). The image of Christ as the head of the body (Eph 1:10; Col 1:18, 16; 2:9–10) is similar to the image of Christ as the vine and believers as the branches (John 15:1). Both pictures demonstrate the intimate relationship between Christ and the church. As head of the body, Christ provides all the nourishment needed for growth and maturity (1 Cor 12:27; Eph 4:12).

- *The bride of Christ.* Just as Israel was called God's bride (Isa 54:5–8; 62:5; Jer 2:2), so also the community of Christ is called his bride (Eph 5:27; Rev 19:7; 21:2). This picture signifies beauty, grandeur and a committed and exclusive relationship. The unique, loving relationship between a bride and groom should not be abused or compromised.

- *The building or temple of God.* In 1 Peter we read that the church is "a spiritual house" made out of "living stones", with Christ as the cornerstone (2:4–6). This image emphasizes that the church is

---

[27] Hans Küng, *The Church* (Tunbridge Wells, Kent: Search Press, 1986), 225.
[28] Millard J. Erickson, *Introducing Christian Doctrine* (Grand Rapids: Baker, 1992), 342.

a living, dynamic and active institution, and that Christ is the one who holds it together and maintains it. The community aspect is highlighted by the way in which the individual stones are joined together to form one single building, which is sustained by God.

- *The household or family of God.* All those who are Christ's are said to be adopted children of God (Rom 8:14–17) and therefore members of his household (Eph 2:10; 1 Tim 3:15). In the ancient world – and in many parts of the world today, including Northern Nigeria – a household is an extended family, including brothers and nephews and their families, all living in close proximity under the leadership of the most senior father or uncle. Likewise, the household of God consists of the whole extended family of believers in Christ.

- *The flock of God.* Just as Israel was God's flock (Pss 80:1; 95:7; Ezek 34:15), so also is the church, with Christ, the Good Shepherd (John 10:1–10), as its chief shepherd (Heb 13:20; 1 Pet 2:25; 5:4). Those who look after his flock are called shepherds, or pastors (John 21:17; Acts 20:28; 1 Pet 5:1–3).

What do all these images add up to? They show that "the church is no mere collection of isolated individuals, but … has a corporate or communal nature which is absolutely essential to its true being".[29] God desires all human beings to live in communion with him and with others.

The Ordinances of the Community of God

An ordinance is "an outward rite instituted by Christ to be administered in the church as a visible sign of the saving truth of the Christian faith".[30] Some churches prefer the word "sacraments" to "ordinances", and some, like the Roman Catholic Church, regard penance, ordination, confirmation and extreme unction as sacraments. Here, however, we will only look at the two ordinances observed in most Protestant churches today, namely water baptism and holy communion.

---

[29] Snyder, *The Community of the King*, 58.
[30] Thiessen, *Lectures in Systematic Theology*, 323.

Water baptism

Water baptism played such a prominent role in the early church that it was unthinkable for a person to be a believer without being baptized. Acts 2:38 records that Peter required new converts to be baptized in order to be saved. True, there were exceptions, like the thief on the cross (Luke 24:43), but these were in exceptional circumstances. Other believers mentioned in the Gospels (like the penitent woman – Luke 7:35–50; the paralyzed man – Matt 9:2; and the tax collector – Luke 18:13–14) are not explicitly said to have been baptized. However, their conversions occurred before Christ's command to baptize (Matt 28:18) and the explicit cases in Acts after the establishment of the church. Moreover, the fact that there are no biblical records of these believers being baptized does not mean that they were not baptized. In general it is true to say that "the idea of an unbaptized Christian is simply not entertained in the NT".[31]

At baptism, the believer is united with Christ in his death and resurrection – this is the symbolic meaning of immersing somebody in water and bringing him or her out of the water (Rom 6:4–5). Though the physical act of being baptized is not what saves the sinner, it is a powerful symbol of the sinner's saving faith in Christ, which is confessed before baptism (Acts 8:37). Baptism also symbolizes the washing of rebirth (Titus 3:5), the forgiveness of sins (Acts 2:38), and initiation into Christ's body, the church (1 Cor 12:12–14).

Baptism is often mentioned in close association with the Holy Spirit (Acts 2:38; 1 Cor 12:12–13). On this F. F. Bruce comments.

> The baptism of the Spirit which it was our Lord's prerogative to bestow was, strictly speaking, something that took place once for all on the day of Pentecost when he poured out the promised gift on his disciples and thus constituted them the people of God in the new age; baptism in water continued to be the visible sign by which those who believed the gospel, repented of their sins and acknowledged Jesus as Lord were publicly incorporated into the Spirit-baptized fellowship of the new people of God.[32]

---

[31] F. F. Bruce, *Commentary on the Book of Acts* (London: Marshall, Morgan & Scott, 1956), 77; see also *New International Commentary on the New Testament* (Grand Rapids: Eerdmans, 1988), 70.
[32] Bruce, *Commentary on the Book of Acts*, 70.

As a rite, "Christian baptism is the first step of participation in the life, death and resurrection of Christ. In baptism Christians are given a new identity. They are defined as children and partners of the triune God, who from all eternity wills to live in solidarity with others."[33]

The question of who may be baptized is one on which Christians disagree. Stanley Grenz summarizes the situation in these words:

> Historically the most volatile aspect of the baptismal controversy focused on the question concerning the subjects of baptism: Who may we properly baptize? Most specifically, should we reserve baptism for those who can make a personal confession of faith through this act (believer's baptism)? Or is this rite also for infants who will only later be able to join the Christian community in its confession?[34]

Believer's baptism

In the New Testament it is those who professed faith in the Lord Jesus Christ who were baptized (Mark 16:16; Acts 2:38; 8:35–38; 16:31–33; Gal 3:26–29; 1 Pet 3:21). Faith and baptism were united, not separated. To quote Grenz again:

> The thrust of the New Testament clearly places a connection between baptism and faith. During the church age, faith expressed in baptism is so closely linked with the new birth that the two are virtually inseparable. ... The apostolic church never separated conversion from baptism, and the early believers always considered inward faith and baptism as its public confession in connection with each other. They saw faith and baptism as two sides of an undivided whole.[35]

Infant baptism (paedobaptism)

While not denying that in New Testament times those who confessed faith in Jesus Christ were the proper recipients of baptism, some theologians also argue in favour of infant baptism.

---

[33] Daniel L. Migliore, *Faith Seeking Understanding: An Introduction to Christian Theology* (Grand Rapids: Eerdmans, 1991), 223.

[34] Stanley Grenz, *Theology for the Community of God* (Grand Rapids: Eerdmans, 2000), 527.

[35] Ibid.

We know little about the early history of infant baptism:

> The point of origin for infant baptism is obscure. It is not in the
> New Testament; 1 Corinthians vii.14 even excludes it. Perhaps
> the growing influence of the heathen mysteries [that is, the
> Greek and Roman mystery religions] helped, since children
> were initiated there. Iraeneus (AD 180) knew of infant baptism.
> But Tertullian (200) was protesting against its adoption. "Why
> hurry the age of innocence to confession of sin?" Then it
> became popular, and its spread was rapid. A generation after it
> was the rule in Africa. Only in the third century, however, did
> it become quite universal, and especially as the church became
> identified with a nation or a whole people.[36]

Many churches practise both adult and infant baptism. They include
Reformed, Anglican, Roman Catholic, Methodist, Lutheran,
Episcopalian and Presbyterian churches. The Roman Catholic Church
teaches that baptism is actually necessary for salvation and brings about
regeneration (new birth). Baptism should therefore be administered to
infants, otherwise infants who die will not enter heaven but will instead
be "consigned to a place called *limbus infantum*. There they do not
suffer the pains and deprivation of hell, but neither do they enjoy the
benefits of the blessedness of heaven."[37] Timothy George has described
limbus infantum (limbo) as "an air-conditioned compartment of hell".[38]
In Roman Catholic dogma, "original sin is washed away at baptism,
although the inclination to sin remains. The baptized child is said to
receive infused faith and love, but such faith is distinguished from the
act of faith which comes later."[39]

Protestant churches that practise infant baptism assert that while in
Scripture "there is no direct command to baptize infants ... there is also
no prohibition".[40] They rely on "the presence of collective (the faith of

---

[36] P. T. Forsyth, *The Church and the Sacraments* (London: Independent Press, 1917), 211.

[37] Erickson, *Introducing Christian Doctrine*, 11.

[38] Timothy George, *Theology of the Reformers* (Nashville, Tenn.: Broadman, 1988), 138. He
continues, "In Zurich the custom had developed of burying unbaptized infants in a certain middle
part of the cemetery, halfway between the profane and the holy ground – a vivid representation of
limbo!" (138).

[39] Donald G. Bloesch, *The Reform of the Church* (Grand Rapids: Eerdmans, 1970), 36.

[40] G. W. Bromiley, "Infant Baptism", in *Evangelical Dictionary of Theology* (ed. Walter A. Elwell;
Grand Rapids: Baker, 1984), 116. He concludes that "once the gospel has gained an entry into a

the baptizing community) or even proxy faith (the faith of the parents or godparents) to legitimize infant baptism".[41] Some speak of "an implanted germ of the new life or an unconscious faith" in the child.[42]

The main argument for infant baptism is the assertion that the church and Israel are identical. Proponents claim that there is continuity between the Testaments and that the church continues as the covenant people of God. Charles Hodge says, "The Church under the new dispensation is identical with that under the old. It is not a new Church, but one and the same. It is the same olive tree (Rom 11:16–17). It is founded on the same covenant, the covenant made with Abraham. ... The conclusion is that God has ever had but one Church in the world."[43] J. Oliver Buswell uses the same logic:

> The God of the New Testament is the God of the Old Testament (cf. Rom 3:29). Moreover, we have one race of fallen sinners; we have one covenant of grace; and we have one relationship of parents and children within the covenant of grace. God, in the Old Testament, explicitly commanded that there should be initiatory rites performed upon the children of godly parents, including their membership in His covenant. ... It follows by inexorable amplification from the data of the Scripture that baptism is to be applied to those to whom the initiatory rites were applied in the Old Testament.[44]

The problem with the position is that the argument holds together only as long as one holds to a continuity of covenants between the

---

family or community, there is good scriptural and theological ground that infant baptism should be the normal practice" (117).

[41] Grenz, *Theology for the Community of God*, 529.

[42] Forsyth, *The Church and the Sacraments*, 213–214, 219. Forsyth explains that baptism "conveys to the child, in God's name, not only a claim but a reality, a membership in the Church; it conveys a right to all its blessings as the soul grows in power to receive them; and in end it imposes the duty to take up personal responsibility and confession. Baptized children are members *in petto*, in reserve. So the Baptism of the child is not its regeneration except in title, but it is a real act of the Church and of Christ in the Church. It is the Church's praise and promise round the child. The Church thanks God for its own regeneration and promises in respect of the child's. It is the objective, and practical, and promissory assurance of it, the committal of the child to it as his Christian destiny. It does not effect the regeneration but intends it" (219–20).

[43] Charles Hodge, *Systematic Theology* (1873; abridged; ed. Edward N. Gross; New Jersey: Presbyterian & Reformed, 1982), 485–487.

[44] J. Oliver Buswell, *Systematic Theology of the Christian Religion* (Grand Rapids: Zondervan, 1962), 262.

Testaments. If one believes that there is a discontinuity between the Testaments, and that the church is not identical with Israel, the whole justification for infant baptism collapses.

One of the most persuasive proponents of infant baptism is Louis Berkhof, a Reformed theologian. He admits that there is no explicit biblical teaching on this issue and believes that when adults are baptized, their baptism must be preceded by a profession of faith. But he also offers the following arguments in support of infant baptism:

1. "The covenant made with Abraham was primarily a spiritual covenant, though it also had a national aspect, and of this spiritual covenant circumcision was a sign and seal."[45] This view is supported by Scripture (Exod 2:24; Lev 26:42; Jer 4:4; 9:25–26; Acts 15:1; Rom 4:16–18; 2 Cor 6:16–18; Gal 3:8–9, 14, 16). The covenant with Abraham also included his children.

2. "This covenant is still in force and is essentially identical with the 'new covenant' of the present dispensation. The unity and continuity of the covenant in both dispensations follows from the fact that the mediator is the same (Acts 4:12; 10:43; 15:10–11; Gal 3:16)."[46] Erickson writes, "As circumcision was the sign of the covenant in the Old Testament, so is baptism in the New Testament. ... Baptism has been substituted for circumcision as the initiatory rite into the covenant."[47] The argument has validity whether or not one accepts Berkhof's view on the continuity of the covenants between the Testaments, an issue over which scholars are divided.[48]

3. "By the appointment of God infants shared in the benefits of the covenant, and therefore received circumcision as a sign and seal. According to the Bible the covenant is clearly an organic concept, and its realization moves along organic and historical lines."[49] This is the most powerful argument for infant baptism. Though, as we

---

[45] Louis Berkhof, *Systematic Theology* (Grand Rapids: Eerdmans, 1996), 632.

[46] Ibid., 633.

[47] Erickson, *Introducing Christian Doctrine*, 1103.

[48] For more on the debate over continuity and discontinuity, see Hans K. LaRondelle, *The Israel of God in Prophecy: Principles of Prophetic Interpretation* (Berrien Springs, Mich.: Andrews University Press, 1983). LaRondelle is a major supporter of continuity between the Testaments. See also John S. Feinberg, ed., *Continuity and Discontinuity: Perspectives on the Relationship Between the Old and New Testaments. Essays in Honor of S. Lewis Johnson, Jr.* (Westchester: Crossway, 1998), which contains serious scholarly discussion of the issue.

[49] Berkhof, *Systematic Theology*, 633.

have seen, the need for adult baptism to be preceded by profession of faith is clearly biblical, the idea of baptizing infants from a covenant perspective is persuasive. Some may see this baptism as equivalent to adult baptism; however, it is actually a powerful symbol of a covenant relationship with believing parents.

> The New Testament repeatedly speaks of the baptism of households, and gives no indication that is regarded as something out of the ordinary, but rather refers to it as a matter of course. [These households include that of Lydia (Acts 16:15), the Philippian jailer (Acts 16:33), Crispus and Gaius (Acts 18:8; 1 Cor 1:14) and Stephanus (1 Cor 1:16).] It is entirely possible, of course, but not very probable, that none of these households contained children. And if there were infants, it is morally certain they were baptized along with the parents.[50]

While this argument for infant baptism can appear reasonable, it is based on possibilities and probabilities, and hence is a theological inference from silence rather than being based on explicit biblical teaching.

To summarize what has been said on this topic: Adult baptism upon confession of faith is the New Testament norm. However, adults do not live their lives alone: they live in families with children who must be brought up in the fear of the Lord. In the Old Testament, all male children were circumcised as a physical sign that they, along with their parents, were contracted to, or covenanted with, God. Today, it is right that parents who come to faith and are baptized desire to bring their children into a relationship with God too. Many churches have a dedication ceremony in which the child is dedicated to God, and this is probably the preferred method of indicating the parents' desire. But churches that believe and practise infant baptism as a covenant bond between their children, themselves and God do not thereby negate the meaning of believer's baptism. These infants are baptized not upon their confession of faith but upon the commitment of their parents and churches to bring them up in the fear of the Lord, leading them towards a personal relationship with the Lord Jesus Christ.

---

[50] Ibid., 634.

What must be avoided is offering a guarantee of salvation without requiring any responsibility from those baptized. Donald Bloesch's warning is appropriate: "It cannot be doubted that baptism, like many other rites of the church, has become the occasion for cheap grace. It is a means by which grace is freely dispensed but without requiring anything in return. It should demand from the believer his very life, but instead it costs him nothing nor does it place any burden of responsibility upon the parents or godparents."[51]

Modes of baptism

Baptism may be carried out in several different ways. It may be done by *pouring*, when water is poured over the candidate's head and body, or by *immersion*, when the candidate is completely immersed in the water. This latter method is closely associated with the root meaning of the Greek word translated *baptism* and is supported by the following Scriptures: Matthew 3:6 – "Confessing their sins, they were baptized by him in the Jordan River"; John 3:23 – "Now John was also baptizing at Aenon near Salim, because there was plenty of water, and people were coming and being baptized"; Acts 8:38–39a – "Then both Philip and the eunuch went down into the water and Philip baptized him. When they came up out of the water ...". Roman Catholics, Methodists and Anglicans practise *sprinkling*, which is especially appropriate for infants and those who are afraid of complete immersion. Sprinkling may also be appropriate where water is in short supply.

The exact manner of baptism is not as important as the theological meaning behind the act. It is a public identification with the death and resurrection in newness of life of Jesus Christ that imposes serious obligations and responsibility on the one baptized.

Holy Communion (the Lord's Supper)

Holy Communion is a rite that dates back to the earliest days of the church. It speaks of our receiving the benefits of Christ's sacrifice (1 Cor 10:16), our spiritual participation in Christ's body (1 Cor 11:24–26) and our fellowship with the people of God (1 Cor 10:17). It is often celebrated with bread and wine, but other elements can be used, including local foods. The major theological question relating to this

---

[51] Bloesch, *The Reform of the Church*, 36.

rite is what exactly Jesus meant at the Last Supper when he "took bread, ... broke it and gave it to his disciples, saying, 'Take and eat; this is my body'" (Matt 26:26), and "This is my body given for you; do this in remembrance of me" (Luke 22:19). Four different answers are given to this question.

1. *Transubstantiation*. Roman Catholic doctrine holds that Christ's words are to be taken literally. The elements of bread and wine actually turn into the real body and blood of Jesus when the priest repeats Jesus' words. Non-Catholics reject this view on the basis that Christ could not have given his own blood and flesh to the first disciples when he was physically present with them. In addition, Jesus would not have encouraged something that was tantamount to cannibalism, a practice abhorred by the Jewish community.

2. *Consubstantiation*. Martin Luther (1483–1546) believed that because Christ is divine and thus omnipresent (present everywhere at the same time), he is present not only in heaven but also on earth, and so he can be "by", "with" and "under" the elements of bread and wine. His divine omnipresence also applies to his human nature, not just as an abstract idea but as a present reality, and thus it can be said that Christ is bodily present in the bread and wine of Communion. The problem with this view is that, although it supposedly rejects the Catholic's insistence on the literal transformation of the bread and wine into the flesh and blood of Jesus, it boils down to much the same thing theologically.

3. *A memorial*. According to the Swiss Reformer Huldrych Zwingli (1484–1531), the Lord's Supper is simply a commemoration of the sacrifice of Christ's body and blood. The elements of bread and wine remind believers of what Christ did for them. Though this view does justice to the second part of the Lord's words, "do this in remembrance of me", it fails to deal with the significance of "this is my body".

4. *Real presence*. Many Reformed theologians hold that, though the elements remain ordinary bread and wine, they nevertheless contain the spiritual presence of Christ.

The Zwinglian position allows for a natural understanding of the text, emphasizing the commemorative aspect without imposing a mystical element. However the Reformed perspective gives greater depth to this view. The Bible affirms that Christ is present everywhere, and the Lord's Supper is one occasion when his presence is commemorated. There seems to be something amiss if Christians believe that the Lord's Supper is merely a reminder of his death without believing, expecting or experiencing his presence within it. Christ's presence is real when he is celebrated. Thus the Lord's Supper is not simply a memorial of what Christ has done; it is indeed a real experience in which believers participate in the Lord's work on the cross.

The Marks of the Community of God

The Nicene Creed identifies four key features of the community of God when it says, "We believe in one, holy, catholic and apostolic church."

1. *One.* Our unity is based on the fact that God is one (Eph 4:1–6). Jesus prayed for the unity of the church (John 17:23), grounding this on the unity between himself and the Father. First Corinthians 12:12 states, "Just as the body is one and has many members, but all its parts form one body, so it is with Christ." Hans Küng explains, "The members of the community ought to be 'one body' ... because they already are 'one body' in Christ."[52]

   This unity does not, however, mean absolute conformity in all practices in all churches throughout the world. For example, there are differences in worship styles (see 1 Cor 14:26) and church government (e.g. presbyterian, episcopalian, and congregational systems; see below). There can even be differences among groups within a local church. For example, the church in Jerusalem included a Hebrew group and a Hellenistic (Greek) group (Acts 6:1–6; see also Gal 6:6–12).

2. *Holy.* Because the church is created by a holy God, holiness must characterize it. In other words, it must be separate from the world and set aside for God. Yes, the church is made up of sinners, but 1 Peter 2:9 states, "you are a chosen people, a royal priesthood, a holy nation, God's special possession". The prayer of Jesus in John 17 also stresses the importance of separation: "My prayer is not that you take them out of the world but that you protect them from the evil one.

---

[52] Küng, *The Church*, 229.

They are not of the world, even as I am not of it. Sanctify them by the truth; your word is truth" (John 17:15–17). Being holy includes behaving morally and ethically as God has commanded.

3. *Catholic.* When the church is described as "catholic", we are not referring to the Roman Catholic Church but to the fact that the church is universal and not merely local. True, churches like the church in Corinth are located in particular places, but each of them is also part of the universal church. "The catholicity of the Church, therefore, consists in a notion of entirety, based on identity and resulting in universality. From this it is clear that unity and catholicity go together; if the Church is one, it must be universal; if it is universal, it must be one. Unity and catholicity are two interwoven dimensions of one and the same Church."[53]

4. *Apostolic.* The church is apostolic because its faith and practice are based on the apostolic teaching of the word. The whole church is built on the foundation of the apostles (Eph 2:20; see also Matt 16:18; Rev 21:14) and must therefore conform to the faith which they entrusted to the saints (Jude 3; see also Acts 2:42).

The Functions of the Community of God

The community of God exists to glorify God by fulfilling all the functions it was made to accomplish, namely worship, evangelism, discipling and prayer. It is therefore of prime importance that we seek to understand these functions and have a clear grasp of what God wants of his church.

Worship

Worship is our private or corporate expression of our reverence for God. The Bible does not prescribe a particular style of Christian worship, but an examination of worship in the Bible reveals that the components of worship include prayers, songs/music, dance, reading and hearing the word of God, rituals, meditation and offerings.

The style in which different churches worship differs widely. Some use traditional songs and music; others mainly choruses. Some like Western musical instruments like organs and guitars; other use

---

[53] Ibid., 303.

indigenous instruments like marimbas, drums and gongs. Some pray formally; others pray informally as the Spirit leads. Some allow prophetic utterances; others discourage them. Some allow members to speak in tongues regularly; others forbid the practice altogether. But in the midst of all this divergence, there are certain biblical principles that govern worship:

1. *Worship is about God, not about us.* The goal of worship is for the worshipper to be moved to adore and magnify God.

2. *Worship should be centred on Jesus Christ.* He should be the centre of gravity in our worship (1 Cor 5:4).

3. *The Holy Spirit empowers Christians to worship God aright* (John 4:24; Phil 3:3). Without the Holy Spirit, worship becomes idolatry and selfishness. We focus more on our own experience than on the God we claim to be worshipping. But when we are in the Spirit, we are enabled to concentrate on spiritual things that honour God. When the Spirit empowers us, we respond by offering true worship directed to God in the name of Jesus Christ (Eph 5:18–20).

4. *The Scriptures should have a central role in worship.* Every aspect of worship should be scrutinized from a scriptural perspective for the Scriptures set the standards and guidelines for the life of the redeemed community. Scripture rather than tradition should be the final judge of what is appropriate. Many excesses would be avoided if the Scriptures were given their proper place. For example, an unbalanced emphasis on Spirit-led worship with total disregard for the word of God often leads to practices that are unbiblical. In New Testament times, new Christians learnt from the synagogues that the reading of the Law and its exposition were central in worship (Luke 4:16–27; Acts 13:14–15). The early church therefore practised public reading and exposition of the Scriptures (Acts 2:42–47; 6:2; Col 4:16; 1 Thess 5:27).

5. *Worship involves a variety of activities.* The Bible mentions a variety of worship activities including praise (Eph 5:18); offerings, baptism, sharing in the Lord's Supper, confession, fellowship (Acts 2:42–47; 4:32–35) and edification, or in other words, the building up and establishing of believers (Eph 4:12, 16). The gifts of the Holy Spirit have been given for this purpose (1 Cor 12–14).

6. *Giving is an essential part of worship.* From the Old Testament days of tithes and offerings on, believers are shown to give willingly and generously (Gen 14:20; Lev 27:30; 1 Chr 29:6; Ezra 1:6; Mal 3:3; 1 Cor 16:1–4; 2 Cor 8–9). However, it is important to note that the money collected was not used to enrich the priests or apostles. In 2 Corinthians 8–9, for example, it was used to help the poor.

In sum, we should not judge others simply because their style or form of worship is different from our own. A Western style of worship is not better or more scriptural than the worship styles of Africans or Asians – and vice versa. Differences in worship reflect the differences that exist within the worldwide community of God, and also indicate that no single Christian community has got everything right!

Evangelism

The church is commanded to reach out to win people to Christ. Jesus said,

> All authority in heaven and on earth has been given to me.
> Therefore go and make disciples of all nations, baptizing them
> in the name of the Father and of the Son and of the Holy Spirit,
> and teaching them to obey everything I have commanded you.
> And surely I am with you always, to the very end of the age.
> (Matt 28:18–20; see also Acts 1:8)

Jesus gave this command not only to pastors, missionaries and evangelists, but to all his disciples, who are all to be witnesses to Christ's offer of salvation to eternal life. The Lausanne Covenant of 1974 declared, "We affirm that Christ sends his redeemed people into the world as the Father sent him, and that this calls for a similar deep and costly penetration of the world. We need to break out of our ecclesiastical ghettos and permeate non-Christian society."[54] The Lausanne Manila Manifesto added, "Every Christian congregation is a local expression of the Body of Christ and has the same responsibilities. ... We believe that the local church bears a primary responsibility for the spread of the gospel."[55]

---

[54] Lausanne Covenant, article 6, "The Church and Evangelism". See www.lausanne.org/covenant.
[55] Manila Manifesto, Article 8, "The Local Church". See www.lausanne.org/all-documents/manila-manifesto.html.

Discipling

At times, we are guilty of carrying out only part of Jesus' Great Commission. We make and baptize converts, but then we neglect the words in Matthew 28:20 that speak of "teaching them to obey everything I have commanded you". This teaching will take place through the preaching and study of God's word, which is not just the task of the church elders or trained pastors but of all church members. Individually and as a community, we should read and seek to understand the word of God.

But reading and an intellectual understanding of the word are not enough. We must also apply it to our own lives, so that others learn what it means to follow Christ by watching how we live. The saying that "more is caught than taught" reflects the importance of modelling in discipleship. The Apostle Paul could point to his own example when appealing to believers, saying "Follow my example, as I follow the example of Christ" (1 Cor 11:1; see also 1 Cor 4:16–17). He also pointed to the lives of ordinary believers and encouraged others to imitate them: "You became imitators of us and of the Lord, for you welcomed the message in the midst of severe suffering with the joy given by the Holy Spirit. And so you became a model to all the believers in Macedonia and Achaia" (1 Thess 1:6–7). He also points to the results of imitating such examples: "For you, brothers and sisters, became imitators of God's churches in Judea, which are in Christ Jesus: You suffered from your own people the same things those churches suffered from the Jews" (1 Thess 2:14; see also Phil 3:17). It is clear from these passages that elders should demonstrate to other believers the kind of lifestyle that is appropriate, and that it is easier to follow the examples of believers who have shared similar experiences.

As part of learning how to follow Christ, the redeemed community must discuss the issues affecting it. It should not be just the trained pastor who makes decisions on these issues. Experienced elders who follow Jesus should also be involved, and with the pastor they should encourage the entire community to participate. For example, the current AIDS epidemic needs to be discussed by each community openly and seriously. In all this, we must demonstrate how the Scriptures comprise "a reliable guide in matters of faith and life".[56] Christian communities must therefore take them seriously.

Prayer

Prayer is an important aspect of the work of the community of God. It includes confession of sins (Ps 32:5; Ezra 10:1; 1 John 1:9), supplication (Ps 30:8; Eph 6:18; Phil 4:6), adoration and thanksgiving (Eph 5:19–20) and intercession (Jas 5:16). Intercession is prayer offered by a believer on behalf of someone else. We can pray effectively for others because the church is a priesthood of believers (Rev 5:10). The New Testament contains many examples of intercessory prayers (Rom 15:5–6; 13; 2 Cor 13:7; Eph 3:16–19; 6:18; 1 Thess 3:10–13; 5:23; 2 Thess 2:17; 3:5–6; Heb 13:21).

The Organization and Government of the Community of God

The New Testament does not prescribe a particular system of church government. It does offer some glimpses of basic forms of organization that were present in the early church, but there is nothing as refined and formalized as church government has become in the course of history.

Basic organization and church officers

The apostles held leadership roles in the early church. When a dispute arose over false teachings, the issue was settled by a meeting of the Jerusalem Council, presided over by the apostles and the elders of the church in Jerusalem (Acts 15). There were also other church officers such as elders (Acts 14:23), stewards (Acts 6:1–7), prophets and teachers (Acts 13:1) and overseers and deacons (1 Tim 3:1–8). The main responsibility of pastors, elders and overseers (or bishops) was the shepherding of the flock (church) of God (Acts 20:27, 38; 1 Pet 5:2–4). At that time, a bishop was simply an elder or pastor, with the same status as every other pastor. Deacons were primarily responsible for serving others (the word "deacon" comes from the Greek *diakonia*, which means "service"). They ministered to and

---

[56] Bruce C. Birch and Larry L. Rasmussen, *Bible Ethics in the Christian Life* (Minneapolis: Augsburg, 1988), 25.

served others (Mark 10:43; Phil 1:1; 1 Tim 3:8). The seven men who were chosen by the apostles to serve tables were called deacons (Acts 6:1–6). Deaconesses were women who served in the same way (Rom 16:1; 1 Tim 3:1–13).

We can also deduce that local churches met at certain times (John 20:19, 26; 1 Cor 16:2). Their meetings were orderly, and those who were not living godly lives were disciplined by the community (Matt 18:17; 1 Cor 5). Offerings were collected (Acts 24:17; 2 Cor 15:15–28). Letters commending believers to other churches were also exchanged (Acts 15:22–29; 18:24–28; 2 Cor 3:1).

All of this indicates that while there were few formal structures in the early church, it was not a disorganized free-for-all.

Forms of church government

Over the centuries, several systems of church government have emerged from the seeds laid down in the early church.

1. *Congregational.* In the congregational system, each local church is governed by its own members. This democratic style of government is favoured by Baptists and other independent churches. They argue that the early churches in Rome (Rom 1:7), Corinth (1 Cor 1:2), Ephesus (Acts 20:17), Colossae (Col 1:2) and Thessalonica (1 Thess 1:1) were all local assemblies with their own members, elders and pastors.

2. *Episcopalian.* In the episcopalian system, local churches are part of a hierarchical organization led by bishops who supervise priests (mainly local clergy), who in turn supervise deacons and deaconesses. This form of government is found in the Anglican, Lutheran and Methodist churches, with minor variations. The Catholic Church practises a special form of the episcopalian system with the pope as the head of the church (or "Christ's vicar on earth") residing in and ruling from Rome.

The main biblical evidence supporting the episcopalian system is the idea that James, the brother of Jesus, was considered the chief elder in the church in Jerusalem (Acts 12:17; 15:13; 21:18; Gal 1:19; 2:9, 12). Some church fathers even referred to him as "the bishop of Jerusalem".[57] However, while the office of bishop did exist in the New Testament church, there is no evidence that bishops had a higher status than other officers such as pastors and elders (Acts 20:17, 28; Phil 1:1; Titus 1:5, 7). Biblical support for this system is thus inferred rather than explicitly taught.

3. *Presbyterian.* The Greek word for "elder" is *presbuteros*, and thus the presbyterian system of church government involves government by elders. It is rooted in the New Testament references to elders being appointed in each local congregation (e.g. 1 Tim 5:17). It appears that a plurality of elders, rather than one single ruling elder, was the norm (Acts 11:30; 14:23; 20:17; Phil 1:1; Jas 5:14). The elders within the presbyterian system are all equal, unlike those in the episcopalian system, which has a hierarchy of leadership.

4. *Independent.* Most independent church movements in Africa have adopted an episcopalian system of government. However, whereas older episcopalian churches have councils or synods and formal structures in place to guide in matters of doctrine, liturgy and administration, in independent churches power usually resides in the founder. This founder is referred to as the general overseer, superintendent or bishop and tends to retain power until he or she dies. Most independent churches claim that the Spirit guides the founder, particularly in regard to the liturgy and preaching, and so they rely solely on the founder in matters of faith, doctrine and sometimes even administration. The founder directs the church according to how he or she feels led, often in a dictatorial fashion.

5. *No government.* Groups such as Quakers (Friends) and Plymouth Brethren refuse to adopt any system of church government on the grounds that no such system is prescribed in the New Testament. Instead, they rely on the inner working of the Holy Spirit to guide them. However, just because a church does not adopt a particular form of government does not mean that it is not organized.

---

[57] John Peter Lange, *Galatians* (vol. 31 of *Commentary on the Holy Scriptures*, trans. Philip Schaff; Grand Rapids: Zondervan, 1957), 91.

The Relationship of the Church to Society

How should the church relate to the world? Should the church participate in the world's affairs, such as politics and economics, or should it concern itself only with matters that are "spiritual"?

As discussed above, one of the key features of the community of God is that it is the *ekklesia*, the people who have been "called out" of the world by God. In this sense the church is separate from the world, and should remain so. However, we are also still living in the world as followers of God (John 17:18–19). As such we are commanded to be "salt and light" in the world (Matt 5:13–14). Even though we are citizens of heaven (Phil 2:21), we are also real citizens of our nations, holders of national passports who enjoy all the rights and privileges of our nations.

The call to be "salt and light" indicates that God sees the world as rotten, corrupt and dark. The task of the community of God is thus to bring light where there is great darkness. In reaching out to the world, the church must be prophetic, speaking out against evil structures, living exemplary lives, and getting involved in both human and social development.[58]

The redeemed community has a public witness to an unbelieving world. Mott believes that the "social order is unredeemed and basically hostile to God and God's standards",[59] but in the midst of this, "the presence of the church as a visible sign of the reign of God produces social change in the surrounding society". We are to be the "light of the world", a town built on a hill that cannot be hidden (Matt 5:14). This image of "a Christian community as a city shedding light in the world seems a fitting picture of the social impact of the church as an alternative social reality".[60]

---

[58] For further discussion of the relationship between church and state, please refer to my book *African Christian Ethics* (Jos, Nairobi and Accra: HippoBooks / Grand Rapids: Zondervan, 2008), 83–106.

[59] Mott, *Biblical Ethics and Social Change*, 116–117.

[60] Ibid., 137.

Questions

1. Describe the various models of the church. Which one(s) best fits the biblical concept of the church? What model does your church follow?
2. Does your church practise adult or infant baptism? Why? What are the theological reasons for choosing one form rather than the other, or for practising both?
3. What are the four marks of the church? If the church is to be holy, how should we deal with sin within the church? How should we handle divisions and splits in the church? Are there ever justifiable reasons for such divisions?
4. What is the difference between Spirit baptism and water baptism? What is the connection between the two?
5. How many ordinances are practised in your church? How does your church practise Holy Communion? What does Holy Communion mean to you?

Further Reading

Avery Dulles. *Models of the Church*. New York: Doubleday, 1978.

Stanley J. Grenz. *Theology for the Community of God*. Grand Rapids: Eerdmans, 1994.

Mark Husbands and Daniel J. Treier, eds. *The Community of the Word: Toward an Evangelical Ecclesiology*. Downers Grove: InterVarsity Press, 2005.

Hans Küng. *The Church*. Tunbridge Wells, Kent: Search Press, 1986.

Samuel Waje Kunhiyop. *African Christian Ethics*. Jos, Nairobi, Accra: HippoBooks / Grand Rapids: Zondervan, 2008.

Robert L. Saucy. *The Church in God's Program*. Chicago: Moody Bible Institute of Chicago, 1972.

Peter Savage. "The Church and Evangelism". In *New Faces of Evangelism: An International Symposium on the Lausanne Covenant*. Edited by C. Rene Padilla. Downers Grove: InterVarsity Press, 1976.

9

BELIEFS AND PRACTICES IN THE COMMUNITY OF GOD

While the Bible is the church's main source for doctrine and practice, churches hold different interpretations of its teaching on particular subjects according to their history and traditions. The following practical issues over which Christians differ are pertinent to African Christianity: spiritual gifts, church discipline, pastoral ordination, the role of women in ministry and the remuneration of church workers.

Spiritual Gifts

Pentecostalism has made a great contribution to the church's increased awareness of the gifts of the Holy Spirit and to the reality of the Spirit's continuing role in the Christian life. It has taught and practised a dynamic Christianity that contrasts with dead orthodoxy. However, it has also provoked controversy around the issue of spiritual gifts. This is nothing new. The gifts of the Spirit – particularly the spectacular gifts such as speaking in tongues – have provoked controversy within the church since New Testament times (see 1 Cor 12–14). So it is important to introduce the topic by pointing out that every believer is "in one sense a charismatic personality, since those who truly believe are indwelt by the Holy Spirit. Every believer should radiate the power of the Spirit and manifest the fruits of the Spirit. Every believer of the body of Christ is a beneficiary of at least some charisma or grace that equips him for kingdom service."[1] In fact one of the key features of the community of God is the presence of spiritual gifts, which are special abilities given by God to members of the body of Christ.

---

[1] Donald G. Bloesch, *The Reform of the Church* (Grand Rapids: Eerdmans, 1970), 120.

The term *spiritual gifts* is a translation of the Greek word *charismata*, which means graces, emphasizing that these gifts are given by the grace of God and are to be used for his own purposes and glory. They are given by the Spirit (hence *spiritual*) as God wills. They are distinct from natural gifts, even though there is sometimes an overlap between the two, and all gifts are given by God. For example, someone may have a natural gift of singing without it necessarily being a spiritual gift. Those who have such natural gifts should use them to serve the church. But sometimes a natural gift is supplemented by God, and then it becomes a spiritual gift. A good example from the Old Testament is Bezalel, who worked on the tabernacle. Exodus 31:3–5 states, "I have filled him [Bezalel] with the Spirit of God, with wisdom, with understanding, with knowledge and with all kinds of skills to make artistic designs for work in gold, silver and bronze, to cut and set stones, to work in wood, and to engage in all kinds of crafts." Bezalel not only had the natural gift of crafting, but he was given the additional gift of knowledge or intelligence, which enhanced his natural gift.

Before looking at individual spiritual gifts, it may be a good idea to look at some general principles regarding why such gifts are given.

The nature and purpose of spiritual gifts

The following five characteristics of spiritual gifts are described in Scripture.[2]

1. *Gifts are given by the Holy Spirit* (1 Cor 12:11). Spiritual gifts are given by the Holy Spirit, not by anointed men or women of God, as is sometimes claimed in some circles. Romans 1:11, 1 Timothy 4:14 and 2 Timothy 1:6 are often quoted as supporting the giving of supernatural gifts by the laying on of hands, but these passages do not explicitly teach this. They more likely refer to the church's recognition of spiritual gifts that had already been given by God.

2. *Gifts are given for the benefit of the body.* Gifts are not intended solely to bless the individual to whom they are given; they are to be used to glorify God and edify the whole church. That is why Paul tells the Corinthian believers, "Now to each one the manifestation of the Spirit is given for the common good (1 Cor 12:7). Peter emphasizes

---

[2] Mal Couch, *A Biblical Theology of the Church* (Grand Rapids: Kregel, 1999).

the same point: "Each of you should use whatever gift you have received to serve others, as faithful stewards of God's grace in its various forms" (1 Pet 4:10).

3. *Gifts are given to every believer.* The Scriptures teach that every believer receives at least one gift for the benefit of the body (1 Cor 12:11; Eph 4:1; 1 Pet 4:10;). Nobody, however, has all the spiritual gifts. It is important that all believers find their gifts and use them, for on the day of judgement we will have to give an account of our stewardship of God's gifts.

4. *Gifts are given at the time of conversion* (Rom 5:5; 8:9; 1 Cor 6:19–20; 12:13). There are some groups that emphasize the bestowal of spiritual gifts by the laying on of hands after conversion (see point 1 above), but it appears that the norm in Scripture is that believers receive their spiritual gifts at the point of conversion rather than later. However, the Holy Spirit may choose to give a spiritual gift at any time when it is needed, possibly even years after conversion.

5. *Gifts are not an indication of holiness or spiritual maturity.* One need only read Paul's letter to the Corinthian church to realize that even a church full of spiritually gifted individuals can still experience abuse, immaturity, pride and boastfulness. We see a similar paradox in Samson in the Old Testament. He was spiritually gifted with supernatural strength, but was evidently an immoral man.

> [Gifts] must not be regarded as evidence of holiness or sanctity, nor should they be viewed as signs or proofs of the indwelling of the Spirit. We are well aware of the fact that many persons who have been both immoral and flagrantly heretical have nevertheless been endowed with special gifts that can be regarded as preternatural. Yet when these gifts are in the hands of those who stand solidly on the scriptural revelation and who seek to use them in the service of Christ, they can be of immense aid to the church in its ministry of reconciliation and redemption.[3]

Clearly, "someone can be spiritually gifted without being spiritual and producing the fruit of the Spirit."[4] Yet spiritual fruit is required of all

---

[3] Bloesch, *The Reform of the Church*, 114.
[4] Ibid., 81.

Christians (1 Cor 12–14; Gal 5:16, 18). Churches and believers who are full of the fruit of the Spirit will demonstrate unity and great spiritual maturity (Gal 5:24).

Specific spiritual gifts

There are five main scriptural passages that mention spiritual gifts:

- *Romans 12:6–8*: prophecy, service, teaching, exhortation, contributing, giving aid, and mercy
- *1 Corinthians 12:8–10*: wisdom, knowledge, faith, healing, working miracles, discernment of spirits, tongues and interpretation of tongues
- *1 Corinthians 12:28–30*: apostles, prophets, teachers, healing, working miracles, helpers, administrators, tongues and interpretation of tongues
- *Ephesians 4:11*: apostles, prophets, evangelists, pastors and teachers
- *1 Peter 4:11*: service and speaking

We can now look at these gifts in slightly more detail.

1. *Apostles, prophets and evangelists.* Apostles were commissioned by Christ and included the twelve disciples and Paul. They were the custodians and writers of the inspired Scriptures. In fact, one of the criteria for determining whether a book could be admitted to the canon of the New Testament was whether or not the book was endorsed by one of the apostles (see chapter 2). Prophets were also part of the early church; their role was to foretell and forth tell, predicting the future and declaring the word of God. Evangelists are preachers of the gospel.

2. *Pastors and teachers.* While a pastor shepherds the flock of God (the church), a teacher primarily teaches the word of God. These gifts may be united in the same person.

3. *Faith.* The word "faith" is used in various ways in the Bible. It may refer to saving faith (Eph 2:8), to the gospel itself ("the faith" – Rom 10:8; see also Acts 6:7; 13:8; 14:22), to faithfulness (Gal 5:22), to trust in God in adversity (Eph 6:16), or to the ability to see the future and trust God to bring it to pass. Most of the heroes of faith fall into this last category: "Now faith is confidence in what we hope for and assurance about what we do not see" (Heb 11:1).

4. *Healings and miracles*. These gifts occupy a prominent place in the church. The early church saw many of the apostles performing miracles, and there is evidence that these gifts have continued in the church since then. Every Christian believes that God can heal and perform miracles through his own people, but some people are specially gifted in this area. The empowering of some by demonic agents to perform fake healings does not negate the fact that certain Christians are empowered by God to perform miracles as a spiritual gift.

5. *Discerning spirits*. Though the gift of discernment is mentioned only in 1 Corinthians 12:10, it is vitally important in contexts like that in Corinth, where there are problems, divisions and heretical teaching. The church is in dire need of those who have the gift of discernment as it faces many complex issues.

6. *Helpers*. Some Christians have the gift of helping or giving. We see this in the church today when such people make financial contributions, provide food to those who need it, help to clean the church, and assist others who require practical assistance.

7. *Leadership*. There is clearly a need for leadership and administration within a local church. Without a Peter, James, Barnabas and Paul, the early church would have struggled. There is great and urgent need for administrators to properly manage both the human and material resources in our churches.

8. *Tongues and interpretation of tongues*. H. Wayne House notes

> Of all the controversial subjects discussed in Christian circles, probably few have received more attention than the subject of glossolalia [speaking in tongues]. Though the material written on the subject is enormous, much confusion still pervades the issue.[5]

Acts 2:1–11 and 1 Corinthians 12–14 both mention speaking in tongues, but they seem to involve different kinds of tongues. In Acts 2 the tongues were intelligible human languages: "When they heard this sound, a crowd came together in bewilderment, because each one heard

---

[5] H. Wayne House, "Tongues and the Mystery Religions of Corinth", in *Vital New Testament Issues: Examining New Testament Passages and Problems* (ed. Roy B. Zuck; Grand Rapids: Kregel, 1996), 132.

their own language being spoken" (2:6). Though some have suggested
that these tongues were interpreted to enable the people present to hear
in their own languages, this is not the plain reading of the text in its
immediate context; rather, these tongues were "indigenous languages
and dialects of their native lands".[6] In 1 Corinthians 14, however, Paul
deals with what seems to be an unknown or heavenly tongue spoken to
God (14:2). The interpretation of such tongues (14:13) is an important
gift that can be used to provide guidance, encouragement and edification.

It is worth noting that Paul writes that tongues are not given to all and
does not list them as among the greatest of spiritual gifts (1 Cor 12:11,
29–30). He even implies that there is limited positive value to speaking
in tongues, particularly if they are not interpreted (1 Cor 14:13). So it
is wrong to insist that every believer should speak in tongues. In fact
believers should be cautious of emphasizing any spiritual gifts more than
others. This leads only to imitation, whereas over the centuries the great
men and women of faith were recognized for their distinctive individual
contributions. Nor should we honour those who have the more
spectacular gifts above those who have more mundane gifts. The one
who has the gift of service is no less spiritually gifted than the one who
has the gift of speaking in tongues. The one who has the gift of healing is
no more a spiritual hero than the one who has the gift of teaching.

Spiritual gifts today

There are some who argue that not all spiritual gifts are still being
given. In particular, they would argue that gifts such as apostleship,
prophecy and speaking in tongues ceased with the apostolic age and are
no longer given to the church. The completion of the New Testament
is understood to have ended the need for such gifts. Those who take
this position argue that the book of Acts is to be interpreted as a purely
historical record and not as a model for the church today. They say
that the spectacular events that happened in the early church were
intended to give credence to the spokesman and the new message being
proclaimed (see Acts 10:24–48; 11:15). They should not be expected to
take place in the church today.

When it comes to the gift of tongues, they would argue that 1
Corinthians 13:8 says, "as for tongues, they will be stilled", which

---

[6] F. F. Bruce, *The Book of the Acts* (rev.; NICNT; Grand Rapids: Eerdmans, 1988), 54.

suggests that this is a transitional gift, given only as the new era of the church began.

Against this position, others argue that God has not changed since New Testament days, and he can and often does still use all the spiritual gifts in the church. He did not cease to work when the apostolic age ended.

The strongest argument against the cessationist position is that the Scriptures contain no explicit statement that spiritual gifts have ceased. Indeed, if one accepts the longer ending to the Gospel of Mark, there is strong biblical evidence that all spiritual gifts should be expected today (Mark 16:9–20). The many records of miracles being performed in both the New Testament (Acts 28:3–6) and in the history of the church provide overwhelming evidence that miraculous gifts are still given today. To say otherwise is to deny reality.

However, acknowledging that the gifts of the Spirit continue is not the same as saying that every believer must have a powerful experience of a miraculous gift of the Holy Spirit subsequent to conversion (see the comments on the baptism of the Spirit in chapter 6). Gordon Fee puts it this way:

> The typical evangelical or reformed exegete who disallows a separate and subsequent experience simply must hide his or her head in the sand, ostrichlike, to deny the reality – the biblical reality – of what has happened to so many Christians. On the other hand, the Pentecostal must be wary of reforming the biblical data to fit his or her own experience.[7]

There are two errors into which Christians can easily fall:

1. *Assuming that the normal experience of the early Christians is still normal today.* It is indisputable that many early converts to Christianity experienced powerful demonstrations of the Holy Spirit at conversion. However, as history progressed, there does seem to have been a lessening of this immediate, powerful experience upon conversion. This may in part be related to the background of those coming to conversion. The early believers had never known Christianity before. In that sense, they were like the first converts

---

[7] Gordon D. Fee, *Gospel and Spirit: Issues in New Testament Hermeneutics* (Peabody: Hendrickson, 1991), 117.

to Christianity in Africa. Their new faith turned their world upside down. However, today there are many second-, third- and fourth-generation Christians who have been baptized as infants and raised with a strong Christian heritage. It is not surprising that their experience of coming to faith is less dramatic. However, this is not to deny that there are many nominal Christians who need to know that conversion should be life-changing. There should not be Christians who know "conversion without empowering, baptism without obedience, grace without love.... That such so-called Christian life exists not only cannot be denied, but one may ruefully admit that it represents the vast majority of believers in the history of the church."[8]

2. *Assuming that everyone else will experience the Spirit in the same way as we do.* Believers tend to interpret their own experiences as normative for all. For example, I know of some young people who went to a youth camp and heard the gospel. They were convicted and wept and prayed as they received Jesus Christ as their Lord and Saviour. On their return home, they set out to preach the gospel to others and demanded that all their converts must also weep and pray as they had done. The problem was that, while their experience was genuine, it was wrong for them to see this as the standard by which they could judge the genuineness of someone's conversion.

What should be emphasized is that, according to the Scriptures, the Holy Spirit empowers all believers for life and evangelism. While there can be no denying that obedience to the word of God and submission to the Holy Spirit will result in radical changes and experiences, we should not expect everyone to have exactly the same experience. Grenz notes,

> This ongoing experience of yielding to the Spirit's control is the key to power for witness and service, and for victorious, godly living (Acts 4:31; Eph 5:19–21). Although we can celebrate with those in whose lives God has chosen to work in such a manner, we dare neither to universalize nor elevate their experience of a supposedly post-conversion encounter with the Spirit into the norm. Rather than seeking a second blessing – a life-changing endowment of the fullness of the divine power –

---

[8] Ibid., 118.

we ought to concentrate our attention on the constant filling of the Spirit.[9]

Fake gifts

Just because somebody is performing a supernatural act in the name of Christ does not automatically mean that they have a spiritual gift. It is not only Christians who can speak in tongues. For example, historians tell us that practitioners of the pagan mystery religions in Corinth were also known to "burst forth into mysterious ejaculations and rapt utterances of the kind described in the New Testament as *glossai lalein*".[10] Similarly in Africa, some are able to perform miracles and healings, having been empowered to do so by the devil. Christians can be drawn in by this and may resort to other ways of getting the power to perform miracles and other supernatural acts such as speaking in tongues and seeing visions. Believers should therefore exercise discernment about those who exercise spiritual gifts. As mentioned earlier, gifts are not a guarantee of spirituality and Christian maturity.

Spiritual gifts must always be used and interpreted in accordance with the word of God, in conjunction with which the Spirit always works. They are never meant to serve as substitutes for reading and understanding the word of God. On the contrary, when the Spirit is made to overshadow the word, it is an indication of an imbalance in understanding God's revelation.

Discipline in the Community of God

When I first went to the USA as a student in the mid-1980s, I was shocked to hear the story of Walter and Maria Nally, a couple who sued a church for a staggering $1 million, alleging malpractice, wrongful death and negligence because their son Kenneth had committed suicide despite receiving counselling from the church. In Nigeria, where I came from, no one would ever even have considered taking court action against the pastor and the church. However, such lawsuits have become increasingly common. Disciplined members may claim that their good

---

[9] Stanley Grenz, *Theology for the Community of God* (Grand Rapids: Eerdmans, 2000), 422.

[10] Martin P. Nilsson, cited in H. Wayne House, "Tongues and the Mystery Religions of Corinth", *Bibliotheca Sacra* 140:558 (Apr 1983).

name, reputation and credibility have been seriously damaged. Some have also sued for reimbursement of expenses incurred for counselling and prescription medication they needed as a result of their experiences with a church.

Such lawsuits are not restricted to the West. A few years ago, a pastor in South Africa was suspended when he admitted his homosexuality. He took the church to court for disciplining him for a lifestyle that was constitutionally legal in South Africa. He won the case, and the church was forced to pay him compensation for the salary he had lost due to his suspension. It is also becoming increasingly common to hear of church members in Africa who have been disciplined for some sin subjecting their pastors to emotional and physical abuse.

Other members who are disciplined simply leave their churches and found new ones. It is a historical fact that many churches in Africa were established not so much because of disagreement over core beliefs but because of disciplinary issues such as taking second wives and alcohol consumption.

The result has been that many Christians and churches are reluctant to apply discipline, or even discuss it. Yet is an indispensible part of the community of God, and without it the church will cease to be an effective source of salt and light in the community.

The decline in church discipline

A number of factors have contributed to the decline of the practice of church discipline in recent years. One major cause is the rise of assertive individualism. Within a community, discipline makes sense. It is impossible to run a household, family, society or military force without some form of discipline. Each member of such a unit has a sense of obligation towards the community, and understands that if these responsibilities are not met, he or she can expect certain sanctions.

In Westernized societies, however, individualism is very strong; people want to live as they please and resent any discipline being imposed on them. Because of the lack of a concept of community, individuals struggle with discipline, feeling emotionally and physically disgraced when it is implemented.

Unfortunately, discipline has also become associated with punishment, which distorts the true purpose of church discipline:

Ecclesiastical discipline is often associated with punishment – sometimes even to the extent of excommunication. However, to take this negative aspect as one's starting point would be incorrect, since discipline must be seen first of all in the framework of deep concern for the church, for preserving her along the way of life. That does not eliminate the aspect of punishment, but it does illuminate its significance.[11]

Some Christians are opposed to church discipline because it suggests that they are judging others. Matthew 7:1–2 is often quoted as a divine command never to do this: "Do not judge, or you too will be judged. For in the same way you judge others, you will be judged, and with the measure you use, it will be measured to you." They also quote Jesus' words to those who brought the woman caught in adultery to him: "Let any one of you who is without sin be the first to throw a stone at her" (John 8:7). Then he said to the woman, "neither do I condemn you. … Go now and leave your life of sin" (John 8:11).

There are four possible responses to this argument:

• The words cited were not uttered in the context of any discussion of church discipline. In Matthew, the focus is on the Pharisees, who were hypocritical in their judgement of Jesus. According to Jesus, final judgement belongs to God; it was not in the Pharisees' power to judge him.

• Jesus was not opposed to all exercise of judgement. He told his followers to beware of false prophets (Matt 7:15–20), which requires them to discern who is a true prophet and who is not. With regard to John 8, it is not true that Jesus did not judge the woman; rather, he instructed her to sin no more, demonstrating that he did not approve of her conduct and was not commending a laissez-faire approach to believers who were committing sin. According to Jesus, the sinner must stop sinning, and the purpose of church discipline is to instruct a person to stop sinning. Paul later called on the Corinthian church to judge its members: "Are you not to judge those inside? God will judge those outside. Expel the wicked person from among you" (1 Cor 5:12–13).

---

[11] G. C. Berkouwer, *Studies in Dogmatics: The Church* (Grand Rapids: Eerdmans, 1976), 363.

- Elsewhere Jesus demanded that people make right judgements (e.g. John 7:24). Matthew 7:2 should be interpreted to mean "that the judgmental person by not being forgiving and loving testifies to his own arrogance and impenitence, by which he shuts himself out from God's forgiveness".[12]

- Passages that do deal explicitly with church discipline (Matt 18:15–19; 1 Cor 5; Heb 12:1–12) clearly teach that believers should not disregard or ignore sinning brothers or sisters but rather should take every step to encourage their repentance and restoration to the church.

Some churches are afraid to practise church discipline because they fear it will drive away church members. Pastors and preachers who fear this outcome will hardly ever preach biblically on subjects such as homosexuality, divorce, witchcraft, ancestral worship, polygamy or living with partners outside marriage.

Foundations of church discipline

To have a good grasp of the need for church discipline, we need to remind ourselves of some foundational issues that have been either forgotten or simply ignored. The first and most important principle is that *church discipline is grounded in the fact that believers and the Christian community are to follow God who is holy*. God's holiness means that no sin, evil or impurity of any kind can be found in him. He required his Old Testament people (Israel) and his New Testament people (the church) to be like him and to "be holy because I, the Lord your God, am holy" (Lev 19:2; see also Matt 5:48; 1 Pet 1:15–16). 2 Peter 1:4 asserts that believers participate in God's divine nature. The New Testament often describes the church or believers in terms of holiness: "a holy priesthood" (1 Pet 2:5); "God's holy people in Colossae" (Col 1:2); "God's holy people in Christ Jesus at Philippi" (Phil 1:1; see also Eph 1:1; Paul addressed even the troubled church in Corinth in a similar way). Though his children cannot be as holy as God, they are required to follow him and to live their lives by standards that are different from those of the world. It is the purpose of church discipline to promote this holiness (sanctification) among believers by rebuking those who err or

---

[12] D. A. Carson, *Matthew* (vol. 8 of *Expositor's Bible Commentary*; ed. Frank E. Gaebelein; Grand Rapids: Zondervan, 1984), 184.

live dishonourable lives. "That is the foundation of all reflection on the holiness of the Church and her discontinuity. There can be no indulgent tolerance of sin in her midst, as if a meaningful place could be conferred on such sin."[13]

The second principle to be remembered is that *the church is an organized community*, with officers to run its affairs. This presupposes discipline, without which there would be chaos. This need for discipline extends to all forms of organized community. As the great sixteenth-century reformer John Calvin noted,

> If no society, nay, no house with even a moderate family, can be kept in a right state without discipline, much more necessary is it in the Church, whose state ought to be the best ordered possible. Hence as the saving doctrine of Christ is the life of church, so discipline is, as it were, its sinews; for to it is owing that the members of the body adhere together, each in its place.[14]

Any church that ceases to exercise discipline will simply cease to exist, as it will have nothing to hold it together. Thus there must be rules of behaviour that are consistent with the nature of a holy God and a holy church. Both the Old and the New Testament list such rules. The Old Testament, for example, insisted on ritual purity for those eating the Passover meal (Exod 12:14-20). It laid down that those who were impure had to offer sacrifices to purify themselves (Lev 5; 17:3–9) and forbade uncircumcised men from entering the temple (Ezek 44:9). During Ezra's time, people were excluded from the assembly because they had married foreign wives (Ezra 10:8). In New Testament times, Paul commanded, "Everything should be done in a fitting and orderly way" (1 Cor 14:40). In 1 Corinthians 6:9–10 Paul lists numerous sins from which believers must abstain, including sexual immorality, idolatry, homosexuality, stealing, drunkenness and slander. The believer is commanded to put off the old self and put on the new self (Rom 6; Eph 4:17–32). These rules of life and conduct are mandatory for believers; those who break them are to be reprimanded by the church in order to

---

[13] Berkouwer, *Studies in Dogmatics: The Church*, 358.

[14] John Calvin, *Institutes of the Christian Religion* (trans. Henry Beveridge; Grand Rapids: Eerdmans, 1989), 2:453.

bring them to repentance and restore them to fellowship with the body of Christ.

Discipline in the Scriptures

In the Scriptures, God is often depicted as a father who disciplines the children he loves. We see this in the way Deuteronomy 8:2–5 describes the physical hardship and emotional trauma the young nation of Israel had undergone for forty years in the desert:

> Remember how the LORD your God led you all the way in the wilderness these forty years, to humble you and to test you in order to know what was in your heart, whether or not you would keep his commands. He humbled you, causing you to hunger and then feeding you with manna, which neither you nor your ancestors had known, to teach you that man does not live on bread alone but on every word that comes from the mouth of the LORD. Your clothes did not wear out and your feet did not swell during these forty years. Know then in your heart that as a man disciplines his son, so the LORD your God disciplines you.

Hebrews 12:5–6 continues this idea for God's New Testament people: "My son, do not make light of the Lord's discipline, and do not lose heart when he rebukes you, because the Lord disciplines the one he loves, and he chastens everyone he accepts as his son." R. Kent Hughes, commenting on verse 6, reminds believers that "discipline is the telltale sign of being loved by God and in family relationship to him.... Discipline is the divinely ordained path to a deepening relationship with God and a growing love with him. It is the only path."[15] Leon Morris reminds us that "God disciplines people he loves, not those he is indifferent to".[16]

Discipline is an important part of bringing up children (Eph 6:4; see also 2 Tim 2:25). Biblical discipline includes instruction and training in righteousness (1 Cor 9:24–27; 1 Tim 4:7–8; Heb 5:14), and will produce the reward of righteousness (Rom 5:3–5; 2 Cor 5:16–18; 2 Tim 3:16; 1 Pet 2:18–21). However, any discipline is incomplete if there are no consequences for wrong actions, and so God's discipline also includes

---

[15] R. Kent Hughes, *Preaching the Word: Hebrews* (Wheaton: Crossway, 1993), 2:169.
[16] Leon Morris, *Hebrews* (vol. 12 of *Expositor's Bible Commentary*, Grand Rapids: Zondervan), 136.

chastisement (Lev 26:23; Ps 94:12; Hos 7:12), correction, reproof (Job 5:17; Prov 6:23) and punishment for wrongs committed. We see this in the fate of Achan and his family (Josh 7). We also see it in the prophet Nathan's confrontation of David, following his adultery with Bathsheba and the murder of Uriah (2 Sam 11–12). David immediately confessed, and Nathan assured him of God's forgiveness. However, David still suffered the consequences of his actions. His child with Bathsheba died, and his own family became very troubled. The supreme example of God's disciplining of his people is his sending Israel into exile for seventy years. This was not vindictive, but was designed to bring them to repentance and restoration (2 Chr 36:15–23; Ezek 11:16–21). Hosea 6:1–2 teaches that, though God disciplines his people, he also provides healing: "Come, let us return to the LORD. He has torn us to pieces but he will heal us; he has injured us but he will bind up our wounds. After two days he will revive us; on the third day he will restore us, that we may live in his presence."

Jesus instituted discipline in the church when he gave his disciples the power to bind and loose those who had committed sins (Matt 18:15–20). He also gave them authority to forgive sins or to retain them (Matt 16:19; 18:18; John 20:23). Paul acted on this authority and taught the churches to do the same (1 Cor 5:2, 7; 13; 2 Cor 2:5–7; 2 Thess 3:14–15; 1 Tim 3:10). The case of handing a sinner over to the devil is exceptional (1 Cor 5:5; 1 Tim 1:20), but this punishment is commensurate with the nature of the sins committed.

Church discipline today

The types of sins that call for church discipline include the following:

- divisions within the church (1 Cor 1:10–11; 11:18–19; see also Gal 5:2–12; Heb 12:15)
- heretical teachings (1 Tim 1:20)
- moral deviations (1 Cor 5:1–13; 1 Thess 3:6–15; 1 Tim 5:19–22; 2 Tim 3:15; Rev 2:2, 14, 20, 24).

The purpose of all disciplinary measures is the restoration of the erring brother or sister. Discipline is not a pleasant experience, for it involves pain and sorrow (2 Cor 2:5–11; Heb 12:11). But properly administered and received, it will result in righteousness and peace.

Those who have to implement discipline must not shrink from doing so, for Christ has instructed us not to ignore the sin of fellow believers (Matt 18:15–20). However, as Jesus indicated, the rebuke can be issued in private. Private sins between two believers should be handled privately, unless there is an unwillingness to repent (Luke 17:3–4; Gal 6:1–5). The rebuke should be gentle and loving (see Matt 7:1–5; 18:21–34; 2 Cor 2:5–11; Eph 4:29–30; Col 3:12–13; 1 Thess 5:14–15).

At times, however, there is a place for public rebuke of public sins (1 Tim 5:20; Gal 2:11–14). Public sins are "not merely sins that are committed in public, but sins that give public and rather general offence".[17] A public rebuke encourages others not to repeat such offences. For example, I remember that the principal of a theological seminary once had to publicly rebuke a graduate of the school who was promoting an allegorical interpretation that lacked any connection to the text of Scripture. The public rebuke was necessary to help students know that this man's teaching was wrong. However, when administering such rebuke, it is important to remember that "as a flower that is pulled from the stem withers, so discipline that is not understood will always disclose its deadly character and wake irritation. For it gives the impression of human meddling and human discrimination!"[18]

Certain offences are so severe that the proper response is excommunication, that is, terminating fellowship with the offending member. This step should only be taken when other methods have been tried and the sinning member has refused to repent (Matt 18:17–18). This is probably what Paul had in mind when he commanded the Corinthian church to hand a sinning man "over to Satan for the destruction of his flesh, so that his spirit may be saved on the day of the Lord" (1 Cor 5:5). Herman Ridderbos explains that "such a person was suspended and in this way the unacceptableness of his behaviour was made clear to him, but brotherly admonition was not withheld."[19]

The exact meaning of the phrase "for the destruction of his flesh" has prompted much debate. In the past, some have understood it to refer to physical death and have used this verse as justification for executing heretics. But this interpretation is very unlikely, not least because this

---

[17] Louis Berkhof, *Systematic Theology* (Grand Rapids: Eerdmans, 1996), 600.

[18] Berkouwer, *Studies in Dogmatics*, 370.

[19] Herman Ridderbos, *Paul: An Outline of His Theology* (Grand Rapids: Eerdmans, 1975), 470.

text says that the man's spirit could be saved. It seems more likely that some

> grave physical affliction, at least affecting the temporal life, is to be thought of, which is to strike the sinner who has been delivered up to Satan (cf. 2 Cor 12:7; Luke 13:16; Job 1, where the suffering too is attributed to Satan). The latter part of the sentence then denotes a possible spiritual turning and salvation arising from this; cf. the similar pronouncement in 1 Timothy 1:20.[20]

The appropriate time and place for the exercise of public discipline seems to be related to the sacraments (1 Cor 11:27), that is, when the church is gathered for Holy Communion. Calvin wrote that serious sins "require a sharper remedy. It is not sufficient verbally to rebuke him, who by some open act of evil example, has grievously offended the church; but he ought for a time to be denied the communion of the Supper, until he gives proof of repentance."[21] A disciplined member who has repented is also restored to fellowship during the Communion service.

When practised appropriately, in gentleness and humility, discipline trains believers in holiness. As Hebrews 12:11 states, "No discipline seems pleasant at the time, but painful. Later on, however, it produces a harvest of righteousness and peace for those who have been trained by it."

Discipline also upholds the honour of Christ, so that

> God may not be insulted by the name of Christian being given to those who lead shameful and flagitious lives, as if his holy Church were a combination of the wicked and abandoned. For seeing that the Church is the body of Christ, she cannot be defiled by such fetid and putrid members, without bringing some disgrace on her Head.[22]

Dissociating ourselves from those whose lives do not honour God will also prevent them having a corrupting influence on the body of Christ. It is very easy to copy bad examples: "For such is our proneness to go astray, that nothing is easier than to seduce us from the right course by

---

[20] Ibid., 471.
[21] Calvin, *Institutes*, 456–457.
[22] Ibid., 455.

bad example."[23] Paul writes, "Don't you know that a little yeast leavens the whole batch of dough? Get rid of the old yeast, so that you may be a new unleavened batch – as you really are" (1 Cor 5:6–7); "Do not be misled. 'Bad company corrupts good character'" (1 Cor 15:33; see also Rom 16:17).

Discipline also serves as a warning to others. Paul explicitly states this when he says, "those elders who are sinning you are to reprove before everyone, so that the others may take warning" (1 Tim 5:20). The following story illustrates how this works in practice:

> A year ago [my marriage] was in trouble. It was about that time that you [pastor] called the church to discipline Max because he would not back off the affair with his secretary. I was just beginning to get involved with someone at my office. When I saw what happened with Max, it shook me up so much that I broke off the relationship and confessed my sin to my wife. She forgave me, and we finally got into the counseling we needed to deal with problems in our marriage.[24]

Pastoral Ordination

The practice of pastoral ordination has a rich history. The Roman Catholic and Orthodox churches include ordination as one of their sacraments. For Roman Catholics, the act of ordination involves the passing on of a supernatural element. At the opposite extreme are the Plymouth Brethren and the Quakers, who argue that the concept of ordination is inconsistent with the biblical teaching of the priesthood of all believers (see below). Thus any member (or in some groups, any male member) who is illuminated by the Spirit can address the church and officiate at the Lord's Supper.

Among most Protestant churches, however, the act of ordination is simply a public acknowledgement of the call of God on an individual for a specific ministry. After the ceremony those who have been ordained often take titles such as "Reverend", "Bishop" or "Superintendent",

---

[23] Ibid., 456.
[24] Ken Sande, "Church Discipline: God's Discipline to Preserve and Heal Marriages", in *Pastoral Leadership for Manhood and Womanhood* (eds. Wayne Grudem and Dennis Rainey; Wheaton: Crossway, 2002), 161–162.

depending on the hierarchical order within their churches. However, there are some who object to the title "Reverend" on the grounds that only God should be revered.

In Africa, the title "Bishop" is often adopted in Pentecostal and Independent churches. It has been found that holders of this title are treated with more respect by civil officials than those who simply have the title "Pastor". However, it is important to remember that the Bible does not teach that a bishop is higher in rank than a pastor. Both words simply mean *shepherd* (see chapter 8).

Pastoral ordination in the Scriptures

Scripture provides many examples of individuals being ordained in the sense of being set apart for a particular vocation or ministry. God tells the prophet Jeremiah, for example, that he was predestined to be a prophet before his birth: "Before I formed you in the womb I knew you, before you were born I set you apart; I appointed you as a prophet to the nations" (Jer 1:5). Other Old Testament leaders were also commissioned for a particular ministry. Thus Moses was commanded by God to "Take Joshua son of Nun, a man in whom is the spirit of leadership, and lay your hand on him. Have him stand before Eleazer the priest and the entire assembly and commission him in their presence" (Num 27:18–19). In a similar ritual, priests, prophets and kings were specially commissioned through anointing with oil.

In the New Testament, Jesus appointed his disciples and called them to share the good news (Mark 3:13–14; 5:18–19). He also called seventy-two disciples whom he set apart for a special work in Luke 10:1–20. Later, the remaining eleven disciples appointed another person to take the place of Judas (Acts 1:21–23). Paul, too, was specially appointed to be an apostle (1 Cor 9:1–2; 15:1–8). Indeed, the word "apostle" means "the sent one". Paul stated, "I have become its [the church's] servant by the commission God gave me to present to you the word of God in its fullness" (Col 1:25).

In Acts 6:1–6, however, we read that the apostles laid hands on seven deacons to set them apart. The same thing happened in Acts 13, when, after praying, the church laid hands on Paul and Barnabas (13:3). It is important to note that it was not the laying on of hands that resulted in their calling. Rather, the laying on hands confirmed what the Holy Spirit was already doing. The seven deacons were "full of the Spirit and wisdom" as a prerequisite to, not a result of, their appointment. Similarly the setting apart of Barnabas and Saul was a public recognition of the Holy Spirit's calling on their lives (Acts 13:2, 4; see also 6:3). The setting apart did not result in a calling, but confirmed God's calling. Paul repeatedly asserted that his calling was from God and not from a human being or institution (1 Cor 1:1; 2 Cor 1:1; Gal 1:1; Eph 1:1; Col 1:1; 1 Tim 1:12; 2 Tim 1:1). Christ chose and appointed the disciples (John 15:16). It was the Holy Spirit who made the elders of Ephesus bishops or overseers (Acts 20:28).

Paul wrote that Timothy had received the "gift which was given through a prophetic message when the body of elders laid their hands on you" (1 Tim 4:14; see also 2 Tim 1:6) – apparently indicating that the supernatural gift was connected to the laying on of hands. But the Bible is clear that the giving of gifts is the divine prerogative of the Holy Spirit (1 Cor 12). Again, the elders, acting on behalf of the triune God by the laying on of hands, were acknowledging publicly what God had already bestowed on Timothy. The fact that the laying on of hands was done specifically by the elders of the church implies that this was a role that was restricted to them.

It is important to note that Timothy himself was warned not to rush to lay hands on people (1 Tim 5:22). Ordination should not be a rushed affair, as it is in some churches.

To sum up what has been said:

> Ordination was related to the gift of the empowering Holy Spirit (1 Tim 4:14; 2 Tim 1:6–7). It marked a public commissioning of the servant of God (Acts 13:3; see also Num 27:18–23). Hence as a public acknowledgment of the Spirit's action, the early church set apart persons whom the sovereign Spirit had selected and endowed for the fulfillment of a special leadership in service to the people of God.[25]

Pastoral ordination and the priesthood of all believers

Sadly, ordination has been abused throughout the history of the church. Many view it as a type of promotion, with a bishop, for example, having a

---

[25] Stanley Grenz, *Theology for the Community of God*, 565. He goes on to explain that "ordination serves the Spirit's intent to provide gifted leadership for the ongoing work of God's people in service to his purposes in the world" (565).

higher rank than a pastor. Such views have resulted in financial incentives for ordination and have given the ordained a privileged social status – and have also promoted corruption within the church. Most seriously, they have obscured the primary meaning of ordination, namely that it is a public declaration by the church that the one ordained has been called and appointed by God. Ordination is not meant to be the means whereby a few privileged individuals can confer titles. To treat it in that way dishonours the Lord.

The practice of ordination has also brought about a division between laity and clergy, denying the doctrine of the priesthood of all believers. In essence this doctrine means that all believers, not just a selected few (the clergy), can approach God to confess sin and can proclaim the gospel. Before the Reformation, the Roman Catholic Church taught that penitent sinners could only approach God through a priest. The realization that the way was open to all was revolutionary!

The priesthood of all believers should, however, be understood in its proper context. Believers are given different gifts by the Holy Spirit for the benefit of their fellow believers (1 Cor 12–14; Eph 4:11). As Donald Bloesch says,

> A church where the priestly role is restricted to the office of the pastor or bishop is a church where the Spirit has been quenched and grieved. All believers are called to be priests and kings with Christ, and this means all are given the privilege of interceding and sacrificing for their brethren; yet the way in which we exercise this ministry will vary depending on how the Spirit chooses to manifest himself in and through us.[26]

While all believers are called to preach the good news (Matt 28:18–20; Acts 1:8), the Holy Spirit has specially gifted some to be teachers, administrators, preachers, prophets and evangelists. Thus biblical ordination does not conflict with the priesthood of all believers. Likewise, the church's abuse of ordination, which ignores the importance of the laity and the equality of all believers in ministry, is not sufficient reason to disregard pastoral ordination.

---

[26] Bloesch, *The Reform of the Church*, 109.

Women in Ministry

Throughout the history of the church women have played very significant roles, yet the question of their status in the church and, in particular, whether they should be ordained has caused much controversy.[27] Many argue that the role of women is equal to that of men and that women should be given recognition for this, rather than being relegated to playing second fiddle to men, as is the practice in many churches.

These discussions are influenced by theological presuppositions, ecclesiastical traditions, biblical interpretation, human bias and plain ignorance of the realities in many churches. How should we understand the role of women in ministry?

The role of women in Scripture

The starting point of any discussion concerning women in the church must be the reaffirmation of the truth that *men and women are created equal.* We are all created in the image of God, which sets us apart from other created beings (Gen 1:27; 2:4–25; 9:6; Jas 3:9), including angels. To treat or see women as holding any lower status than this is unacceptable.

---

[27] Some of the most important literature on the subject is as follows: Ronald W. Pierce and Rebecca Merrill Groothuis, *Discovering Biblical Equality: Complementarity Without Hierarchy* (Downers Grove: IVP, 2005); Elizabeth A. Clark, *Women in the Early Church* (vol. 13 of *Message of the Fathers of the Church*; Wilmington: University of Pennsylvania Press, 1993); William M. Swartley, *Case Issues in Biblical Interpretation: Slavery, Sabbath, War and Women* (Scottdale: Herald Press, 1983); Stephen B. Clark, *Man and Woman in Christ: An Examination of the Roles of Men and Women in Light of Scripture and Social Sciences* (Ann Arbor: Servant Books, 1980); Paul K. Jewett, *Man as Male and Female: A Study in Sexual Relationships from a Theological Point of View* (Grand Rapids: Eerdmans, 1974); Perry Yoder, "Woman's Place in the Creation Accounts", in *Study Guide on Women* (ed. Herta Funk; Newton, Kan.: Faith & Life Press, 1975); Charles Ryrie, *The Place of Women in the Church* (New York: Macmillan, 1958); George Knight III, *The New Testament Teaching on the Role Relationship of Men and Women* (Grand Rapids: Baker, 1979); Fritz Zerbst, *The Office of Women in the Church: A Study in Practical Theology* (trans. Albert G. Merkens; St. Louis: Concordia, 1955); Wayne Grudem, *The Gift of Prophecy in the New Testament and Today* (Eastbourne: Kingsway 1998); John Piper and Wayne Grudem, eds., *Recovering Biblical Manhood and Womanhood: A Response to Evangelical Feminism* (Wheaton: Crossway, 1991); Robert L. Saucy and Judith K. TenElshof, eds., *Women and Men in Ministry: A Complementary Perspective* (Chicago: Moody, 2001); Patria Hill, *The World Their Household: The American Woman's Foreign Missions Movement and Cultural Transformation, 1870–1920* (Ann Arbor: University of Michigan, 1985); Ruth A. Tucker and Walter L. Liefield, *Daughters of the Church: Women and Ministry from New Testament Times to the Present* (Grand Rapids: Zondervan/Academic, 1987); Wayne Grudem and Dennis Rainey, eds., *Pastoral Leadership for Manhood and Womanhood* (Wheaton: Crossway, 2002).

Secondly, we need to recognize that *the redemption of Christ has had a great impact on the status and role of women in the church.* He did away with all discrimination on political, sociological, biological and spiritual grounds. Practical evidence of this equality was provided by baptism, which throughout the church's history has been given to both men and women (Acts 8:12; 16:15). Through baptism men and women are equally incorporated into the body of Christ (1 Cor 12:13).

> From the very beginning the community of Christ baptized men and women alike and put them on equal footing through *the one baptism.* That is undisputed, and has never been called in question. By doing so it recognized without qualification the fellowship with Christ and the experience of the Spirit of both women and men.[28]

As Galatians 3:28–29 states, "There is neither Jew nor Gentile, neither slave nor free, nor is there male and female, for you are all one in Christ Jesus. If you belong to Christ, then you are Abraham's seed, and heirs according to the promise." Or as Moltmann puts it,

> The person whom God "justifies" he installs as his child with the "right to inherit" eternal life in his kingdom. The new beginning out of grace makes the women and men concerned citizens of the coming kingdom of God, with equal rights. They have equal rights before God and towards one another, and are not bound to the positions assigned to them by the patriarchal rule of this world.[29]

Before redemption in Christ, these distinctions really mattered and people were treated according to their political, religious, sexual and social status. But Christ has reformulated our human identity. This does not mean the obliteration of distinctions such as national identity or human sexuality, but it does mean that discrimination on such grounds is not acceptable. Maleness or femaleness is no longer a decisive factor, and believers are not to build a theology that seeks to discriminate on the basis of gender. Gordon Fee puts it like this:

---

[28] Jürgen Moltmann, *Experiences in Theology* (Minneapolis: Augsberg Fortress, 2000), 285.
[29] Ibid., 284.

Paul does not tear down existing structures, but neither does he sanctify them. Everything for him begins with Christ, his death and resurrection, whereby he established the new order, the new creation. In the new creation, two things happen: the relationship must be lived out under the paradigm of the cross. In Christ Jesus there is neither male or female, not meaning that differentiation has ceased, but that both alike enter the new creation on the same footing, and thus serve one another and the rest of the church in the same way their Lord did – by giving themselves to the other(s) out of love. Ministry is thus the result of God's gifting and has nothing to do with being male or female, any more than it has to do with being Jew or Gentile, slave or free.[30]

Michael Green also comments on these verses:

This totally upsets the Jewish assumption of male superiority, in which, by the way, Paul himself had been reared. Man and woman are completely equal before God. But he means more than this: That equality has to have practical outworking. ... If all are indeed one in Christ, the agelong prejudices must be abolished. Galatians 3:28 is the fundamental presupposition against which all Paul's other teachings about women must be seen.[31]

Krister Stendahl also demonstrates from this passage that Christ has transcended all three divisions, namely Jew and Greek, slave and free, and male and female:

1) The boundary line between Jews and Greeks has been abolished, the wall of partition which God himself had raised through the Law, the foundation of Israel's glory and faith. 2) The boundary line between slave and free, which also is well attested in the Law and belonged to the order of life in the Gentile world, is overcome. 3) And, finally, the most primary division of God's creation is overcome, that between male and female – the terminology points directly back to Genesis 1:27

---

[30] Gordon D. Fee, *Listening to the Spirit in the Text* (Grand Rapids: Eerdmans, 2000), 76.
[31] Michael Green, *Freed to Serve* (London: Hodder & Stoughton, 1983), 87.

and the direction of man as the image of God, beyond the division into male and female.[32]

Moreover, it is clear that the Holy Spirit does not discriminate between women and men. On the day of Pentecost, men and women participated together and both received the filling of the Holy Spirit, as is made clear by Acts 2:17–21, which describes the fulfilment of the prophecy of Joel 2:28–32: "In the last days, God says, I will pour out my Spirit on all people. Your sons and daughters will prophesy, your young men will see visions, your old men will dream dreams. Even on my servants, both men and women, I will pour out my Spirit in those days, and they will prophesy."

Both women and men are also recipients of the gifts of the Holy Spirit, who gives them to whomsoever he pleases (1 Cor 12:4), empowering believers for ministry regardless of their sexual identity. Women had the ministry of prophecy (Acts 2:18; 21:9; 1 Cor 11:5). Widows were encouraged to be teachers (1 Tim 5:3, 16) and were co-workers with the Apostle Paul (Rom 16; Phil 4:3). Priscilla worked with her husband (Acts 18:18–19, 26), and Phoebe was a deacon in the church. The Greek word for "deacon" is often correctly translated "minister" (Eph 6:21; Col 1:7; 1 Tim 4:6), so women occupied leadership positions in the early church.

The third point that needs to be made is that the doctrine of the priesthood of all believers means that both women and men can approach God and have been called to be evangelists, teachers and preachers. The Old Testament described Israel as a "kingdom of priests and a holy nation" (Exod 19:6) and "a people holy to the LORD your God" (Deut 7:6), and the New Testament broadens this to all believers (1 Pet 2:9–10; Rev 1:5–6; 5:10; see also 20:6). The Aaronic priestly office, which belonged to just a few men, has now been extended to every tribe and nation of the world.

The early church believed that the church was made up not only of "distinguished members, but [that] all the members of the body of Christ are important and play their part. They all have their own dignity and their own functions, on the basis ... of fundamental equality."[33]

---

[32] Krister Stendahl, *The Bible and the Role of Women: A Case Study in Hermeneutics* (trans. Emilie T. Sander; Philadelphia: Fortress Press, 1966), 32.

[33] Hans Küng, *The Church* (Tunbridge Wells, Kent: Search Press, 1986), 370.

Küng explains, "The priesthood of all believers includes not only the witness of actions, of one's whole life spent in loving self-sacrifice, but also the specific witness of the word (cf. Heb 13:15). The preaching of the word of God is entrusted to all, not just a few."[34] Thus believing men and women are equally priests of God in the new church age. Though the argument has been rightly made that the priesthood of all believers does not equate to the eldership of all believers, it does nevertheless have implications regarding the role of women in the church.

Finally, *both the Old and New Testaments underscore the dignity and honour of women in the building of God's kingdom.* In Genesis, for example, the creation of Eve completed the meaning of what it is to be human. Adam was lonely and incomplete without her. There are also a number of examples of women who were leaders:

- Miriam, a prophetess (Exod 15:20), was a recognized leader alongside her two brothers, Moses and Aaron. Micah 6:4 confirms this: "I brought you up out of Egypt and redeemed you from the land of slavery. I sent Moses to lead you, also Aaron and Miriam."

- Deborah the judge and prophetess (Judg 4:4).

- Huldah the prophetess (2 Kgs 22:14; see also 2 Chr 34:22).

- Phoebe, a deacon (minister) (Rom 16:1–2).

- Priscilla, wife of Aquila (Acts 18:2–4, 18, 26; 1 Cor 16:19). She and her husband were Paul's companions and helpers, and they were both recognized as leaders by Paul and the church.

- Lydia and Nympha, both women who had churches that met in their homes (Acts 16:14–15, 40; Col 4:15). "To put it plainly, the church is not likely to gather in a person's house unless the householder also functioned as its natural leader. Thus Lydia would have held the same role in the church as she did as master of the household."[35]

- Euodia and Syntyche (Phil 4:2–3); Paul said that these women "contended at my side in the cause of the gospel" (4:3).

- Junia is one of those described as "outstanding among the apostles" (Rom 16:7).

---

[34] Ibid., 375.
[35] Fee, *Listening to the Spirit in the Text*, 73.

In addition, women such as Rahab, Naomi, Ruth and especially Mary played key roles in the history of redemption. It is significant that Jesus came into the world through a woman. Protestants often pay little attention to the words addressed to Mary by Gabriel, one of the highest in the angelic hierarchy, who said to her, "Greetings, you who are highly favoured! The Lord is with you" (Luke 1:28). Similarly, Elizabeth, the mother of John the Baptist, declared, "Blessed are you among women, and blessed is the child you will bear" (Luke 1:42). If God chose to give Mary a position of honour within redemptive history, we should not dishonour women by assigning them roles that are subordinate to those of men.

> It is clear that the Scripture provides for women a place of unusual dignity and significance. It never demeans the activities in which primarily women are engaged, such as their functions as wife, homebuilder, mother, educator of children. To engage in these notable activities according to Scripture is not to choose some second-best option, manifestly inferior to the pursuit of an independent career.... there is no scriptural reason to consider women as inferior, as too often has been done in human culture.[36]

What then are we to make of other biblical statements that seem to assign women subordinate roles? These passages must be taken seriously, but they must not be interpreted in isolation from the rest of Scripture. A number of passages in the New Testament, especially in the letters of Paul and Peter (1 Cor 7; 11:3–16; 14:33–36; Eph 5:22–33; 1 Tim 2:9–15; 1 Pet 3:1–7), seem to support the view that women are subordinate to men and should not hold leadership positions among them. However, we need to take contemporary cultural and sociological factors into account if we are to understand these passages correctly. In other words, it is possible that these assertions about the role of women reflect the contemporary situation rather than being statements that are intended to be binding on all people at all times.

Some would argue that this constitutes special pleading, but a similar approach has to be followed in order to understand the Bible's

---

[36] R. Nicole, "The Biblical Concept of Women", in *Evangelical Dictionary of Theology* (ed. Walter A. Elwell; Grand Rapids: Baker, 1984), 1180.

treatment of slavery. While the Bible presents slavery as normal and even exhorts slaves to be subordinate to their masters, no serious Bible scholar would argue that slavery should be a universal practice among all peoples. Slavery is not merely unethical – it is criminal. In other words, one must not take every biblical statement as rule for universal practice.

There is no space in this book to go into great detail on these passages. Nor is it necessary to do so, for there are many excellent expositions of them from different theological perspectives.[37] Even though we may not be able to reach a consensus on their precise meaning, the same general approach that should be followed in interpreting all Scripture can also be followed here: namely, difficult passages should be interpreted in the light of straightforward passages. The general teaching of Scripture is that women are not subordinate to men but do differ, for example, in terms of their roles in the home. As far as ministry is concerned, women are indwelt by the Holy Spirit and are called to preach and minister the good news just as men are.

With regard to 1 Corinthians 14:33–36, and in particular verse 34 ("Women should remain silent"), Stendahl explains, "The context (14:35) makes it clear that the silence here stands in contrast to 'asking questions', not to preaching, teaching or prophesying. That being so, there is no tension between this passage and the clear reference in chapter 11 to the fact that women may prophesy."[38]

The role of women in the church, past and present

Over the centuries women have held influential leadership positions in the church. They have gone out as missionaries to preach and win people to Christ, and many have paid for their devotion with their lives. Among the first of these were Perpetua and Felicitas, who were martyred in AD 202. It is impossible to mention all the great women in church history, but here are a few names:

---

[37] See, for example, E. M. Howe, *Women and Church Leadership* (Grand Rapids: Zondervan, 1982); P. K. Jewett, *The Ordination of Women* (Grand Rapids: Eerdmans, 1980); J. J. Davis, "Ordination of Women Reconsidered: Discussion of 1 Timothy 2:8–15", in *Presbyterian Communique* 12:6 (Nov.–Dec. 1979); D. W. and L. S. Dayton, "Women as Preachers: Evangelical Precedents", *Christianity Today* (May 23, 1975); Mercy Amba Oduyoye and Musimbi R. A. Kanyoro, eds., *The Will to Arise: Women, Tradition, and the Church in Africa* (Maryknoll: Orbis, 1995); R. Modupe Owanikin, "The Priesthood of Church Women in the Nigerian Context" in Oduyoye and Kanyoro, *The Will to Arise*, 206–219.

[38] Stendahl, *The Bible and the Role of Women*, 30.

- Monica shaped the life of her son, the great theologian Augustine of Hippo in North Africa.

- Katharina von Bora married Martin Luther and was described by him as "the first lady" of the Reformation.

- Argula von Stauffer (1492–1552) and Katherine Zell were significant reformers in their own right.

- Susannah Wesley, the mother of John and Charles Wesley, has been regarded as the "the Mother of Methodism".

- Mary Slessor (1848–1915), a Scottish missionary to Nigeria, worked in Calabar to eradicate the wicked practices of killing twins and cannibalism.

- Ellen G. White played a significant leadership role in the founding of the Seventh-Day Adventist Movement.

- Agnes Gonxha Bojaxhiu, popularly known as Mother Teresa (1910–1997), a Catholic nun from Albania, founded the Missionaries of Charity in Calcutta, India, and became famous for her service to the poor of India.

There have been great female Christian Bible teachers who have taught pastors, evangelists, missionaries, and teachers. Many of us, including myself, have been privileged to be taught at the feet of great female missionary teachers such as Grace Archibald and Faye Anderson. There are also great women preachers like Joyce Meyer, the most popular female preacher in the USA, and Juanita Bynum, a popular African-American preacher. Matilda Banda and Doreen Mwanza were recently ordained as the first female pastors by the Evangelical Church of Zambia.

Women have played key roles in planting and leading churches all over the world. In Kenya, Bishop Dr Margaret Wanjiru is the founder and presiding bishop of the Jesus Is Alive Ministries (JIAM) headquartered in Nairobi, Kenya. It is one of the fastest-growing churches in Africa. In Nigeria, the Family Worship Centre in Abuja is led by Pastor Sarah Omakwu; Bimbo Odukoya was a powerful female preacher; Margaret Idahosa, the presiding bishop of the Church of God Mission International, manages more than 3,000 churches worldwide; Nkechi Anayo Iloputaife is general overseer of the Victory Christian Church in Lagos; and Evangelist Ukpabio is the founder of Liberty Gospel Church. Churches in other parts of the continent have similar leadership.

While we may not endorse all the teachings and practices of these women (like all other preachers, they must be tested by the Scriptures), it is clear that without the active leadership of these women, many churches would struggle to survive. Though only a few churches currently ordain women, the situation is likely to change in the years to come. Whether or not we accept women as leaders in the church, the fact of the matter is that these women pastors are accepted and appreciated as pastors in their own churches.

It is also worth noting that women play a prominent role in the church by their commitment and devotion. Women are the backbone of many churches. Eighty per cent of the members of black South African churches are women! These women support their pastors and send missionaries to the field. Failure to acknowledge their significant role in ministry results in an incomplete history of the church.

Handling disagreements

Though we may disagree on this issue, it does not mean that those who differ from us are necessarily wrong. It is important to be sensitive to cultural contexts and ecclesiastical traditions. Some denominations, such as the Brethren, take 1 Timothy 3:2 as referring exclusively to men and do not believe that women should occupy pastoral leadership positions, although they do permit them to teach and carry out other ministries. This does not mean that other Christian communities are not justified in seeing things differently. All positions are searching for the truth, which can seem different depending on one's viewpoint. Thomas Kuhn makes a similar observation concerning scientists:

> The proponents of competing paradigms practice their trades in different worlds. ... [They] see different things when they look from the same point in the same direction. Again, that is not to say that they can see anything they please. Both are looking at the world, and what they look at has not changed. But in some areas they see different things, and they see them in different relations, one to the other.[39]

---

[39] Thomas S. Kuhn, *The Structure of Scientific Revolutions* (2nd ed.; Chicago: University of Chicago Press, 1970), 150.

Anne Firor Scott explains how this relates to the fact that historians often overlook the role of women:

> It is a truism, yet one easy to forget, that people see most easily things they are prepared to see and overlook those they do not expect to encounter. ... Because our minds are clouded, we do not see things that are before our eyes. What clouds our minds is, of course, the culture that at any time teaches us what to see and what not to see.[40]

As Christians we have the same source (the Scriptures), but our traditions often influence our interpretation. No human being is completely free of biases.

We therefore need to listen to and learn from one another. No position has completely grasped the whole truth; hence the need to listen to and learn from one another so that our position can be based on a more thorough understanding of God's word. This has particular application to men, who are used to being in charge and writing all the theologies concerning the issue of men and women. German theologian Jürgen Moltmann has described how his exposure to feminist theologies, liberation theologies and Third World theologies deeply affected him. He states that in order to overcome patriarchal traditions, "the power game must stop, the master in the man must vanish, power must be distributed justly and equally, so that everyone, men and women alike, get the chance to fulfil their talents and callings, so that they can be used".[41]

We all need to recognize that discussion on the role of women in ministry is still ongoing. We should not be satisfied with our position on women. We need to study more and continue to listen with both ears to what the Spirit is saying. Karl Rahner writes from a Roman Catholic perspective,

> The discussion must and can be extended to all the aspects and questions which have been more explicitly or freshly involved in the theological discussion of the last decades. These include questions about the sociological emancipation of woman in theory and practice; questions about the consequences

---

[40] Anne Firor Scott, "On Seeing and Not Seeing: A Case of Historical Invisibility", *Journal of American History*, 71: 1 (June 1984): 7, 19.
[41] Jürgen Moltmann, *Experiences in Theology: Ways and Forms of Christian Theology* (trans. Margaret Kohl; London: SCM, 2000), 271.

of women's sociological emancipation in the life of the church (questions which are there anyway); questions about overcoming discrimination against women in the church (a discrimination which is still far from being eliminated, even if we disregard our main theme); questions about the authentic and integral essential image of the priest, which cannot be restricted to his purely sacramental power; questions about present-day requirements for the structure of a Christian congregation and about the function of women in the Church as determined by the structure; questions about the concrete methods and measures by which the discrimination against women in Church and society persisting before and after merely theoretical ideals can be effectively overcome in life and society and about the different requirements in different cultural groups; questions about ways and means of educating and changing the consciousness of the Church as a whole, where the causes of such a change of consciousness are to be found and what are the factors preventing it, how and in what form due consideration can and must be given. ... Consequently the discussion must continue. Cautiously, with mutual respect, critical of bad arguments on both sides, critical of irrelevant emotionalism expressly or tacitly influencing both sides, but also with that courage for historical change which is part of the fidelity which the Church owes to its Lord.[42]

Though traditions are hard to discard, it is important to challenge beliefs, perceptions and practices regularly to see if our position is consistent with biblical revelation or is merely an ecclesiastical tradition that seeks endorsement from the Scriptures. As Albert Einstein once noted, "It is harder to smash prejudices than atoms",[43] but when they have been smashed and biblical views put in their place, they will "release forces that can move mountains, perhaps even in the Church".[44]

It is also important to be obedient to the leading and illumination of the Holy Spirit with regard to the meaning of Scripture. The Holy

---

[42] Karl Rahner, *Concern for the Church* (trans. Edward Quinn; New York: Crossroad, 1986), 46–47.
[43] Quoted in Hans Küng, *Theology for the Third Millennium: An Ecumenical View* (trans. Peter Heinegg; New York: Doubleday, 1988), 152.
[44] Ibid.

Spirit is at work today, and believers need to recognize that he appoints men and women to his ministry. If he has decided to commission certain women to provide leadership or service in any way, we should not oppose it but rather give God the glory and honour. Even if we know of women who have abused their position, that should not make us conclude that God does not use women in the church. Bishop Alma White, founder of the Pillar of Fire Church, has said that "so long as the Holy Spirit operates in the world, women must necessarily preach the gospel".[45] It is insensitive to the work of the Holy Spirit to assume that he gives certain gifts only to men and not to women, who are equal members in the body of Christ.

Remuneration of Church Workers

The question regarding the payment of ministers of the gospel (e.g. pastors, elders and missionaries) is an important one. Should they be paid? If so, how much? The history of the church indicates a diversity of beliefs and practices in this regard.

In Africa, thinking on this issue is shaped by the fact that historically Western missionaries came to Africa with their own support and so did not have to deal with the issue of remuneration. This has resulted in Africans having the following views regarding remuneration for those working for God:

- *God's workers should trust God to meet their needs.* Ministers work for God and therefore do not need to be paid in the same way as those working for human institutions. God will reward them. The missionaries have been held up as models to be followed – forgetting that missionaries receive total support for themselves and their families. Their children are schooled in private institutions and do not have to pay for their tuition and board. In contrast, local church workers have to pay for the tuition of their children.

- *God's workers are promised an eternal reward.* While those in secular fields work for material rewards, God's workers work for rewards that will be given in heaven or after death at the throne of Christ. It was common in the past to hear the phrase "Our reward is in heaven".

---

[45] Quoted in Janette Hassey, *No Time for Silence: Evangelical Women in Public Ministry Around the Turn of the Century* (Grand Rapids: Academie Books, 1986), 46.

The idea of hoping for any reward "here and now" may be seen as worldly and inappropriate for God's minister.

- *An eternal reward is more important than a material reward.* The crown of righteousness is more important than a salary or a better lifestyle. Verses such as "What good is it for someone to gain the whole world, yet forfeit their soul?" (Mark 8:36) are cited as proof of the importance of seeking spiritual rewards rather than material satisfaction.

- *Living in material want is the ultimate cost of serving God.* To be materially poor is synonymous with being God's worker. A truly spiritual pastor should expect to live in poverty.

- *God's workers should accept whatever remuneration is offered, no matter how small, without complaint.* Anyone who complains of poor wages is unsuitable for the ministry.

In recent times, some churches and television evangelists have challenged these presuppositions and pay their workers very well. Some pastors are rich and powerful. Some own their own planes and expensive cars, and have large salaries and beautiful homes. They offer the following arguments to justify their high salaries:

- *God's workers have been promised a present reward* as well as a future one (Matt 6:33).

- *God's workers are God's ambassadors on earth.* As such, they must live in a style that is consistent with such a position. The child of God should not live a wretched life because God is not a poor God, but owns everything in the world.

- *God's workers have the same physical needs as all other human beings.* They need to eat, clothe themselves and have places to live like everyone else.

- *The Scriptures teach that adequate remuneration of God's ministers is appropriate* (1 Tim 5:17–18).

- *Prosperity is not inconsistent with being a minister.* Living well is now perceived as a blessing from God. In many churches, the last verse of Psalm 23 is used as the benediction: "Surely your goodness and love will follow me all the days of my life, and I will dwell in the house of the LORD for ever." The "goodness" and "love" are understood to mean the good things of life, which will be with the child of God throughout life.

Given these two dramatically different approaches to remuneration, it is important to establish what the Scriptures actually teach on this issue.

Remuneration in the Scriptures

First of all, the Bible states the fact that God's workers need and deserve financial support. In 1 Corinthians 9, Paul demonstrates this using the examples of career soldiers, vine growers and shepherds (9:7), oxen (9:9), farmers (9:10) and the Old Testament priests (9:13).

Not only should God's workers be paid, but elders need special payment. This point emerges clearly if we look at different translations of 1 Timothy 5:17:

- "Pastors who do their work well should be paid well and should be highly appreciated, especially those who work hard at preaching and teaching" (Life Application Bible).

- "Give a bonus to leaders who do a good job, especially those who work hard at preaching and teaching" (The Message).

- "Elders who do well as leaders should be reckoned worthy of a double stipend, in particular those who labour at preaching and teaching" (New English Bible).

Clearly the phrase translated "double honour" in the NIV denotes both respect and remuneration. This point is driven home by the next verse. As A. Duane Litfin explains, "For their oversight all elders received a stipend; but those who excelled in this ministry of leadership were to be considered 'worthy of double honor', or twice the remuneration as the rest. Especially was this true of those who labored in preaching and teaching."[46] Some will receive higher wages than others simply because of the nature of their work (Gal 6:6).

Given that workers are entitled to be paid, they are within their rights to demand remuneration. Paul asserts that he has the right to demand compensation (1 Cor 9:15, 18; see also Acts 18:13). He also encourages the compensation of God's workers (1 Cor 16:18; 1 Thess 5:12).

---

[46] A. Duane Litfin, "1 Timothy", in *The Bible Knowledge Commentary: New Testament* (eds. John F. Walvoord and Roy B. Zuck; Colorado Springs: Cook Communications Ministries, 2004), 744.

Refusal to pay fair wages is unethical and cruel (1 Tim 5:18). In particular, to claim that God's workers are working for God and will therefore receive their reward after death flies in the face of the clear instruction to pay God's ministers.

That said, God's servants may voluntarily choose to forgo their right to compensation. Paul did this in Corinth (1 Cor 9:15, 18; see Acts 18:3) and Thessalonica (1 Thess 2:9; 2 Thess 3:8). But note that this was a voluntary abstention. The church has no right to impose a meagre salary on God's workers and should do its utmost to avoid using a lack of funds as an excuse for paying low wages.

Churches should also be warned that failure to pay fair wages will have consequences for the church (Gal 6:6–7). It can result in a financial crisis for the church.

Concluding remarks and recommendations

The Bible teaches that proper compensation of God's workers is not merely appropriate but mandatory. God's workers should be paid for their services. Some will get more than others according to what they do for the church. Still others may forgo their wages because of certain circumstances (e.g. a church may be too small to be able to support its workers).

Remuneration of God's workers should be seen not only in terms of financial payment but as part of the total care of pastors and their families. Some pastors, evangelists and ministers and their families live in appalling conditions, in dilapidated buildings with worn-out furniture and a lack of medical care. This is unacceptable.

At the opposite extreme, however, are pastors who have taken matters into their own hands, enriching themselves through ingenious and often devious interpretations of Scripture. They talk about principles of "seed faith", "hundredfold return", "first fruit", "the Melchizedek offering" and "the blessings of Abraham".

> At its worst, the gospel of prosperity permits corrupt clergy to get away with virtually anything. Not only can they coerce the faithful to pay their obligations through a kind of scriptural terrorism, but the belief system allows them to excuse malpractice. If the pastor drives a limousine, this is only just

recompense for his outstanding faith. And critics must either
be lacking in their faith, or else they serve as agents of evil.[47]

Though it is proper for members to give, it is immoral to coerce
members to give through shaky and selective use of Scripture rooted in
sinful motives. In most instances, such practices show what the ministers
are really after. We would do well to heed the warning issued by Sir
Roger L'Estrange in the seventeenth century: "He that serves God for
money will serve the Devil for better wages." Believers need to be wary
of those who serve God for financial and material benefits, and who use
the pulpit to enrich themselves by asking members, even poor members,
to give generously to meet their selfish needs.

Questions

1. Explain the difference between the gift of the Holy Spirit and the
   gifts of the Holy Spirit.
2. What do you understand by "spiritual gifts"? Does every believer
   have a particular spiritual gift?
3. Why do you think there has been an explosion in the emphasis on
   spiritual gifts in the church?
4. What is the relationship between spiritual gifts, the fruit of the Spirit,
   and spirituality?
5. Discuss Paul's words in 1 Corinthians 14:1 about desiring spiritual
   gifts. Should every believer have the gift of speaking in tongues and
   interpretation? Why or why not?
6. Evaluate your church's views on church discipline in light of the
   Bible's teaching on the subject.
7. Church discipline sometimes results in division within churches. Why
   is this the case? Do you know of a church where this has happened?
   Does this mean that church discipline should be abandoned, or
   does its practice need to be revised in order to reduce negative
   consequences?

---

[47] Philip Jenkins, *The New Faces of Christianity: Believing the Bible in the Global South* (London:
Oxford University Press, 2006), 92.

8. Evaluate your church's views on pastoral ordination in light of biblical teaching.
9. What is the position of your church regarding the role of women in ministry? Evaluate the position in light of biblical teaching.
10. What is the position of your church regarding the remuneration of church workers? Evaluate the position in light of biblical teaching.

Further Reading

Funso Afolayan. *Culture and Customs of South Africa*. Westport: Greenwood Publishing, 2004.

Efrain Agosto. *Servant Leadership: Jesus & Paul*. Danvers: Chalice Press, 2005.

Gilbert Bilezikian. *Beyond Sex Roles: What the Bible Says about a Woman's Place in Church and Family*. Grand Rapids: Baker Academic, 2006.

John Piper and Wayne Grudem. *Recovering Biblical Manhood and Womanhood*. Wheaton: Crossway, 2006.

Gordon D. Fee. *Listening to the Spirit in the Text*. Grand Rapids: Eerdmans, 2000.

Ginger Gabriel. *Being a Woman of God*. Rev. and exp. ed. Nashville: Thomas Nelson, 1993.

Wayne Grudem. *Evangelical Feminism: A New Path to Liberalism?* Wheaton: Crossway, 2006.

Patricia Gundry. *Women Be Free*. Grand Rapids: Zondervan, 1977.

Carl F. H. Henry. *God Who Speaks and Shows*. Vol. 4 of *God, Revelation and Authority*. Waco: Word, 1979.

Craig Keener. *Gift & Giver: The Holy Spirit for Today*. Grand Rapids: Baker, 2001.

Jürgen Moltmann. *Experiences in Theology: Ways and Forms of Christian Theology*. Translated by Margaret Kohl. London: SCM, 2000.

Wilbur O'Donovan. *Biblical Christianity in African Perspective*. Carlisle: Paternoster, 2000.

Mercy Amba Oduyoye and Misimbi R. A. Kanyoro, eds. *The Will to Arise: Women, Tradition, and the Church in Africa*. Maryknoll: Orbis, 1995.

10

DEATH, JUDGEMENT AND ETERNITY

Time and the future have been prominent in the writings of African theologians. John Mbiti summarizes one understanding of the traditional African concept of time in the following words:

> According to traditional concepts, time is a two-dimensional phenomenon, with a long past, a present and virtually no future. The linear concept of time in Western thought, with an indefinite past, present and infinite future, is practically foreign to African thinking. The future is virtually absent because events which lie in it have not taken place, they have not been realized and cannot, therefore, constitute time.[1]

Mbiti uses two words in the Swahili language of East Africa to explain this concept of time. "*Sasa* covers the 'now-period'. ... *Sasa* has the sense of immediacy, nearness, and 'now-ness', and this is the period of immediate concern for the people, since that is 'where' or 'when' they exist. ... *Zamani* overlaps with *sasa,* and the two are not separable.[2] But *zamani* is bigger than *sasa*. It embraces the remote past and envelops the present. It is the sense of time that we need if we are to learn from the past so as to be able to live wisely in the present in order to have a better future.

Though there are valuable insights in these fine distinctions, what is most worrisome in Mbiti's thesis is his extreme statement that Africans lack a concept of the future. Many African scholars, such as Byang Kato

---

[1] John Mbiti, *African Religions and Philosophy* (2nd ed.; Oxford: Heinemann, 1990), 17. Mbiti's other books on theology are *Concepts of God in Africa* (1970) and *New Testament Eschatology in an African Background* (1971).

[2] Ibid., 21–22.

in *Theological Pitfalls in Africa*, have argued convincingly that Mbiti has overstated his case. Citing examples from the Jaba, Urhobo, Igbo and others, Kato argues that these African tribes and many others do have concrete ideas about the future. He concludes, "From the African point of view, a belief in the future is an attested fact. ... Africans' strong belief in creation is itself indicative of their belief in linear time."[3] He adds, "While the *sasa* [present] and the *zamani* [past] concepts are stronger than the future concept, this does not mean that African peoples do not think of the distant future."[4]

One of the evidences of the concreteness of the future in African thought is the African concept of death and the afterlife. Traditional African beliefs concerning the future may not be as detailed as the teaching found in the Bible. Yet they are real, and the subject has great promise when it comes to developing a Christian theology that is African.

Eschatology

The end of life and what happens thereafter is a matter of ultimate concern for every human being in the entire universe. Millions people have been born, lived and died, and death is the lot of all those now living and yet to be born. To know about the end of life and respond appropriately to its demands is therefore important for a meaningful life. This is the subject of the field of theology known as eschatology. It derives its name from the Greek word *eschaton*, which refers to the coming end of the present world.

A few decades ago the study of the end times was a dominant theme within theological circles, with much attention focused on the books of Revelation, Daniel and Ezekiel. But this is no longer the case; other issues have taken centre stage. Erickson is right when he warns that two extremes have to be avoided. The first is what he calls an "intensive preoccupation with eschatology"– "eschatomania"– which "makes eschatology the whole of theology". The other extreme is "eschatophobia", which "is a fear or aversion to eschatology".[5] We cannot afford to be overly consumed about the end times, but neither

---

[3] Byang H. Kato, *Theological Pitfalls in Africa* (Kisumu, Kenya: Evangel, 1975), 63.
[4] Ibid., 62.
[5] Millard J. Erickson, *Introducing Christian Doctrine* (Grand Rapids: Baker Academic, 1992), 374.

should we ignore the fact that the end times forms a key part of the Bible's teaching. As such, we cannot afford to neglect it.

The theology of the end times is complex, with many difficult theological debates. You may wonder why it is necessary to study them in so much detail. Here are some compelling reasons:

1. *We should understand what the Bible teaches about the end times.* As complicated as it is, this teaching is part of the Bible, and Christians are commanded to read and obey the word of God. In 2 Timothy 3:16 Paul asserts the inspiration and authority of all the words of Scripture. This means that it is imperative for Christians to seek to understand it all, including those parts that are concerned with the end of human history.

2. *Our understanding of the Bible's teaching on the end times affects our understanding of the present and the future.* For example, has God finished with Israel? Should the prophecies concerning Israel in the Old Testament be interpreted literally, as being fulfilled in the future, or are they only to be fulfilled in the church, the new Israel? Should the book of Revelation be interpreted symbolically, seeing that most of it is presented in symbolic form? If so, what does the symbolism mean? To what extent should our interpretation be consistent with other biblical revelation on the end times? What does the kingdom of God mean in this age and in the age to come? Does God's reign in human hearts, through Christ, exhaust the meaning of the future kingdom of God on earth?

3. *It is important to understand the reasons for different opinions regarding the end times.* Some aspects of eschatology are straightforward. For example, the Bible clearly teaches that Christ will return. However, the details of when and how he will return are not so easy to understand. The Bible describes events that will precede or coincide with Christ's second coming, and it is the attempt to explain and fit all the events and personalities mentioned into the chronology of the end times that makes eschatology difficult and results in differences of opinion. Bible students need to understand and attempt to deal with these different theological positions.

4. *The study of the end times provides an important perspective on life.* We have the tendency to occupy our minds with the here and now and with material things, but the study of the end times reminds us

that these things will come to an end. The Bible asserts that, instead of being occupied with temporal matters, we should rather occupy ourselves with that which lasts – eternity.

> Since everything will be destroyed in this way, what kind of people ought you to be? You ought to live holy and godly lives as you look forward to the day of God and speed its coming. That day will bring about the destruction of the heavens by fire, and the elements will melt in the heat. But in keeping with his promise we are looking forward to a new heaven and a new earth, where righteousness dwells. (2 Pet 3:11–13)

This awareness provides a balance in our earthly human existence and the pursuit of the kingdom of God. We are told to "seek first his kingdom and his righteousness, and all these things will be given to you as well" (Matt 6:33). Often people seek earthly things first and append the kingdom of God, which becomes a footnote in their lives. The study of the end times helps us to check our priorities. Ours should be to seek the kingdom and righteousness.

5. *A rich reward is promised for those who study the Scriptures with regard to prophecy and future events.* Revelation 1:3 states, "Blessed is the one who reads aloud the words of this prophecy, and blessed are those who hear it and take to heart what is written in it, because the time is near." Reading, hearing, pondering and obeying all of God's word, including prophecy, will result in blessing.

We turn now to discuss some important aspects of eschatology.

Death, Burial and the Afterlife

Death comes for all. That fact is never disputed. But what happens after death? How should the dead be disposed of? And where do they remain as they await the day of judgement? These are important questions that every person and every religion has to deal with in one way or another.

The African view of death

Death and the afterlife loom large in the African world view. At death, one moves into the presence of the ancestors, and so while living here on earth one is taught how to prepare to meet them. There is no clear, systematic teaching regarding judgement after death, but it is generally understood that a good life will result in being joined with the ancestors after death, while an evil life will result in total oblivion, the idea of which is utterly abhorrent to Africans.

It is common for Africans to talk about their deceased loved ones as now being among "the living dead". Death, especially of the elderly, is considered to be the end of one journey (life on earth) and the beginning of another journey into the world of the living ancestors. It is a transition, a comma, a beginning, moving from one life to the other. The dead become visibly absent but invisibly present among their family members, and they become visibly present among the ancestors. The ceremonies or rituals attached to this very special event vividly demonstrate this belief. For example, during the ceremony the corpse may be addressed in words like this: "Leave us, O Father, leave us; here is your stool; here is your tobacco, chew it; this is your milk, drink it; ... this is your feather holder, take it. Here is your oil, drink it; this is your meat, eat it. Father, help us now and give us life, make us rich and give us food."[6] Most African peoples use somewhat similar words in traditional funeral ceremonies. Some continue to provide meals for the deceased after the funeral. In the past, servants were sometimes buried alongside a dead ruler to provide him with service after death. Money and other precious articles may also be buried to meet the person's needs in the afterlife.

But while the death of the elderly is felt to be the next step on a journey, the death of a young person is a completely different matter! Such deaths are always considered premature. It is common to read the following kinds of announcements in newspapers: "We regret to announce the sudden and premature passing away of ..."; "We deeply regret the sudden and unexpected death of ..."; "We announce with deep sorrow that the cruel hands of death snatched prematurely our dearly beloved ...". These statements reveal not only the grief and sorrow that death brings, but also the deep conviction that some die before their ordained time. The death of infants and the termination of innocent life by murderers or through accidents fall into this category of premature death. In such cases the death is traditionally ascribed to

---

[6] A. Barrett, *Dying and Death among the Turkuna, Part II* (Eldoret: Gaba Publications, 1987), 13.

witchcraft and demonic activities.[7] It is felt that a person who has not lived long enough to have offspring is cut off from his or her place among the ancestors.

Of course, it is not only traditional believers who are deeply affected by premature death. Christians too are beset by questions and doubts when a young and productive person suddenly dies. If God is a loving and caring Father who would not want to cause pain to his children, it is assumed that there must be some other power behind a premature death. And such deaths are all too common. Accidents and HIV/AIDS have been claiming millions of young lives. Christian leaders have been affected too. When the well-known African evangelical theologian Dr Byang H. Kato met his death while swimming in Kenya in 1973, he left behind a wife and young children. Did he die prematurely? Many people thought so. More recently, the deaths of Drs Kwame Bediako (2009) and Tokunboh Adeyemo (2010) left many Christians wondering why these productive African theologians were struck down by cancer and died while they were in the process of making huge contributions to the church.

Of course, such cases are not unique to Africa. Keith Green, an American Christian musician and "prophet" who won the hearts of many Americans, died suddenly and tragically in a plane crash in 1982. We even find cases in the Bible: the deaths of Absalom, Saul, Job's children, and David's son with Bathsheba can all be said to be premature in the sense that these people did not live out their full lifespan. What good does it serve when potentially productive people die unexpectedly in the prime of their lives?

To many, it seems that the devil and evil forces gain by such deaths, and that God, the families of the bereaved and the church lose out. One author wrote that "Death remains [a] hideous, cruel executioner, alien to man and to God."[8] Rabbi Kushner, who lost his young son, has a similarly disturbing understanding of the issue of pain, disease, death and God: "God wants the righteous to live peaceful, happy lives; but sometimes even he cannot bring that about. It is difficult even for God to keep cruelty and chaos from claiming their innocent victims."[9]

---

[7] My previous book, *African Christian Ethics* (Jos, Nairobi and Accra: HippoBooks / Grand Rapids: Zondervan, 2008), offers biblical and theological perspectives on the issue of witchcraft.

[8] Alvin N. Rogness, *Appointment with Death* (Nashville: Thomas Nelson, 1972), 83.

[9] Harold S. Kushner, *When Bad Things Happen to Good People* (New York: Avon, 1983), 43.

The book in which he wrote those words was a bestseller. There is thus not such a vast gulf between this view and the African view that death is caused by forces opposed to God. Both traditions teach that God's omnipotence is limited by pain, suffering and death. But such a belief contradicts the Scriptures.

Scriptural teaching on death

Death is first mentioned in Genesis 3:3, when Eve reported God's command not to eat of the forbidden fruit. Failure to abide by this explicit command would result in death. When Adam and Eve disobeyed God by eating the fruit, the sentence of death was pronounced: "By the sweat of your brow you will eat your food until you return to the ground, since from it you were taken; for dust you are and to dust you will return" (Gen 3:19). The events in Genesis reveal that death was not part of God's original plan for humankind; it is an intrusion. The Bible elsewhere speaks of death as an enemy that will be conquered at the final resurrection (1 Cor 15:54–57). It was sin that introduced death into human existence, and this death was not only physical, but also spiritual and eternal.

Physical death

Physical death is the departure of life from the material body. This is referred to many times in Scripture, for example, in Genesis 35:18, "As she breathed her last – for she was dying". It is often spoken of in terms of the spirit (the immaterial part of us) separating from the body (the physical part of us). Thus the writer of Ecclesiastes says, "the dust returns to the ground it came from, and the spirit returns to God who gave it" (Eccl 12:7). Jesus is said to have given up his spirit (Luke 24:4; John 19:30;). Stephen said, "Lord Jesus, receive my spirit" (Acts 7:59). James uses this as a metaphor when he says that "as the body without the spirit is dead, so faith without deeds is dead" (Jas 2:26).

The causes of physical death include the following:

* *Natural causes, such as old age, as well as accidents and disease.* As creatures, we are subject to the natural laws of the universe we live in. The second law of thermodynamics states that everything decays. Thus from the time of our birth we begin to die slowly until we breathe our last breath. We cannot, by nature, live for ever. Psalm

90:10 states that "our days may come to seventy years, or eighty, if our strength endures." This does not mean that eighty is the maximum number of years we can live, but that there is a limit on the number of years of life for every human being. Psalm 103:15–16 also teaches that our lives are fleeting compared with the life of the everlasting God.

- *Moral choices.* The moral decisions we make can have disastrous consequences. For example, those who decide to drink and drive can easily cause serious injuries to themselves and others. Smoking contributes to developing lung cancer. Promiscuity increases one's chances of contracting HIV/AIDS.

- *A divine cause.* Ultimately, as stated above, death is a divine appointment made by God for all human beings (Job 1:21; Luke 12:5; Rev 1:18). It is closely related to judgement, as we saw in the account of the fall in Genesis 3. Hebrews 9:27 specifically states that "people are destined to die once, and after that to face judgement".

In Africa, witchcraft is often understood to be a major cause of death. But death would still reign even if all witches and wizards were eliminated. This is so because sin, not witchcraft, is the primary cause of death. Physical death came about as a result of the sin of Adam and Eve (Gen 3:3, 22–23; 1 Cor 15:21). Because humankind has sinned, humankind dies. If there had been no sin, there would be no death. Believers and unbelievers, the righteous and the evil, young and old, adults and infants: all are sinners and therefore face death.

Spiritual death

Spiritual death is the separation of humanity from God. This spiritual death, which is different from physical death, is also a result of Adam's sin: "Your iniquities have separated you from your God; your sins have hidden his face from you, so that he will not hear" (Isa 59:2); "As for you, you were dead in your transgressions and sins" (Eph 2:1).

Eternal death

Eternal death is ultimate and eternal separation from God. This is "the second death", the fate of those who do not accept his free gift of salvation in Christ and who perform acts contrary to his will (Rev 21:8). Eternal death is the "final destiny of the unbelieving in a state of separation from his life".[10] This death, often called the second death (Rev 20:13–15; 21:8; 2 Thess 1:8–9), will occur at the end of the age, when God will put away, for eternity, all those who refuse to accept Jesus Christ as their personal Lord and Saviour.

Christ's victory over death

Death is a reality for both unbelievers and believers. All must suffer death. And there may not seem to be significant difference between the manner and time of death of a believer and an unbeliever. But the Christian faith brings a new and refreshing aspect to death, for "at the very heart of the Christian faith is the claim that God has intervened in the world of death through the death and resurrection of this one man [Jesus Christ]".[11] What has Christ achieved?

1. *Christ's death and resurrection rendered death powerless.* Hebrews 2:14 states this truth powerfully: "Since the children have flesh and blood, he too shared in their humanity so that by his death he might break the power of him who holds the power of death – that is, the devil." The Greek word translated "break the power" is *katargese*, meaning to render inoperative or inactive. The same word is used in Romans 6:13 and 2 Timothy 1:10. Christ's death rendered Satan's hold over sin, which is equated with death, inoperative.

2. *Christ substituted life for death.* In 2 Timothy 1:10 Paul speaks of the work of Christ in this respect: The grace given to us by Jesus "has now been revealed through the appearing of our Saviour, Christ Jesus, who has destroyed death and has brought life and immortality to light through the gospel". Not only did Jesus Christ, through his death, render death inoperative, he also substituted it with life. While the devil wields death as a weapon, Christ conquered it and offered life. Those who have trusted the Lord Jesus Christ have passed from death to real life (John 5:24). "I have come that they may have life and have it to the full" (John 10:10). This is the whole thrust of the Easter message: Jesus is alive. Death has been conquered, and now there is life!

3. *Through his death, Christ delivered believers from the fear of death.* Hebrews 2:15 explains that Christ's death was necessary not only to

[10] W. Robert Cook, *Systematic Theology in Outline Form* (Portland: Western Conservative Baptist Seminary, 1970), 726.

[11] Ray S. Anderson, *Theology, Death and Dying* (New York: Basil Blackwell, 1986), 85.

render death powerless, but also to "free those who all their lives were held in slavery by their fear of death". Reinecker and Rogers point out that *apallaso*, the Greek word translated "free", was used "for the release from a place of responsibility, e.g., marriage contract, the superintendence of land under lease, or the release from a municipal office".[12] The Lord Jesus Christ, through his death, has released believers from the burden of being slaves to the fear of death.

4. *Through his death, Christ judged death, and its destruction is now certain.* Paul states, "The last enemy to be destroyed is death" (1 Cor 15:26). Though death is still present as an effect of sin, it has been sentenced to destruction. The last book of the Bible announces the execution of this judgement: "Then death and Hades were thrown into the lake of fire" (Rev 20:14). It is God, not death, who has the last word.

New Testament descriptions of death

The New Testament pictures death in the following ways:

1. *A transition into the presence of Christ.* In Philippians 1:21–23 the Apostle Paul says confidently, "For to me, to live is Christ and to die is gain. ... I am torn between the two: I desire to depart and be with Christ, which is better by far." The word translated "depart" comes from the Greek *analusai*, which means "to undo". It was used of "loosening a ship from its moorings, of breaking camp, and of death".[13] The apostle looked upon death as loosening him so that he could be with Christ and in his presence.

The Apostle Peter had the same optimistic outlook. In 2 Peter 1:15 he spoke of his death as his "departure", using the same Greek word translated as "exodus", with all the hope that holds of moving on towards the promised land. He also spoke of his body as a tent that he would soon put aside (2 Pet 1:13–14). Paul too referred to the body as a "tent":

> For we know that if the earthly tent we live in is destroyed,
> we have a building from God, an eternal house in heaven, not
> built by human hands. Meanwhile we groan, longing to be
> clothed instead with our heavenly dwelling, because when we

---

[12] Fritz Reinecker and Cleon Rogers, *Linguistic Key to the Greek New Testament* (Grand Rapids: Zondervan, 1980), 670.

[13] Ibid., 547.

are clothed, we will not be found naked. For while we are in this tent, we groan and are burdened, because we do not wish to be unclothed but to be clothed instead with our heavenly dwelling, so that what is mortal may be swallowed up by life. (2 Cor 5:1–4)

It is significant that Peter and Paul did not view death as a bad or horrible thing to be feared or avoided, but as something that God would use to bring them into the glorious presence of their Lord and Saviour.

2. *A continuation of our relationship with the Lord Jesus Christ.* Paul in Romans 8:38–39 states categorically that not even death can separate the believer from the love of God. Since death does not alter the believer's position, there is absolutely no reason to fear or abhor death.

3. *A victory.* In 1 Corinthians 15:55–57 we read, "'Where O death, is your victory? Where O death, is your sting?' ... Thanks be to God! He gives us the victory through our Lord Jesus Christ." Death is not victorious over the believer; it is the believer who, through the Lord Jesus, is triumphant and sings the song of victory.

4. *"Falling asleep" and dying "in Christ"* (John 11:11; 1 Cor 15:18; 1 Thess 4:13, 16).

5. *A source of hope instead of a cause of dread.* While unbelievers are still under the bondage of the fear of death, believers have been delivered from this and can be hopeful even in death. Carl F. H. Henry writes,

> Authentic hope is possible only if one accepts death as part of the present human condition, faces the future with the assurance that physical death is not the end of individual being, and believes that one can and must in fact share even in a quality of spiritual life fit for eternity as the alternative to a terrible destiny.[14]

Because of what Christ has accomplished, the believer's perspective on death is radically transformed. However, as much as this is a profound theological truth, it has caused some to stumble. Some Christians feel that the manner and time of a believer's death should be different from

---

[14] Carl F. H. Henry, *God, Revelation and Authority* (vol. 4 of *God Who Speaks and Shows*, Waco: Word, 1979), 513.

those of an unbeliever. But we need to remember that while we need no longer fear spiritual death (we have been made alive through Jesus Christ – Eph 2:1–3), nor eternal death (we already have eternal life in Christ Jesus), we must still face physical death (Acts 7:60; Rom 8:38–39; 2 Cor 5:1–4; 1 Thess 4:13–17; 2 Pet 1:13–14). This is true even of great leaders: John the Baptist was beheaded while in prison (Matt 14:10). Stephen was stoned to death (Acts 7:55–56). James the brother of John was slain by a sword (Acts 12:2). Millard Erickson states,

> although the eternal consequences of our own individual sins are nullified when we are forgiven, the temporal consequences, or at least some of them, may linger on. ... [Death] is now a part of life, as much so as birth, growth and suffering, which ultimately also takes its origin from sin.[15]

Lloyd R. Bailey puts it slightly differently: "Death has been defeated, although temporarily it continues to manifest itself biologically."[16]

Dealing with death

When we face death ourselves, or see our loved ones die, we need to remember that life and death are in God's hand. He sets the time of death for everybody, young and old (Job 14:5; Heb 9:27). When and where is never revealed to us; it is always a mystery. Some deaths may appear to be premature, but that is only from our perspective. No death is premature as far as God is concerned.

In fact the very words "premature death" might be best avoided. They imply that God intended the person to live but was overpowered by the force of death. Yet God is omnipotent in all things, including death. He knows the exact number of days allotted to each of us, and when and how we will die. So we must not jump to the conclusion that the death of a young person is the result of some curse or witchcraft. What is important is not when the person died, but what they did with their life.

---

[15] Millard J. Erickson, *Introducing Christian Theology* (Grand Rapids: Baker Academic, 1992), 1179.

[16] Lloyd R. Bailey, *Biblical Perspectives on Death* (Philadelphia: Fortress, 1979), 89.

True, we deeply grieve the death of the young, but rather than looking for revenge, we should pray for comfort and focus on the life beyond.

Burial or cremation?

Around the world, the dead are disposed of in many ways. The ancient Egyptians used to embalm their noble dead before burial. Some throw corpses into the sea for the fish to devour. Zoroastrians place corpses in a Tower of Silence, where vultures and other flesh-eating birds dispose of them. Tibetan Buddhists may expose corpses to scavenger birds in what they call "giving alms to the birds". Others burn the corpse to ashes, an ancient method that has been practised throughout the world for centuries. Still others bury the corpse in the earth. This is probably the most common method, and the one generally preferred in Africa. A rare method is excarnation (defleshing), in which after the skin, muscles and organs have been stripped or rotted away, the bones are buried or stored elsewhere. This was practised in ancient Israel and by Native Americans.

Some people, before their deaths, arrange to donate useful organs like their kidneys, liver, heart and corneas to those who need transplants. Others donate their entire body to medical research. The remains are usually cremated after medical students have completed their work.

The method chosen is affected by religious, cultural, economic, sociological and ecological factors. For example, in some areas there is not enough land to bury the dead, which means that it is necessary to find alternative methods of disposing of corpses. Also, it is always cheaper to cremate than to bury a corpse.

But what does the Bible say? Are there theological issues surrounding how we deal with the dead?

Genesis 3:19 states that at death, as a consequence of the first sin of Adam and Eve, humanity will "return to the ground, since from it you were taken; for dust you are and to dust you will return". It is obvious that all the dead decompose, no matter how we dispose of them. Does that mean, then, that we are free to dispose of bodies in any way we please?

In both the Old and New Testaments, burial was the normal means of disposing of bodies. The dying Joseph explicitly commanded his descendants to "carry my bones up from this place" (Gen 50:25).

Moses later carried out his wishes and buried them in the promised land (Exod 13:19; Josh 24:32). John the Baptist was buried (Matt 14:12), as was Jesus (Matt 27:57–60; Mark 14:42–46; Luke 23:50–53; John 19:38–42). The Jewish authorities used the money that Judas received for betraying Jesus to purchase a place to bury foreigners (Matt 27:57). The early church also continued the practice of burying the dead (Acts 5:6–10; 8:2) and Paul's teaching on the resurrection of the dead uses images closely linked to the idea of burial (Rom 6; 1 Cor 15).

Not receiving a proper burial was considered a matter of great shame (Isa 14:18–20; Jer 16:14). Thus it was a sign of respect when some Israelites retrieved the bodies of King Saul and his son Jonathan from the Philistines and gave them proper burial (1 Sam 31:10–13; 2 Sam 21:13–14). The passage also notes that the bodies of Saul and Jonathan were burnt before their bones were buried. Though this implies cremation of some sort, it should be noted that the bones were not burnt to ashes, unlike cremation as it is carried out today.

2 Kings 23 presents a scene in which the burning of bones is clearly intended as an insult to the deceased. As part of his religious reformation to cleanse Israel of all idol worship, King Josiah removed human bones from the tombs in areas associated with idol worship and had them "burned on the [pagan] altar to defile it" (2 Kgs 23:15–16). But this incident is not really an example of cremation as usually practised.

However, although burial is the norm in the Bible, it is never explicitly commanded. And Paul's use of a burial as a metaphor when talking of resurrection does not mean that those whose bodies have been cremated will not also be resurrected. They will receive new bodies, just like those whose bodies have decomposed, or who have been drowned, eaten by animals or burned in fires. This also means that there is no scriptural reason for refusing to donate organs or to accept donated organs.

The critical issue around death is not the method of burial but the spiritual condition of the deceased. If the deceased person was a believer at death, that person is eternally saved and goes into the presence of the Lord, regardless of how his or her body is disposed of. If, on the other hand, the deceased was an unbeliever, he or she is eternally lost.

Funerals

Even though the body will return to dust, it is still a body that was created by God. It should therefore be treated with respect, whatever method of disposal is used. The decision about what should be done is the prerogative of the deceased and his or her family. Their wishes should be respected.

Some churches have gone so far as to discourage or even ban funeral and memorial services. They argue that these ceremonies can impose a heavy financial burden on the bereaved family, who have to purchase an expensive coffin and provide abundant food for mourners for days. More importantly, they argue that the rituals that go along with funeral ceremonies sometimes reflect traditional cultural and religious beliefs that are contrary to the teaching of Scripture. For example, mourners may call on the spirit of the deceased or make offerings to the ancestral spirits. Such practices are forbidden in Scripture (Deut 18:11; 1 Sam 28:7–20; 1 Chr 10:13). Moreover, in the case of accidental or so-called premature death, a widow may be forced to undergo harmful rituals, such as being made to drink the water used to bathe the corpse of her deceased husband.

However, banning funeral rites is perhaps not the best way to handle these problems. Funeral ceremonies are important for bringing closure to grieving families. A better approach would be to Christianize the rituals, replacing the old ceremonies with clear Bible teaching on death, dying and salvation. This has been done successfully with other anti-biblical practices. For example, drums, flutes and other musical instruments used in traditional worship of ancestral spirits are now frequently used in Christian worship.

The Intermediate State

Though we believe that life continues for the dead, there is less certainly about the nature of their existence between the day they die and the day of resurrection. This period is often referred to as "the intermediate state". The Bible does not give much information on this, but we do have sufficient information to distinguish what happens to unbelievers and believers.

- *The unbelieving dead.* The Bible is clear that, at death, the unbelieving go to a place of torment. In the story of Lazarus and the rich man, we are told that after his death, the rich man went to a place of mental anguish (Luke 16:23). Only those who are conscious are capable of experiencing such torment. This place is not called hell; it is nevertheless a place that is separated from God. Though the unbelieving may wish to reverse their state and even warn their relatives on earth, this desire is not granted by God. It is clearly a place of punishment for unbelievers (Heb 9:27). It is not purgatorial: it is not a place where sinners are purified before going to heaven.

- *The believing dead.* Those who believe in the Lord go, at death, straight into the presence of the Lord and enjoy bliss with him there, as illustrated by the story of Lazarus in Luke 16 (see also Luke 23:43; 2 Cor 5:1–8). There they enjoy rest (Eccl 12:7; Heb 12:23; Rev 6:9–11; 14:13). This state is preferable to being alive in the body on earth (Phil 1:23). The believing dead remain in this state until the second coming of Jesus, when they will reign with him for ever and ever.

Soul sleep

There are some who hold that on death the soul goes into a state of unconsciousness or sleep. Several passages are cited in support of this view:

- Matthew 9:24 states that Jesus told the people in the noisy crowd to go away, saying, "The girl is not dead but asleep." According to the proponents of soul sleep, Jesus was teaching that death is equivalent to falling asleep.

- In John 11:11 we read, "Our friend Lazarus has fallen asleep; but I am going there to wake him up." Because the disciples did not understand him clearly, Jesus went on to explain to them that "Lazarus is dead" (11:14).

- A Pauline perspective is given in 1 Thessalonians 4:13: "Brothers and sisters, we do not want you to be uninformed about those who sleep in death, so that you do not grieve like the rest of mankind, who have no hope." It is argued that Paul, like Jesus, also taught that death was the same as sleeping.

- Stephen's death is also described as sleep: "When he had said this, he fell asleep" (Acts 7:60). Other relevant passages include Psalm 146:4,

Ecclesiastes 9:5–6, 10; Isaiah 38:18; Acts 13:36; 1 Corinthians 15:6, 18, 20, 51.

Seventh-Day Adventists, who hold this position, explain their scriptural justification as follows:

> (1) Those who fall asleep are unconscious. "The dead know nothing" (Eccl. 9:5). (2) In sleep conscious thinking ceases: "His breath goeth forth ... in that very day his thoughts perish," (Ps. 146:4, KJV). (3) Sleep brings an end to all the day's activities. "There is no work or device or knowledge or wisdom in the grave where you are going" (Eccl. 9:10). (4) Sleep disassociates us from those who are awake, and from their activities: "Nevermore will they have a share in anything done under the sun" (Eccl. 9:6). (5) Normal sleep renders the emotions inactive: "their love, their hatred, and their envy have now perished" (Ps. 115:17). (6) In sleep men do not praise God. "The dead do not praise the Lord" (Ps. 115:17). (7) Sleep presupposes an awakening: "The hour is coming in which all who are in the graves will hear His voice and come forth" (John 5:28, 29).[17]

At first glance, this argument may seem convincing. But we must always be cautious about building a doctrine on selected passages; we must always look at the entire teaching of Scripture on a particular subject.

For example, one of the key principles of soul sleep is that a human is basically an indivisible unit, not made up of a separate body, soul and spirit. When a person dies, the entire person thus ceases to exist.

> Body and soul only exist together; they form an indivisible union. ... At death ... the dust of the ground minus the breath of life yields a dead person or dead soul without any consciousness (Ps 146:4). The elements that make up the body return to the earth from which they came (Gen 3:19).
>
> The soul has no conscious existence apart from the body, and no Scripture indicates that at death the soul survives as a conscious entity. Indeed, "the soul who sins shall die" (Eze 18:20).[18]

---

[17] *Seventh-day Adventists Believe ... A Biblical Exposition of 27 Fundamental Doctrines* (Washington DC: All-Africa Publications, 1988), 352.

[18] Ibid.

Yes, it is true that the body returns to dust, but the Scriptures are abundantly clear that there is a definite consciousness after death. If there were no consciousness between death and the resurrection, why did Christ talk to the dying thief on the cross about entering paradise that day (Luke 23:42–43)? The thief clearly knew that life was going to continue right after his physical death, and Jesus affirmed that. There was no indication that he was going to enter a prolonged sleep until the resurrection.

In Jesus' parable about the rich man and Lazarus, both are presented after death as conscious human beings who can express their emotions (Luke 16:19–31). Jesus also talked with both Moses and Elijah on the Mount of Transfiguration (Matt 17:3). This was not the final resurrection for these saints, yet they were obviously conscious. Stephen, when faced with death, said, "Lord Jesus, receive my spirit" (Acts 7:59).

The biblical passages on death, though using imagery of sleep, clearly present the dead as having conscious existence. Though they do not yet have resurrected bodies, they must have some bodily form so that they can express the emotions and sensibilities of being fully human

Purgatory

The Roman Catholic and Greek Orthodox Churches believe that only believers who have attained perfection go straight to heaven after death. All other believers go to purgatory, where they are punished for their sins in order to be purified and cleansed before being ushered into heaven. The severity and length of time spent in purgatory depends on the nature of the sins committed while on earth; the time could range from hours to many years in great torment. In addition, "Gifts or services rendered to the Church, prayers by priests and Masses provided by relatives or friends in behalf of the deceased can shorten, alleviate or eliminate the sojourn of the soul in purgatory."[19]

The following texts are used to support this belief:

* *1 Corinthians 3:12–15*. This passage includes these words: "and the fire will test the quality of each person's work. If what has been built survives, the builder will receive a reward. If it is burned up, the builder will suffer loss but yet will be saved – even though only as

---

[19] Loraine Boettner, "Purgatory", in *Evangelical Dictionary of Theology* (ed. Walter A. Elwell; Grand Rapids: Baker, 1984), 897.

one escaping through the flames" (1 Cor 3:13b–15). However, in context these verses are talking about receiving or losing rewards for work done on earth. A temporary stay between hell and heaven is not at issue. The Scriptures explicitly teach that at death all those who have received the gift of God through Christ will go straight to heaven, without receiving temporal punishment to cleanse them of their sins (Luke 23:43; John 3:16, 18; Rom 5:1; 8:1, 33–39).

- *2 Maccabees 12:39–45.* This apocryphal book mentions that after a battle the leader "had this atonement sacrifice offered for the dead, so that they might be released from their sin" (12:44–45). Evangelicals do not believe that the apocryphal books are inspired (see chapter 2). They believe that these books contradict the Bible's teaching on salvation by grace through faith in Jesus Christ. It is a legalistic mentality that holds that salvation is attained by works.

Thus the concept of purgatory has no scriptural justification but is based on legalistic perspectives, speculative philosophy and non-canonical texts. It is legalistic in that it implies that there are some believers who have attained perfection while others need to go through purgatory to be cleansed of their sins. But the Bible teaches that we are all sinners, and that we are all saved in the same way, that is, only by grace through faith (Eph 2:9–10). The Scriptures make it abundantly clear that, after death, unbelievers go to a place of suffering, and believers go straight into the presence of God.

Annihilationism

Annihilationism holds that the unsaved cease to have any conscious existence at the point of death. The unbeliever, according to this view, simply goes out of existence or is deleted from conscious existence forever. The fact that Scripture uses terms such as "perish," "destruction" and "death" in describing their fate is used to support this position (John 3:16; 8:51; Rom 9:22; 3 Pet 3:8). But the Scriptures make it clear that the unsaved or wicked will continue to exist forever (Eccl 12:7; Matt 25:46; Rom 2:5–10; Rev 14:11). Moreover, the fact that all must appear before God for judgement indicates that the unsaved live on after physical death (Dan 12:3; Acts 24:15; Rev 2:11; 20:14; 15; 21:8). Life does not come to an end at death but continues forever.

A second chance

While purgatory is presented as awaiting imperfect Christians, the doctrine of the second chance deals with the afterlife of unbelievers. It teaches that they will be given a second opportunity to hear the gospel and respond. Support for this view is derived from those texts which teach that God loves everybody, does not want anybody to be lost, and has extended his invitation to all (Matt 12:32; John 3:16, 18, 36; 1 Pet 3:19, 46).

Those who hold to this doctrine argue that it would not be fair of God to send to hell people who did not have an opportunity to respond to the call to salvation in Christ. It is reasonable, therefore, that these people be given another chance, even after death, to respond to the gospel. Clark Pinnock, who supports this view, writes,

> God does not cease to be gracious to sinners just because they are no longer living. The God that sinners meet after death remains the same one who sent his Son to die for the sins of the world. Jesus, who was the friend of sinners, has not suddenly become their enemy after death. God has not abruptly ceased to desire that salvation of sinners, or that they come to a knowledge of the truth.[20]

Though these arguments are appealing, they are not persuasive when stacked against the complete witness of Scripture. Hebrews 9:27 says, "people are destined to die once, and after that to face judgement." To return to the story of the rich man and Lazarus, the rich man begged for a second chance to go back to earth and do things right, but his request was denied (Luke 16). The biblical evidence is clear: men and women have the chance to respond to the gospel only while they are alive; after death, their destiny is fixed by the choice they made while they lived.

---

[20] Clark H. Pinnock, *A Wideness in God's Mercy: the Finality of Jesus Christ in a World of Religions* (Grand Rapids: Zondervan, 1992), 170. He continues, "Scripture does not require us to hold that the window of opportunity is slammed shut at death. The fate of some may be sealed at death; those, for example, who heard the gospel and declined the offer of salvation. But the fate of others is not sealed; babies, for example, who die in infancy. No one holds that death is the end of opportunity for them" (171).

The Second Coming of Christ

The second coming of Jesus Christ – his return to this earth – will be the most spectacular global event of all time. Unlike his first coming, which was local to Israel and the early church, the second coming will be universal and earth-shaking. It will be noticed by everybody and everything. Nothing will be left untouched by it.

The nature of his second coming

Although there is much that we do not know about the second coming, there are five things we can be certain of.

1. *It will be personal.* In Acts 1:11 the disciples were told, "This same Jesus, who has been taken from you into heaven, will come back in the same way you have seen him go into heaven." Jesus will return as the God-man – in his real body, not just as a spirit. The Apostle John confirms this: "we shall see him as he is" (1 John 3:2).

2. *It will be unexpected.* The language used to talk of the second coming – "a thief in the night" (1 Thess 5:2); "the Son of Man will come at an hour when you do not expect him" (Matt 24:44) – shows that Christ's coming will be unexpected and will catch many unprepared. Though signs of his coming are described, no fixed date of his return is given. Many theologians and Bible students have attempted to work out the date, but this is mere guesswork with no theological justification whatsoever. Even Jesus himself claimed ignorance about the exact date or hour of his coming (Mark 13:32). Because of the unexpected nature of his return, Christians are urged to watch and pray.

3. *It will be glorious and triumphant.* Christ will come "with power and great glory" (Matt 24:30). Though his first coming was in obscure and humble circumstances, his second coming will be marked with signs in the skies (Dan 7:13; Matt 24:30; Rev 1:7). No king or monarch in the history of humankind will have been part of such a glorious event.

4. *It will be visible.* Just as Christ's departure was visible to the disciples, so his second coming will be visible (Matt 24:30; Acts 1:11).

5. *It will be the consummation of history.* At Christ's second coming, "the end will come" (1 Cor 15:24). It will mark the end of history and the beginning of another era in which God will be acknowledged as the ultimate and final ruler.

The purpose of his second coming

Why will Christ come again? Once again, we can list five reasons:

1. *To make salvation complete.* Though Christ has already provided salvation, the full benefits of that redemption will only be realized when he returns. In this world, we are faced with trials and temptations, pain, sickness and death, poverty, oppression and the like. When Christ comes, he will free his people from these things (1 Cor 15:22–28, 42–57).

2. *To bring the devil and all demonic activity to an end.* The devil is currently active in opposing the work of God, but when Christ comes, he will bring this to an end.

3. *To raise the dead.* Some will rise to be with God; others will be sent to eternal condemnation (John 5:28).

4. *To judge the world* (2 Tim 4:1). All will be judged at Christ's second coming.

5. *To claim his bride, the church* (Matt 25:1–13; Rev 19:7–8). Christ will deliver the church from the enemy and give it a permanent dwelling place with himself.

Events, groups and personalities involved

Israel

No matter how we read the Scriptures, the nation of Israel features significantly in the events of the second coming. What role will Israel play?

A literal approach to interpreting the Scriptures suggests that the prophecies concerning Israel will be fulfilled in literal terms. So, just as the Old Testament prophets prophesied that Israel would be returned to the promised land, and that happened exactly as prophesied, so Israel will literally fulfil all the remaining prophecies concerning it. Though the New Testament church is called the Israel of God, the nation of Israel still has a part to play in God's future plans.

The church

A main reason for Christ's coming is to take his bride, the church, to be with himself. All those who are in Christ will be raised to meet him in the air. They will then reign with him during the millennial kingdom (see below).

The Antichrist

Opposition to God by evil beings is a common theme in both Old and New Testaments. Those who deny Jesus Christ and the Father are called antichrists (1 John 2:18, 22; 4:3), as are false teachers. In the time between the foundation of the early church and the second coming of Christ, "there were to be many antichrists, many manifestations of malignant opposition to the person and to the work of Christ, many attempts to cast off His authority and to overthrow His Kingdom".[21] The Apostle John writes, "Many deceivers, who do not acknowledge Jesus Christ as coming in the flesh, have gone out into the world. Any such person is the deceiver and the antichrist" (2 John 1:7). Jesus himself said, "For false messiahs and false prophets will appear and perform great signs and wonders to deceive, if possible, even the elect" (Matt 24:24; see also 1 Tim 4:1).

During the end times, however, one specific Antichrist will play a prominent role. What do the Scriptures say about him?

- The Antichrist is first mentioned in Daniel 7, in which the beast with the little horn is described as abolishing the burning of offerings in the temple and erecting his own "abomination of desolation" there (Dan 11:31; Matt 24:15; Mark 13:14; Rev 13:14–15).

- The apocalyptic beast that emerges from the sea in Revelation 13 has strong similarities to the beast with the little horn mentioned in Daniel 7:8 and 8:9 He is identified as a world power opposed to God (Dan 9:27; Rev 17:11).

- He will exalt himself to the position of deity (Dan 11:3–39; 2 Thess 2:3–4). He will claim to be the Christ, performing wonders which will deceive many (2 Thess 2:9–10). Just as Christ performed miracles through the power of God, so this Antichrist will perform miracles through the power of Satan (Matt 12:24–29).

---

[21] Charles Hodge, *Systematic Theology* (abridged; ed. Edward N. Gross; New Jersey: Presbyterian & Reformed, 1982), 529.

- He is not divine but is a human being with supernatural abilities who will play a crucial role in deceiving the nations and in the battle at the end times.

- He is described as "the man of lawlessness" (or "man of sin") and the "lawless one" (2 Thess 2:3, 8–9; compare Dan 7:25).

- He is also described as the man "doomed to destruction" (2 Thess 2:3; compare John 17:12). This indicates that he will be destroyed by the power of Christ (2 Thess 2:8; Rev 19:15, 20; compare Isa 11:4). His end will be in the lake of fire, along with Satan and God's enemies.

The Tribulation

"Tribulation" is a word that refers to the suffering of God's people. In the Old Testament it refers to "inner turmoil (Pss 25:17; 120:1; Job 7:11), the pain of childbirth (Jer 4:31; 49:24), anguish (Job 15:24; Jer 6:24) and punishment (1 Sam 2:32; Jer 6:24)".[22] The tribulation of Israel as a nation is conveyed in Deuteronomy 4:30 and Psalm 37:39.

In the New Testament, tribulation is understood as being "the experience of all believers and includes persecution (1 Thess 1:6), imprisonment (Acts 20:23), derision (Heb 10:33), poverty (2 Cor 11:13), sickness (Rev 2:22), and inner distress and sorrow (Phil 1:17; 2 Cor 2:4)".[23]

However, the Scriptures also refer to a future period of "great tribulation" or "great distress" (Matt 24:21; Luke 21:23; Rev 2:22; 7:14), which will be unlike any other tribulation that has been experienced. On the basis of the "sevens" in Daniel 9:24–27 (which some translations call "weeks" – NASB, ESV, HCSB), many argue that this period will last seven years. The references in the book of Revelation to "a time, times and half a time" (Rev 12:14) are taken to refer to the final three and a half years of this period, which will be filled with even more intense tribulation. This interpretation of the "times" is supported by Revelation 11:2 and 13:5, which refer to a period of "forty-two months", and Revelation 12:6–7, which refers to 1,260 days. Both periods work out to three and a half years.

---

[22] W. H. Baker, "Tribulation", in *Evangelical Dictionary of Theology* (ed. Walter A. Elwell; Grand Rapids: Baker, 1984), 1110.

[23] Ibid.

Daniel 9:27 prophesied the desecration of the temple by one who is probably to be identified as the "man of lawlessness" in 2 Thessalonians 2:3–4. Matthew 24:15 also mentions the period of the "abomination that causes desolation" in the chapter in which Jesus specifically discusses the intensity of the tribulation and its effects on all the inhabitants of the earth. He specifically links this tribulation to the second coming of Christ: "Immediately after the distress [tribulation] of those days ... will appear the sign of the Son of Man in heaven. And then all the peoples of the earth will mourn when they see the Son of Man coming on the clouds of heaven, with power and great glory" (Matt 24:29–30).

The timing of the great tribulation is according to God's programme. Who will experience it is the subject of serious debate. The theological positions Christians take concerning the timing of the rapture of the church are determined by their theology of the great tribulation.

The purpose of the tribulation is to bring about the conversion of Israel to God through God's disciplining of his own people (Jer 30:7; Ezek 20:37; Dan 12:1; Zech 13:8-9). The tribulation also represents the outpouring of God's wrath and judgement upon evil and unbelieving peoples and nations (Isa 26:21; Jer 25:32-33; 2 Thess 2:12).

The Resurrection of the Dead

The resurrection of the dead is one of the cardinal beliefs of Christianity. Both Old and New Testaments speak of the dead being raised to life, either to face judgement and enter an eternal rest with God in heaven or to be sent to a place of punishment and torment.

In the Old Testament, David spoke of waking up in the presence of God (Ps 17:15). Korah expressed a similar hope of being rescued from the power of death (Ps 49:15). Other passages which speak about the hope of the resurrection of the dead include Psalm 73:24–25 and Isaiah 2:19. Daniel 12:1–2 explicitly connects the resurrection with the judgement and reward of the dead.

In the New Testament, the Gospels speak of the power of God to raise the dead to life (Matt 22:29; Mark 12:24–27; Luke 20:34–38). John 5:28–29 echoes the fact that the dead will hear the voice of Christ and be raised to life – some to eternal life, others to judgement (compare Dan 12:2). Other relevant passages are John 6:39–40, 44, 54; 11:25–26. In 1 Corinthians 15:17 Paul presents the resurrection of the dead as foundational to the Christian faith (see also Acts 2:31; 4:2, 33; 17:18; 2 Tim 2:18; Rev 20:4–5).

The Rapture of the Church

The main text that teaches the rapture of the church is 1 Thessalonians 4:15–17, which states,

> According to the Lord's word, we tell you that we who are still alive, who are left until the coming of the Lord, will certainly not precede those who have fallen asleep. For the Lord himself will come down from heaven, with a loud command, with the voice of the archangel and with the trumpet call of God, and the dead in Christ will rise first. After that, we who are still alive and are left will be caught up together with them in the clouds to meet the Lord in the air. And so we will be with the Lord for ever.

The question is, when will the church or believers be "caught up" (the root meaning of the world "rapture") to meet the Lord in the air? Christians hold different views on this, ranging from pre-tribulation rapture to mid-tribulation rapture, post-tribulation rapture and partial tribulation rapture.[24]

Pre-tribulation rapture

Some believe that Christ's second coming is imminent, that it will occur before the tribulation, and that the rapture of the church will take place at that time. In this view, the great tribulation is understood as being unique, unlike any other suffering the world has seen before. Christ will come before it begins and will take the church to be with him (1 Thess 4:17). Thus the purpose of the rapture is to deliver the church from the tribulation, which is understood as God's wrath poured out on the earth (1 Thess 5:9–10). The rapture is held to be secret in the sense that Christ comes only for the church. In other words, nobody else will notice this event, and God's other people, the nation of Israel, will continue to exist throughout the tribulation.

---

[24] For a thorough presentation and critique of the three major views, I strongly recommend *Three Views on the Rapture: Pre-, Mid-, or Post-Tribulation* (ed. Stanley N. Gundry; Grand Rapids: Zondervan, 1996). The three views are exegetically and theologically argued by three prominent biblical and theological scholars, namely Gleason Archer (mid-tribulation), Paul D. Feinberg (pre-tribulation) and Douglas Moo (post-tribulation).

The main scriptural support for this position is Revelation 3:10: "Since you have kept my command to endure patiently, I will also keep you from the hour of trial that is going to come on the whole world to test the inhabitants of the earth."

Mid-tribulation rapture

Some argue that the second coming will take place in the middle of general tribulation, just before the great tribulation which will affect the entire earth and all its inhabitants. The wrath of God will be poured out only upon the world and not upon the church (Rev 16–18). However, the church will have to endure the tyrannical rule of the Antichrist for three and a half years (Dan 9:27).

Passages used to support this position are Revelation 12:14 and the Olivet Discourse (Matt 24; Mark 13; Luke 12). The view argues against a secret rapture as posited by the pre-tribulationists since, according to Matthew 24:10–27, Christ's coming will be accompanied by a great shout and a trumpet blast (2 Thess 4:16; Rev 11:15; 14:2; 7:9, 14).

Post-tribulation rapture

Others argue that the church and God's people have always experienced tribulation and that all believers will go through the great tribulation, although they will not experience the wrath of God. There will be no secret rapture (see above); instead Christ will rapture his saints and establish his millennial rule at the same time.

The Scripture used to support this view is Matthew 24:27–29, which teaches that Christ's return will be public and will follow the tribulation.

Partial tribulation rapture

Some (like the writers of the *Left Behind* novels) hold that faithful believers will be raptured at the beginning of the tribulation. Thus believers who have been faithful and have been watching for the day of the Lord will escape the tribulation, but nominal Christians and those who have been unfaithful will have to endure it. The partial rapture position also holds that other believers will be taken from time to time when they are ready for the Lord. In this view the rapture will happen more than once. Passages used to support this view include Luke 21:36 ("Be always on the watch, and pray that you may be able to escape all that is about to happen, and that you may be able to stand before the

Son of Man") and Matthew 24:40 ("Then two men will be in the field; one will be taken and the other left"). Matthew 25:31-46 and Hebrews 9:28 are also used to support the partial rapture position.

The seven-year tribulation period refers to what the Bible describes as a period of intense suffering unlike anything the world has ever seen. This suffering is still in the future. This period is generally agreed to be seven years (Dan 9:24–27; 12:7; Rev 11:1–2; 12:6, 14; 13:5) with its second half of three and a half years being filled with more intense tribulation.

Conclusion

Holders of all four of these views appeal to Scripture to justify their positions. The view that Christians take depends on their interpretation of the Scriptures. For example, a dispensational approach, which sees a radical distinction between Israel in the Old Testament and the church in the New Testament, will most likely end up with a pre-tribulation position if it is to be able to explain how Israel continues to exist while the church is absent during the end times.

From a normal reading of Scripture it seems most likely that the church will go through the tribulation, though it will be protected (post-tribulationism). After all, throughout church history, Christians have gone through many trials and tribulations, and in some instances, intense persecution. However, this does not mean that the other views are to be rejected as unbiblical and a reason for schism in the church of Jesus Christ. The proponents of all views work hard to interpret the Scriptures properly, which may indicate that no single position has the whole answer. As brothers and sisters, differences of opinion should not divide us; rather, they should motivate us to appreciate the diversity within the church of Jesus Christ.

The Millennial Kingdom

Revelation 20:2–3 states, "He seized the dragon, that ancient serpent, who is the devil, or Satan, and bound him for a thousand years. He threw him into the Abyss, and locked and sealed it over him, to keep him from deceiving the nations any more until the thousand years were ended. After that, he must be set free for a short time." This period of a thousand years – the millennium – has attracted a lot of attention and has led to the following different theological positions.

Premillennialism

Those who hold to a premillennial position expect that after a period of unique and intense suffering (the great tribulation), Christ will return to earth, bodily and personally, to establish his kingdom on earth. He will rule with the saints from Jerusalem for a literal period of one thousand years. This millennial rule will precede the judgement and the eternal state.

This view is based on a literal reading of Revelation 20:1–4. Proponents also appeal to 1 Corinthians 15:23–28 where Christ is depicted as handing the kingdom of God to the Father after destroying all rule, authority and power. They also take literally the many Old Testament prophets who speak about the restoration of the glory of Israel, in which Jerusalem will become the centre of power characterized by peace and prosperity (Ps 48:2; Isa 2:3; 26:1–4; Zech 2:4, 23). Other Old Testament prophesies that contribute to the premillenial understanding of Israel's future include the promise of land to Abraham's descendents (Gen 15:18–21); the restoration of this land to Israel and the forgiveness of their sins (Isa 49:8; Ezek 36:27–38; 37:14; Amos 9:11–15); a massive ingathering of the Jewish people (Zech 10:6; 13:9; Rev 9–11); and the Messiah's rule on earth, as promised to King David (2 Sam 7:12–16). The millennial kingdom is the only means of fulfilling this promise of theocratic, messianic rule (Dan 7:14; Rev 19:15–16; 20:1–6).

Premillenialism is characteristic of the dispensationalist approach, which sees a basic distinction between the church and Israel in the present age and right up to the end times. Classical premillennialists see the church going through the tribulation, but dispensational premillennialists believe that the church will be taken away (raptured) before the beginning of the millennial kingdom.

Within the early church, Justin Martyr, Irenaeus, Methodius, Tertullian and Montanus were premillennialists. The best-known dispensationalist is probably John Nelson Darby of the Plymouth Brethren in the nineteenth century. Others include R. A. Torrey, D. L. Moody and C. I. Scofield, the last of whom popularized this position through his Scofield Reference Bible. More recent advocates of dispensationalism include John Walvoord, Charles Ryrie, Hal Lindsey, J. Dwight Pentecost, Lewis S. Chafer, Arno Gaebelein and Rene Pache.

Classical dispensationalism has also been promoted by George Eldon Ladd, Oscar Cullmann, Hans Bietenhard and G. R. Beasley-Murray.

This view has the strength that it takes biblical prophecies seriously and does not spiritualize those that concern the future. It believes that God's promises to Israel will be fulfilled literally in the same way that prophecies about Christ's first coming were fulfilled. They would, for example, point to the fact that God promised that Israel would be brought back as a nation to its original land, and that this actually happened in 1948. This view also takes seriously the minute details about future events and looks forward to the imminent return of Christ, which is a strong theme in the biblical teaching concerning the second coming of Christ.

However, premillennialism does tend to exaggerate distinctions in order to fit everything into its scheme of things. For example, dispensationalism originally insisted that God has two programmes (or purposes), one for Israel and one for the church. Some adherents even understood this to mean that God has two ways of salvation, one for Israel and one for the church. The original Scofield Reference Bible seems to endorse this radical distinction, but progressive dispensationalists have denied this view as unsupported by Scripture.

Premillenialists have also been accused of being pessimistic about the future, which can lead to a lack of concern about addressing present problems. They see the world as only getting worse and never better, and predict that people will become more wicked and more evil, nations will continue to rise up against nations, and devil worship and demonic activity will increase.

A common allegation against premillennialism is that it relies only on Revelation 20. However, as demonstrated above, this is not the case.

Amillennialism

Those who hold to the amillennial position believe that Revelation 20:4–6 is to be interpreted symbolically. The "thousand years" does not mean a literal thousand-year rule of Christ but refers to the reign of Christ in the present age, during which Satan is bound. The "kingdom of God is now present in the world as the victorious Christ rules his people by the Word and Spirit".[25] Thus this view does not deny that

---

[25] Donald G. Bloesch, *Essentials of Evangelical Theology* (Peabody: Prince Press, 2001), 191.

there is any millennium, but believes that it is fulfilled entirely in this present, church age. They also claim that the tribulation and the great tribulation are a reality which Christians experience now; there will not be a specific great tribulation in the future. God's eternal kingdom will be inaugurated immediately at the consummation of this present age.

Unlike dispensationalists, amillennialists believe that the second coming, the resurrection, the last judgement and the end of the world will all happen at about the same time, as a single event. Amillennialism is in agreement with postmillennialism in this regard.

Notable proponents of this view in the early church were Origen and Augustine. More recently, support has come from Louis Berkhof, G. C. Berkouwer, Emil Brunner, George L. Murray, Anthony Hoekema and Leon Morris.

The strength of this view is that it reminds us that the binding of Satan in the Gospels (Matt 12:22–28) is related to the binding of Satan in Revelation 20. It also maintains a biblical balance in its view of the kingdom of God. Within the premillennial scheme "the kingdom" is often given a political or nationalistic emphasis. Moreover, with its simple and straightforward focus, amillennialism is not as complex and involved as premillennialism. It is thus easy to understand.

However, amillennialism tends to over-spiritualize the kingdom of God, ignoring its physical or literal aspects. Details regarding the imminent return of Christ, judgement and the Antichrist are thus ignored or forced into the mould of spiritual concept of the kingdom of God. But the true kingdom of God, as described in the New Testament, also involves this material, physical world. In its desire to be simple and straightforward, amillennialism lacks thoroughness in dealing with details regarding the great tribulation, the rapture, and the literal future of Israel.

The strength of amillenialism lies in its negation of the overly literal premillennial position regarding issues such as the literal thousand-year rule of Christ on earth, the rapture and the judgements. However, beyond that it has very little to say regarding future events. It also reduces or minimizes expectancy of the return of Christ because it emphasizes his kingdom in the present more than the second coming.

The main problem with amillennialism is that it fails to deal honestly with the biblical passages that teach a literal period of Christ's rule on earth. It is very hard to interpret all of Revelation in symbolic terms, robbing it of any literal fulfilment. The inherent weaknesses of the amillennial system are also evident in postmillennialism.

Postmillennialism

Postmillennialists maintain that there will not be a literal thousand-year rule of Christ. Instead, they say, the preaching of Christ will bring many to conversion. The rule of Christ in the hearts of regenerate men and women will be complete and universal (Ezek 36:27–38; Matt 24:14) and will result in total peace and righteousness on earth, leading to a better society (the golden age). Christ will return once the gospel has been fully presented to all and human hearts have returned to God. The following passages are quoted in support of this view: Psalms 47, 72, 100; Isaiah 45:22–25; and Hosea 2:23.

Some of the more prominent proponents of this view include Philip Spener, John Owen, Jonathan Edwards, John and Charles Wesley, Samuel Rutherford, Charles Hodge, B. B. Warfield, A. H. Strong, James Orr and Greg L. Bahnsen.

The strength of this position is that it recognizes the link between the binding of Satan in the New Testament and the work of mission. It also provides great motivation for evangelizing the nations and is very optimistic about evangelistic ventures.

However, the idea of a golden age of mass conversion is not supported by the New Testament. It is not surprising that postmillennialism was particularly popular before the First World War, as this was a period of great technological and industrial development and optimism. Many Christians thought that if more people were converted, things would become better and better and that this would promote the kingdom of God and the return of Christ. However, the destructive effects of the First World War (and later the Second World War and the subsequent threat of nuclear war) indicated that this optimistic perception was in error. Although Christ does indeed change human hearts, and this should be evidenced in people's lifestyles and therefore in society, the Bible demonstrates that human hearts are not completely cleansed of the tendency to do evil.

The socio-economic and political realities of our world today, even among so-called Christian nations or communities, indicate that postmillennialism is built on false foundations and shaky theology.

Scripture teaches not only a spiritual transformation of the human heart, but also a literal kingdom of God in Christ for a definite and literal period in human history.

Summary

In my opinion, the premillennial position, though not perfect, best fits the Bible's teaching. The strongest case for premillennialism is that it attempts to deal with all aspects of God's kingdom on earth and the prophecies made to Israel and the church. Though the church is the new Israel, it has not taken over the promises that were made specifically to Israel. Kingdom promises to Israel are not inconsistent with promises made to the church.

That said, as with the rapture, all millennial positions should be respected because their proponents have studied the Scriptures and put forward the views that best fit their understanding. It is important that differences of opinion on these matters do not undermine fellowship. Our differences of opinion should motivate us to study the Scriptures more and to respect each other's positions.

Judgement

Judgement is a critical aspect of the end of history. All forms of evil actions by evil people, Satan, evil angels, all nations, the Gentiles, and all Israel will be judged (Isa 13:9; Joel 3:2; Amos 1:2; 9:1–4; Mal 3:2–5). There will also be a judgement of believers, not in terms of condemnation but in terms of whether they will be rewarded for what they have done on earth. Judgement is in fact a prominent theme in the New Testament. Jesus taught about the judgement, which will result in the separation of the righteous from the wicked (e.g. Matt 13:41–43; 47–50; 25:31–46). Present human actions and decisions will be judged. Paul wrote about many aspects of the last judgement (Rom 2:1; 14:10; 1 Cor 6:2–3; 15:22–25; 2 Cor 5:10; 2 Tim 4:1). Jude and 2 Peter give powerful symbols of the judgement (2 Pet 3:3–7, 11–13; Jude 3–4). Above all, Revelation provides a graphic depiction of the final judgement.

From these Scriptures we learn the following:

1. *Christ is the judge* (Matt 25:31–33). Though God is spoken of as the ultimate Judge, he has handed this work over to the Son (John 5:22, 27; Acts 10:42). Believers are also included among those who will judge the

world (1 Cor 6:2–3; Rev 3:21; 20:4). We have a foretaste of this when believers are called upon to deal with moral issues and other disputes in the church (1 Cor 5:1–13). However, this position is not to be abused and used as an excuse to lord it over others (2 Cor 1:24; 1 Pet 5:3).

2. *The basis of judgement* will be what people have done while on earth (2 Cor 5:10). Those who reject Jesus Christ will be judged according to that decision.

The judgement of believers

Paul writes in 2 Corinthians 5:10 that "we must all appear before the judgement seat of Christ, so that each of us may receive what is due to us for the things done while in the body, whether good or bad." This judgement will take place when Christ returns (1 Cor 4:5). It will not determine whether we will enter heaven or not, but whether the works we have done in the body deserve rewards or not. Our motives will reveal why certain works were done. Some believers will receive rewards (1 Cor 3:10–15); others will receive nothing (1 Cor 3:14; 1 John 2:28; 2 John 8; Rev 3:11). Some will shine as bright as the stars in heavens (Dan 12:1–3) and will receive exceptional privileges and positions of royal honour (Matt 10:32; Luke 12:8; 1 Cor 2:9; Rev 3:4–5), described as crowns of righteousness (1 Cor 9:25–27; 2 Tim 4:7–8), a crown of rejoicing (Dan 12:1–31; Thess 2:19–20), a crown of life (Jas 1:12; Rev 2:10) and a crown of glory (1 Pet 5:4).

The judgement of Israel

Many prophecies indicate that Israel will face a judgement before the establishment of the Davidic kingdom (Ps 50:1–7; Isa 1:2, 24–26; Ezek 20:30–38). Israel will be judged at the return of the Lord (Mal 3:2–5).

The judgement of Satan and his angels

During the tribulation, Satan, who is the source of all evil, and his angels will be cast down to the earth (Rev 12:7–9, 12; 20:1–3). Satan will be temporarily imprisoned for a thousand years (Rev 20:1–5) and will then be finally and eternally cast into the lake of fire with all the wicked (20:10).

The judgement of unbelievers

All the unbelieving dead will be judged for their sins and will be sent to the lake of fire, or hell (Rev 21). The devil and his armies will be judged at this time and will also be sent to eternal condemnation. The Bible also describes the judgement of the nations, which is similar to the judgement of unbelievers (Joel 3:11–17; Matt 25:31–46; 2 Thess 1:7–10).

Annihilation and universalism

Some people question why a loving God should send unbelievers, or the wicked, to suffer in hell for eternity, believing that it is unworthy of him. Clark H. Pinnock, for example, says,

> Just ask yourself: How can one reconcile this doctrine with the revelation of God in Jesus Christ? Is he not a God of boundless mercy? How then can we project a deity of such cruelty and vindictiveness? Torturing people without end is not the sort of thing the "Abba" Father or Jesus would do. Would God who tells us to love our enemies be intending to wreak vengeance on his enemies for all eternity?[26]

To avoid the problem, some have put forward the doctrines of universalism and annihilation. *Universalism* teaches that, because God is loving and compassionate, all people will be saved from the eternal lake of fire. *Annihilationism* is the view that the unsaved cease to have any conscious existence at all after death. Unbelievers simply go out of existence for ever. Supporters of annihilationism argue that Scripture's use of terms such as "perish", "destruction" and "death" to describe the fate of unbelievers (John 3:16; 8:51; Rom 9:22; 2 Pet 2:12) suggest that consciousness does not continue for ever. Some also argue that there is a sense in which words like "everlasting" and "eternal" refer to an age or dispensation, rather than to a particular length of time. They suggest that Scripture indicates that the eternal destiny of the wicked will one day come to an end.

However, while prominent theologians have promoted both these views, they do not fit the Bible's teaching.

- The love and compassion of God must be squared with the justice of God. It is the love and compassion of God that made him send his Son to die a terrible death in order to provide salvation for all who

---

[26] Clark H. Pinnock, "The Conditional View", in *Four Views on Hell* (eds. John F. Walvoord, William V. Crocket, Zachary J. Hayes and Clark H. Pinnock; Grand Rapids: Zondervan, 1996), 140.

will believe (John 3:16). Is it unworthy of him to cause those who reject his Son to suffer the consequences of their actions?

- God does indeed desire that none should perish (1 Pet 3:9), but that does not mean that none will perish.

- The Scriptures do teach that the unsaved (the wicked) will continue to exist forever (Eccl 12:7; Matt 25:46; Rom 2:5–10; Rev 14:11). The fact that all must appear before God for judgement indicates that unsaved people live on after physical death (Dan 12:3; Acts 24:15; Heb 9:27; Rev 2:11; 20:14–15; 21:8). Life does not come to an end at death but continues for ever and ever.

- The "eternal bliss" of the righteous is generally accepted as unending. If this is so, why should we understand the "eternal punishment" of the wicked as coming to an end? What holds for one must also hold for the other. The righteous will live for eternity (no end), and the wicked will live for eternity (no end). Powerful descriptions of suffering in hell, such as "weeping and gnashing of teeth" (Matt 8:12; 13:42, 50; 22:13; 24:51; 25:30; Luke 13:28), "the fire never goes out" (Mark 9:43) and "the worms that eat them do not die" (Mark 9:48) clearly indicate that the state of punishment has no end. Luke 16:23 and 26 describe the permanent gulf fixed between the saint and the wicked, indicating that this state is everlasting (see also Matt 11:22, 24; Luke 12:47, 20:17; Rev 14:11; 21:8).

- The Bible verses cited above also show that the wicked are fully conscious of their existence in the lake of fire.

Hell

There is great reluctance to talk about hell today, even among Christians and theologians. Yet the Scriptures speak of hell as a very real place. It is where the wicked will continue to exist and where they will be punished after death (Matt 24:5; 25:30, 46; Luke 16:19–31).

The word *hell* comes from the Hebrew word *Sheol* and the Greek word *Hades*, both of which can also be translated as "grave" or "pit". In the Old Testament, Sheol is used in the sense of "grave" in Job 17:13, Psalm 1:10 and Isaiah 38:10. It is also often used to refer to the place where both the wicked and the righteous go immediately after death (Gen 37:35; Num 13:33; Job 14:13; Ps 55:15; Prov 9:18). Some have thus concluded that Sheol has two compartments – one for hell and another for heaven.

The New Testament use of Hades seems to follow a similar pattern to the Old Testament use of Sheol. It is the place to which all the departed go – the place of the intermediate state and the future resurrection of both the wicked and the righteous (Acts 2:27, 31).

In the New Testament the word *gehenna* is used to refer to the eternal state or place of punishment and condemnation for the wicked. It is described as a place of "unquenchable fire" (Matt 3:12; compare 5:22; 18:9), a "lake of fire" (Rev 20:14–15), a "blazing furnace" (Matt 13:42, 50), a "fiery lake of burning sulphur" (Rev 21:8), "the outer darkness" (Matt 8:12), a place where the wicked are "tormented" (Rev 14:10), the "second death" (Rev 21:8), and "a place prepared for the devil and his angels"(Matt 25:41).[27] In summary, the final state of the wicked is "the loss of all good, whether physical or spiritual, the misery of an evil conscience, banished from God and from the society of the holy, and dwelling under God's positive curse forever".[28]

Heaven

The term *heaven* is also used in many ways. It comes from the Hebrew word *shamayin*, which simply means the "heights". Similarly, the Greek word *ouranos* can simply mean "sky" or "air", the sphere above the earth. However, in Scripture the word has three other possible meanings:[29]

1. *The entire universe.* Genesis 1:1 states that "in the beginning God created the heavens and the earth". Jesus similarly said that, "until heaven and earth disappear, not the smallest letter, not the least stroke of a pen, will by any means disappear from the Law until everything is accomplished" (Matt 5:18; Luke 1:17). Heaven is also the location of the sun, moon and stars (Gen 1:17; Matt 24:29).

2. *A synonym for God.* The prodigal son said to his father, "I have sinned against heaven and against you" (Luke 15:18, 21). John the Baptist

---

[27] R. P. Lightner, "Hell", in *Evangelical Dictionary of Theology* (ed. Walter A. Elwell; Grand Rapids: Baker, 1984), 506.

[28] Emery H. Bancroft, *Christian Theology: Systematic and Biblical* (Grand Rapids: Zondervan, 1961), 398. For further reading on hell, see Walvoord, Crocket, Hayes and Pinnock's *Four Views on Hell.*

[29] Erickson, *Introducing Christian Theology*, 1126–27.

said, "A person can receive only what is given them from heaven" (John 3:27). In Matthew the phrase "kingdom of heaven" clearly refers to God's kingdom, and Luke uses the same expression.

3. *The abode or dwelling place of God*. Jesus taught his disciples to pray, "Our Father in heaven" (Matt 6:9). He also spoke of "your Father in heaven" (Matt 5:16, 45; 6:1; 7:11; 18:14) and "my Father who is in heaven" (Matt 7:21; 10:32–33; 12:50; 18:10, 19).

The Scriptures make it abundantly clear that the dwelling place of God is the final and eternal destiny of the righteous. Jesus told his disciples that he was going to prepare a place for them. That place was in his Father's house, where he and all the disciples (believers) will one day be (John 14:2–3; see also 1 Thess 4:17; Heb 9:24). Scripture states that for believers, to be away from the body is to be with Christ, and to be with Christ is to be with God.

How does the Bible describe heaven?

- *A literal place*. Revelation depicts heaven as the new Jerusalem (Rev 21:2–22), with gates, walls and streets. The inhabitants of this city will have places to live (rooms), according to John 14.

- *A new heaven and new earth* (Isa 65:22; Rev 21:1–4). The current heaven and earth will be regenerated, renewed and transformed into a beautiful new state (Matt 19:28; 2 Pet 3:10–13).

- *The dwelling place of God*. In Revelation 21:3 heaven is likened to a tabernacle that God indwells: "And I heard a loud voice from the throne saying, 'Look! God's dwelling place is now among the people, and he will dwell with them. They will be his people, and God himself will be with them and be their God.'" The presence of God means that believers will have perfect knowledge (1 Cor 13:9–12; 1 John 3:2).

- *Devoid of all evil and suffering*. The devil, demons, evildoers and false prophets will be banished from the presence of God and will be tormented in the lake of fire (Rev 20:10). As a result, there will be no sickness, death or suffering of any kind in heaven (1 Cor 15:24; Rev 21:4; 22:3).

- *Full of God's light*, because of the glory and splendour of God (Rev 21:23–25; 22:5). The inhabitants will live constantly in this light.

- *A place of splendour and glory*, made of pure gold and precious stones (Rev 21:18–21).

- *A place of fellowship and celebration.* The metaphors of heaven as the place of the "wedding of the Lamb" and the church (Rev 19:7) and as "a feast" (Matt 8:11) describe the total enjoyment of God's presence.
- *A place of rest* from the drudgery of earthly life (Heb 4:9–11).
- *A place of worship of God and the Lamb* (Rev 19:1–4). Those in the presence of God always render to him songs appropriate to his nature (Isa 6:3).

Summary

When pursued to their logical conclusion, African concepts of death and eternity lead to hopelessness and despair. Belief in death as a transition from one life to another, though true, is not an adequate explanation of all that surrounds death, including the judgement of both the righteous and the wicked, their final destiny with God in heaven or damned in hell on the basis of whether or not they received or rejected eternal life through the sacrificial and substitutionary death and resurrection of the Lord Jesus Christ. It is the Bible alone, the inspired and authoritative word of God, that provides the true understanding of these serious issues.

To God be the glory!

Questions

1. Define the concept of time. What does "futurity" mean in your community? How does this compare with the meaning of eternity in Scripture?
2. Explain your community's beliefs about the dead and life after death. Compare this with the Bible's teaching.
3. Discuss the various methods of disposing of bodies. Does the Bible give a preference to any particular method?
4. Give examples of people who died "prematurely". How does the idea of premature death square with the doctrine of God's sovereignty over death?
5. Discuss the doctrines of purgatory and the second chance in light of the Bible's teaching.

6. List the key Bible passages dealing with the resurrection of believers. What do you understand these passages to be saying? Compare and contrast the different interpretations of the tribulation and the millennium.

7. What is the rapture? Which Bible passages support this teaching?

8. How do God's justice and mercy relate to hell?

9. What is heaven like? Describe it, using Bible references.

Further Reading

Randy Alcorn. *Heaven*. Wheaton: Tyndale House Publishers, 2004.

Donald G. Bloesch. *Essentials of Evangelical Theology*. Peabody: Hendrickson, 2006.

Robert G. Clouse, ed. *The Meaning of the Millennium: Four Views* by George Eldon Ladd, Herman A. Hoyt, Loraine Boettner and Anthony A. Hoekema. Downers Grove: InterVarsity Press, 1977.

Millard J. Erickson. *Introducing Christian Doctrine*. Grand Rapids: Baker, 1992.

Stanley N. Gundry, ed. *Three Views on the Rapture: Pre-, Mid-, or Post-Tribulation*. Grand Rapids: Zondervan, 1996.

Charles Hodge. *Systematic Theology*. Abridged edition; originally published in 3 volumes in 1871–1873. Phillipsburg, NJ: Presbyterian & Reformed, 1997.

Anthony A. Hoekema. *The Bible and the Future*. Grand Rapids: Eerdmans, 1994.

George E. Ladd. *The Blessed Hope*. Reprint of 1956 edition. Grand Rapids: Eerdmans, 1990.

Clark H. Pinnock. *A Wideness in God's Mercy: The Finality of Jesus Christ in a World of Religions*. Grand Rapids: Zondervan, 1992.

John F. Walvoord, William V. Crockett, Zachary J. Hayes and Clark Pinnock, eds. *Four Views on Hell*. Grand Rapids: Zondervan, 1996.

APPENDIX
GENERAL THEOLOGIES

The following are examples of general theologies that can be consulted for further reading on the topics covered in this book.

Louis Berkhof. *Systematic Theology*. 1938. Rev. ed. Grand Rapids: Eerdmans, 1979.

Donald G. Bloesch. *Essentials of Evangelical Theology*. Peabody: Hendrickson, 2005.

James M. Boice. *Foundations of the Christian Faith*. 2nd ed. Downers Grove: InterVarsity Press, 1986.

Millard J. Erickson. *Introducing Christian Doctrine*. 2nd ed. Grand Rapids: Baker, 2001.

Stanley J. Grenz. *Theology for the Community of God*. Grand Rapids: Eerdmans, 1994.

Wayne Grudem, *Systematic Theology*. Grand Rapids: Zondervan, 1994.

Charles Hodge. *Systematic Theology*. 3 vols; originally published 1871–1873. Peabody: Hendrickson, 1999.

Peter Hodgson and Robert H. King, eds. *Christian Theology: An Introduction to Its Traditions and Tasks*. Rev. ed. Philadelphia: Fortress, 1994.

Daniel L. Migliore. *Faith Seeking Understanding: An Introduction to Christian Theology*. 2nd ed. Grand Rapids: Eerdmans, 1991.

Bruce Milne. *Know the Truth*. 3rd ed. Leicester: InterVarsity Press, 2009.

Richard A. Muller. *The Study of Theology: From Biblical Interpretation to Contemporary Formulation*. Grand Rapids: Zondervan, 1991.

John Theodore Mueller. *Christian Dogmatics*. St. Louis: Concordia, 1934. Reprinted 2003.

Wilbur O'Donovan. *Biblical Christianity in African Perspective*. Carlisle: Paternoster Press, 1996.

Charles Ryrie. *Basic Theology*. Wheaton, Ill: Victor, 1986.

Augustine H. Strong. *Systematic Theology*. Valley Forge: Judson Press, 1907. Reprinted and updated, 2010.

Charles R. Swindoll and Roy B. Zucks, eds. *Understanding Christian Theology*. Nashville: Thomas Nelson, 2003.

Henry C. Thiessen, rev. by Vernon D. Doerksen. *Lectures in Systematic Theology*. Grand Rapids: Eerdmans, 2006.